VISUAL ATHLETICS

VISUALIZATIONS FOR PEAK SPORTS PERFORMANCE

KAY PORTER, Ph.D.

JUDY FOSTER

Foreword by
Shane M. Murphy, Ph.D.
Head of the Sport Psychology Program
United States Olympic Committee

Wm. C. Brown Publishers

Book Team

Editor *Ed Bartell*
Production Coordinator *Peggy Selle*

 Wm. C. Brown Publishers

President *G. Franklin Lewis*
Vice President, Publisher *George Wm. Bergquist*
Vice President, Publisher, *Thomas E. Doran*
Vice President, Operations and Production *Beverly Kolz*
National Sales Manager *Virginia S. Moffat*
Advertising Manager *Ann M. Knepper*
Marketing Manager *Kathleen Nietzke*
Production Editorial Manager *Colleen A. Yonda*
Production Editorial Manager *Julie A. Kennedy*
Publishing Services Manager *Karen J. Slaght*
Manager of Visuals and Design *Faye M. Schilling*

Cover design by Jeanne Marie Regan
Inset photo © David Madison 1989
Silhouette image by Michael Dean, Photographer
Text art by Yvonne McCauley

Library of Congress Catalog Card Number: 89–83368

ISBN 0–697–10987–9

Printed in the United States of America by Wm. C. Brown Publishers,
2460 Kerper Boulevard, Dubuque, IA 52001

10 9 8 7 6 5 4 3 2 1

Visual Athletics

■

Visual Athletics begins where the best-selling *The Mental Athlete* by Porter and Foster left off. It features

- over fifty individual and team-guided visualizations
- the most complete visualizations for football and basketball ever written
- how to deal with fear and anger in competition
- step-by-step mental training programs for high schools and colleges
- visualizations for stress reduction, relaxation, and sleep improvement
- visualizations for overcoming pain and healing of injuries
- new information on how to unset goals and deal with disappointment in athletic competition
- helpful information for recreational as well as elite athletes in every sport

About the Authors

■

Kay Porter, Ph.D., owns Porter Performance Systems, a sports and organizational counseling firm in Eugene, Oregon. She and Judy Foster have taught mental training techniques to athletes, teams, businesses, and school districts and have offered sport psychology consulting to the University of Oregon Athletic Department. They have presented their program at the Olympic Scientific Congress; the Women's Olympic Marathon Trials; the Seaside Wellness Conference; Seattle's Women Plus Business Conference; the Boston, Houston/Tenneco, and Pittsburgh Marathons; Health & Hospital Services Corporation; Eugene and Beaverton, Oregon, and Rochester, New York, school districts; and the University of Washington Athletic Department. They have also taught courses on self-concept; death and dying; and mind, body, spirit at the community college and university level.

They are the authors of *The Mental Athlete: Inner Training for Peak Performance*, Ballantine Books, 1987; have coproduced two teaching videotapes, "The Mental Athlete" and "Change Your Mind!! Inner Training for Women in Business"; and co-created six audiotapes of specific guided visualizations for goal achievement, stress reduction, and healing injuries in sports. They have written and published over thirty articles for national magazines and journals such as *Physician and Sports Medicine, Runner's World,* and *World Tennis.* They are now working on a new book for women, *Be the Heart and Live the Knowing,* for Ballantine Books, 1991.

Dr. Kay Porter holds her Ph.D. in Human Developmental Psychology from the University of Oregon and was a professor at the University of Oregon Center for Gerontology for eight years. She is an appointed member of the United States Olympic Committee Sport Psychology Registry and a sport psychologist for the Athletics Congress and the U.S. Tennis Association. She was a competitive athlete in tennis while in high school and college and is now a competitive masters runner, having completed seven marathons.

Judy Foster holds a B.A. in English Literature and Creative Writing from the University of Oregon. She is an artist and an athlete who has taught skiing, swimming, and fiber art in the Pacific Northwest. Judy is a masters sprinter and is the owner of J Bear, Inc., a manufacturer of jewelry, clothing, and accessories in Eugene, Oregon.

For more information on athletic, business/corporate, and personal seminars, clinics, and workshops, call Dr. Kay Porter at (503) 342–6875 or write

Porter Performance Systems
P. O. Box 5584
Eugene, OR 97405

Dedication

■

To the athletes and teams who have talked to us, shared with us, laughed and cried with us—they are the true teachers, giving us the inspiration to continue in this work.

Contents

■

Foreword

■

When I first began working with Olympic athletes, I was struck by how many of them naturally used imagery techniques. My lectures on visualization immediately struck a responsive chord with this group of young people—we were speaking the same language. By listening carefully to athletes, I have discovered many fascinating and useful ideas concerning the use of imagery in sports. Although my role is the sport psychologist, I often learn just as much from the athletes as they learn from me. Working together, we often come up with exciting new ideas about how to tap the power of the human imagination. But often I hear the question, "I know how important visualization is in sports, but how can I utilize my own imagination more effectively?"

This book shows you how—how to relax before a visualization, how to create an effective visualization for peak performance, how to use your imagination to help your body heal. Kay Porter and Judy Foster's first book, *The Mental Athlete,* was a shining beacon for those young athletes struggling to learn more about the psychological side of sports and to integrate that knowledge into their training. In this book, they remain at the vanguard of sport psychology and break new ground in several important areas. Two subjects in this book are especially exciting to me. One is the chapter on health and healing. As a clinical psychologist, I have been very excited about the new findings coming from the field of psychoneuroimmunology. At last, the artificial barrier between mind and body in modern medicine is breaking down. In very practical ways, Kay and Judy show you how to put this new knowledge to work for you. Any athlete, serious or recreational, struggling with injury or illness should read this chapter—and read it again!

The other must-read section for all serious athletes is on unsetting goals. This section offers many excellent suggestions for athletes who are facing the prospect of leaving competitive sports behind but who may be uncertain about the future. This is a difficult period for a good athlete, but in the U.S.A., we minimize the impact of this transitional period. After the 1988 Olympics, many athletes told me how bad it was to suddenly stop training. As Kay and Judy suggest, there is no need to stop training once competitive goals have been reached. The body needs time to "detrain," and all of us who work with athletes need to learn how to help them detrain more effectively. Once again, Kay and Judy are pointing the way.

There is something in this book for everyone. Athletes of all types will find themselves challenged and stimulated by the ideas in this book. Most important, Kay and Judy show you how to use your own imagination most effectively. They provide the tools for understanding the imagination. Using those tools, each of us can take responsibility for working with our powers of imagination to enrich our lives. It is a lifelong journey. This is your book. Enjoy!

Shane M. Murphy, Ph.D.
Head of the Sport Psychology Program
United States Olympic Committee

Preface

■

Since the publication of our first book, *The Mental Athlete,* five years ago, we've taught hundreds of athletes and coaches our five-step approach to mental training for peak performance. We've found that the results can be exceptional in some cases and merely good in others. But in all cases, mental training has been positive and highly effective.

In addition to the evidence we've witnessed firsthand, we've received letters from numerous readers who acknowledge their excitement, successes, and joy. They feel they're now able to think in positive and productive ways, no longer controlled by negative thoughts and feelings.

It has always been important for us to "walk our talk" and practice concepts we discuss in our books and workshops. We can honestly say that mental training has fundamentally affected us, too. Both of us have found these principles and techniques have application beyond athletic peak performance, into the realm of personal and professional realities.

We've encountered major life changes in the last few years, and mental training has enabled both of us to face these transitions with grace and conviction.

Mental training is as useful as it is powerful. And we're only at the forefront of discovering its potential.

Visual Athletics is a natural outgrowth of *The Mental Athlete.* It includes more than fifty general sports' visualizations and answers to most of the questions and comments we've received from our students and readers over the years. It also includes chapters on health and healing, unsetting goals, overcoming fear and anger, and moving on to new choices and opportunities.

In *The Mental Athlete,* you learned how to use mental training to attain your fitness goals. With *Visual Athletics,* you will learn how to deal with some of life's emotional aspects in addition to meeting your athletic objectives.

We hope you will find that mental training, especially affirmations and visualizations, is a dynamic initiative for change and success in all areas of your life.

Kay Porter, Ph.D.
Eugene, Oregon

Judy Foster
Eugene, Oregon

VISUAL ATHLETICS

VISUALIZATIONS FOR
PEAK SPORTS PERFORMANCE

Chapter ■ One

Mental Training: The Winning Edge in the 1990s

The purpose of life is to grow.

—Kay Porter

In the five years since we wrote *The Mental Athlete* (Ballantine Books), we have talked to hundreds of elite and recreational athletes from all over the country. We have seen a tremendous shift in awareness about mental training and sport psychology. In the early 1980s, we spent hours explaining to athletes and teams the importance of mental training techniques and skills. Today, it is a given. Athletes are hungry to learn how to improve their competitive or winning edge. In the 1990s, that competitive edge is *mental*—a legal competitive edge, at that!

In two athletes of equal and often unequal ability, the athlete with the mental edge most often emerges as the winner. The good news is that these skills are simple and fairly easy to learn. The rest of the news is that mental training takes a commitment to train one's mind with the same dedication that one trains the body. Daily mental practice prepares the athlete for all possibilities and helps him or her cope positively with the unexpected, rather than being psyched out. Most sport psychologists practicing in the U.S. use some variation of a five-step approach: mental log keeping, goal setting, positive self-talk or affirmations, relaxation, and visualization/mental rehearsal.

We have found that by using these skills the athlete can create a positive mental state before, during, and after competition. By using mental training strategies, the athlete creates more personal control over what happens in competition. The athlete is not only ready physically, he or she is mentally tough and ready—completely prepared in mind, body, and spirit.

Many of the elite athletes whom we interviewed before the 1984 Olympics said they had used various types of mental training techniques for years: generally positive self-talk, relaxation, and visualization. They always had goals for the season and for periods of up to four years ahead. Most had done so instinctively, often never discussing it with others. They simply assumed that everyone did it, and most athletes do—however, not always in a positive way. As athletes began to work with sport psychologists, they learned to use their mental powers in a *positive* and powerful way; and they improved significantly.

The mental side of athletics is an exciting new area, and athletes are enjoying it. It is something new and different, something to be explored, and they can see and feel it working. In the 1990s, we will see great strides and acceptance in sport psychology. We have already seen and heard the talk of sports commentators during the 1980s Olympics. With each passing year, they are talking more and more about athletes working on their mental edges and what they might be doing to mentally prepare and psych themselves up. Athletes are now ready for new ideas that will help them be the best they can be. Athletes are no longer worried about being seen as a "head case" if they work with a sport psychologist. They know that if they are physically fit and ready, they can perform even better by using their positive mental skills. Many athletes are open in talking about their mental preparation and have discussed it in depth with the media and the public. This openness has helped sport psychologists gain popularity and acceptance and has increased public awareness and interest in the field.

In *The Mental Athlete,* we describe the five steps to mental success in great detail, devoting a chapter to each step. In this book, we will go over the details once, lightly.

We want to make sure you, the reader, know that this mental training program is an *educational* process. It is not meant to cure any deep psychological blocks or problems. If such problems exist, they must be worked on with the help of a trained professional therapist. Many deep-seated psychological issues may be responsible for poor performance. This program can assist in helping the athlete approach competition with a more positive and enthusiastic frame of mind; it cannot cure deep psychological trauma.

We have written this book from a wellness viewpoint, rather than from a pathological one. In other words, we believe that people can, indeed, create their own reality—by what they think, feel, and expect. There is a quantity of sport psychology research showing that goal-setting, affirmations, and visualization processes work in creating a positive outcome. We believe the process of striving to achieve is as important as the accomplishment of the goal or vision. So, it is important to remember that this work is of an educational and learning nature. The process may be therapeutic, but it is not therapy.

There is an excellent book that I feel describes the nature of the American culture of the 1980s. *Healing the Shame That Binds You* (Health Communications, Inc. 1988) by John Bradshaw, a counselor in Texas, is a riveting account of the problems of addiction in our culture. Fortunately, three chapters describe the problem, and nine chapters are devoted to the solution. Basically, what he says is that toxic shame is what deprives us of being able to acknowledge our successes and appreciate our accomplishments. Toxic shame is shame that has been hidden and that we keep hidden. We are so busy striving for perfection that we forget to enjoy who we are, what we have, and what we have done. Most of his book centers on transforming toxic shame into healthy shame. Healthy shame is momentary embarrassment. When we are open and honest, shame loses its power. When we hide it, it becomes toxic and takes our power from us.

The fear of losing face in our culture, of making mistakes, and of being wrong are huge issues for us. With these issues of perfection and being perfect, we as a people, and athletes in particular, face difficulties in self-acceptance, in pride in achieving, and in the acknowledgment of our successes. Instead, we keep on driving ourselves, upping the bar, rather than patting ourselves on the back. It is OK to believe in ourselves; we don't have to be arrogant. Athletes, especially younger ones, have trouble knowing the difference.

It is our purpose, here, to create awareness in you, the readers, of what your processes are, so you can choose to change them if they are not working for you any more. The purpose of our books is to help supply ways for you to create success, excellence, and improvement in your sport and in life.

We think in terms of *opportunities* for learning and growth, rather than in failures, blocks, and negativity. Yes, it is important to acknowledge and mourn your losses, feel your feelings, get them out of your body the best you can, and then go on with life—learning from your experiences, letting go of your losses, and healing your pain. I have always tried to see life as supplying me with opportunities to grow—personally, professionally, and emotionally. At times it is difficult to see things in that way; yet I believe we are here to grow.

In our work with athletes, we encourage them to use these techniques as tools for discovery, not for escape from reality. A few of the visualizations use dissociative imagery, i.e., thinking about something else in order to relax and sooth the pain or heal the injury. However, most of these visualizations are based firmly in the process and content of the event—the details of the race, game, or match. They are written this way to engage the conscious mind, the mind we compete with—the mind that serves us during our waking hours.

We believe it is important to cultivate a state of internal peacefulness—a resourcefulness that helps us to *respond,* rather than *react.* We, as athletes, can then respond from a solid core, rather than react from a turbulent state of being. We strive to create a state of balance—balance between heart and mind, body and spirit. So as athletes, we can play with passion, desire, and spirit, coming from a great reserve of inner peace and harmony.

The Basic Program

The basic program of our five steps to mental success is easy, powerful, and simple to use. The five steps are

Mental Log Keeping
Effective Goal Setting
Positive Self-Talk or Affirmations
Relaxation
Visualization or Imagery

We have found that in order to change behavior, athletes must be willing to

1. Make change a priority
2. Be willing to risk
3. Make a personal commitment
4. Take Action
    a. Do something different
    b. Take a risk
    c. Be willing to lose face

If you decide to take steps to improve your mental edge, priority, willingness, risk, commitment, and action will be extremely important in the achievement of your goals and dreams.

Liz Bradley, a member of the 1988 Olympic rowing team, made her first selection camp in 1984, made the 1986, 1987, and 1988 teams and placed fourth, fourth, and fifth in the world. She wrote us a letter after the Olympics about using our methods.

"This is an 'I made the Olympic team after using your methods' letter. Two of us who eventually made the Olympic team went to the seminar that you held at the University of Washington in April, 1988. The seminar was great. It felt like you two were just giving names and recognizable faces to demons that were haunting me— and when you have the names and faces, you can fight them! I bought your book (*The Mental Athlete*) and worked through it. The exercises hit so close to home that it was an effort of will to make myself finish many of them. I used your techniques, adapting some of them according to what worked for me and the advice of my consultant. The most helpful technique was the index cards with affirmations and the most helpful concept was that of focusing on the positive. The mental log was useful in identifying the things that needed to go on the index cards. When it came time to perform, the visualized scenarios all played themselves out like a movie I'd been rehearsing; each time that happened, I became more confident in my abilities to alter my performance. I ended up doing the best rowing of my career and making the team with room to spare.

"Then I turned the techniques to the task of medalling in Seoul. Our whole boat (four with coxswain) did group visualizations and several of us added our own individual programs. It contributed greatly to our racing performance: the group staff implanted our race plan in our heads, and my own work made me absolutely ready and eager to race for the first time in my life."

Liz's letter was exciting for us to read, and it represents many of the letters we have received in the last five years. Certainly not all from Olympians; most of them are from the mainstream of America. We have continued to teach the five-step process, supplemented by focusing and concentration exercises. In working with athletes since 1983, we have found that an athlete's competitive concentration improves through listening to guided visualization tapes about the event itself. Thus, this book was born, consisting of many visualizations that can be taped by athletes for their own improvement. If an athlete chooses only a few of the steps, the most important are goals, affirmations, and visualizations.

Chapter ■ *Two*

The Basics

After working with many athletes over a four-year period, we found that the order of the five steps was more effective when we began working with the mental log first. Although the original book and our video, *The Mental Athlete,* both have the mental log at the end, it has proved much more effective to use it first.

The Mental Log

The mental log, or mental training diary/journal, is kept by the athlete after each important workout or competition. The purpose is for the athlete to write down everything that happened in his or her mind during the event or competition. What were the positive and negative thoughts that were coming up in the brain? The mental log contains the good, the bad, and the ugly! All the things you were saying to yourself that helped you, all the things you were saying that got in your way—all your confidence, all your self-doubt. Each performance is described within twenty-four hours after the competition, while the information is still complete in your mind.

The purpose of this log is to help you analyze your thinking patterns and their strengths and weaknesses. The log builds self-awareness of the mental and emotional beliefs and reactions you carry into the game. It helps you see on paper what words you say to yourself during the stress of competition. You become aware of when you feel powerful, in control, and at your peak; you also begin to see when you feel powerless, self-defeating, and out of control.

For example: You are a basketball player beginning the first game of the season. You are not too sure how you will do; you have been chosen to start, even though it is your first year after redshirting. What is happening in your head? Are you breathing?

As you begin playing, how do you feel? Are you relaxed? Are you afraid of getting the ball? When you get the ball, are you smooth in passing it or shooting it? Are you focusing on the game or on what other people are thinking about your performance? What are you saying to yourself? "Boy, that was a dumb move!" "Hey, Kyle, that was a good one! Good going!" Whatever you are saying to yourself or thinking about, you will write in your mental log within twenty-four hours.

Write it down fully, being honest and clear, writing the good and the bad. You may have been thinking, "Oh, no! That guy is a full five inches taller than I am! It's going to be a long night!" or "OK, Kyle. This guy is tall; you are faster and quicker than he is. Let's run his legs off tonight!"

We recommend writing this for three to four weeks during your training and competitions to look for patterns in your thinking processes. We often use the logs when helping athletes formulate game goals or goals for the entire season. The patterns we see are important in our working on meaningful goals for the short, medium, or long term.

Mental Training Log

Event: Date:
Finishing Place/Score: My goals:

General Feelings, Successes, Doubts:

Positive Thoughts and Feelings and What They Did for Me:

Negative Thoughts and Feelings and How They Hindered Me:

How I Overcame These Negative Thoughts:

Three Things I Need to Work on Mentally for the Next Game, Competition, or Training Session:

    1.
    2.
    3.

After noticing your thought patterns, it will be easy for you to work on goals for improving your mental toughness on the court or in the game.

Your mental log is also a place to write down all the anger, frustration, and negativity you might have after a poor performance. It can be used as a starting point for a new attitude and a way of letting go of your frustration, negativity, and self-doubt, so you can start building a more positive and confident mental attitude. It will help you use the competition as a learning experience—your first step toward excellence.

Goal Setting

Most athletes are aware that they need to have goals: each month, each competition, each season, each year. As most athletes know, goals guide their training and competition. Many don't know, however, that it is important to write down goals. They should be written as clearly and specifically as possible so the athlete knows what he or she is asking for. Goals are anything we wish for, desire, or dream about achieving. They are our dreams for the future.

Say yes to your dreams.

In *The Mental Athlete,* chapter 2 describes goals in detail. Briefly, goals can be short, medium, and long range. Short-range, or short-term, goals are very clear and specific for the next week or month of training and competition. Medium or intermediate goals are from two to six months in duration. Long-term goals may be anywhere from one year to four years.

It is important to be as specific as you can in writing your goals. Longitudinal research studies on goal setting and goal achievement have shown that when the groups studied have written out their goals, the achievement rate is about 75 to 80 percent. One twenty-five-year follow-up study at a major eastern university found that of the group studied, only 3 percent had written goals. However, that 3 percent controlled more monetary wealth than the other 97 percent of the group. They definitely knew what they wanted and went after it!

Begin to write down your goals for each game or competition, each month, and each season. For example, a young tennis player we worked with wrote the following goals:

Short-term goals
1. Between points—let go of the last point and think about strategy, get ready for the next shot, think about serve and where to place it.
2. When I'm ahead, I'm aggressive in closing out the point, game, set, or match.
3. If I'm behind, I play aggressively and well.
4. Maintain my composure on the court (keep my temper under control).
5. Be mentally tough for and during my matches.

Medium-term goals
1. Go to state this year.
2. Make it through the third round or better at state this year.
3. Be ranked in tournaments in sixteen and under this year.
4. Go to Bolliteri tennis camp next year.

Long-term goals
1. Get sponsored to play—free clothing, racquets.
2. Turn pro with a contract.

It can be argued whether these are reasonable goals. It is our belief that if we want something, we should "put it out there" with our intention and our energy behind it. Reasonable or realistic are such value judgments that they are hard to assess. In chapter 7 of this book, we discuss unsetting goals that we don't reach or that no longer work for us. We think it is important for all of us, athletes or not, to have dreams and visions for the future. Who is to say what is realistic and what isn't? Sports are full of inspirational stories of athletes who overcame unbelievable odds to succeed at the national or international level. Instead of asking, Why me? we urge athletes to ask, Why not me? We urge you:

Dare to dream and have a vision.

Positive Self-Statements/Affirmations

Of the five steps in this program, what you say to yourself is probably *the second* most important step. Our lives are spent thinking, even if we are not aware of the thinking. Our minds have about ten million thoughts per day. Isn't that staggering? And you can be sure many of them are negative. We are taught both positive and negative beliefs about ourselves and others. These belief systems help us and hinder us. Whatever we learned, we can unlearn, or relearn. As Chekhov said, "Man is what he believes." And woman is also what she believes. All of us are realizing that what our families might have told us about ourselves may not be altogether true—especially the negative.

Most of us have feelings of self-doubt and worry—about performance, appearance, intelligence—and our minds are busy with thoughts such as "That was stupid," "What if I'm not good enough?" and "Can I really do it?" If our best friends said to us what we say to ourselves, we would never speak to them again. While the mental log helps us look at our positive and negative self-talk, affirmations help change the negative to the positive.

A simple exercise for you is to list what you say to yourself during competition. Sort out the positive from the negative. For each negative thought, write an affirmation to correct the negative. For example: A young soccer player on scholarship may have worries about being deserving enough, not wanting to let the coaches down, how he looks in games (how he is playing).

These negative thoughts can be devastating. Something as simple as "I am good enough to be here" or "I belong here" can help the insecure athlete feel more comfortable.

NEGATIVE THOUGHTS	POSITIVE THOUGHTS
Do I deserve to be here?	I belong here. I am good enough!
I don't want to let Coach Smith down.	Coach Smith believes in me; I believe in myself.
I look terrible.	I look and feel good on the field.
Boy, I'm really a klutz.	I am smooth and powerful in my plays.
I'm too slow.	I am fit and fast.
I don't want people to think I'm conceited.	I give back to others the responsibility for their opinions.
What if I make a mistake and blow it?	It is OK to make mistakes.
	If I make a mistake, I let it go easily.

After making a list of negative thoughts and writing affirmations (which are always in the present tense, are always positive, and begin with "I"), burn, tear up, or destroy the negative list. Write the five to ten affirmations that are most important on four-by-six index cards and put them on your nightstand, on the mirror in the bathroom, on your desk, in your car—wherever you will read them during the day. It is important to read the affirmations a couple of times per day, especially in the beginning. In the morning when you wake up and at night just before sleep are good times. Your subconscious is more receptive at these times. During practice or in a game, say them to yourself whenever you are uptight or in a sticky situation.

Another way of writing affirmations is to make a list of strengths and weaknesses, again on separate pages. A tennis player we worked with made the following list:

STRENGTHS	WEAKNESSES
First serve strong and accurate.	I choke a lot; I get tight around the end of the set
Backhand solid.	Can't see self closing it out.
Hit and place well.	Don't take chances; I play it too safe.
Net game-sound.	Forehand erratic.
All-court player.	I don't stick to my game plan when things go wrong
Sound overhead.	Timing and footwork for forehand need improvement.
Endurance.	I stop hustling when I choke; I put my head down.

She changed her weaknesses with the following affirmations:

I am aggressive on the court whether I am winning or losing.
I am good at closing out a point, game, set, match.
I risk and take chances to close out the set.
I enjoy visualizing myself closing it out.
I stop playing it safe.
I play strong, powerfully, and accurately under pressure.
I stick to my game plan.
My timing and footwork for my forehand are excellent.
I hustle when I am behind.
I encourage myself on the court.
I say positive things to myself when I am playing.
I hold my head high; I am proud of myself.

It is important to remember that your subconscious doesn't have a sense of humor. It doesn't know you are kidding when you say, "Well, Kent; you are an idiot today. You are so stupid!" Affirmations change the internal negative tapes that we play in our heads. Don't even kid yourself or others in a self-deprecating way. It's no joke! The joke will be on you, because all affirmations, both positive and negative, become self-fulfilling prophecies.

Saying nice things to yourself is not bragging or showing false pride. It is building a solid sense of self-worth and self-acceptance. It is part of being on your own team. Acknowledgment of yourself and your abilities is important in supporting your self-confidence as an athlete.

In order to be a great champion,
You must believe that you are the best. . . .
And if you're not,
Pretend that you are

Muhammad Ali

Although the great fighter Muhammad Ali was not always the most humble of athletes, he believed in himself. He had one of the best affirmations of all time: **"I am the greatest!"** And he was!

Remember that some of the best affirmations for you might be the biggest bald-faced lies when you first start to say them. They are stretches for you; they are what you want to be true in the future. It is important that you say them as if they are already true; the more you say them, the more they will be true. Saying them under pressure will relax you and give you something to think about besides how freaked out you are! They give you focus and concentration; they calm your troubled and negative mind.

We love to tell the story of our Pittsburgh Marathon affirmation. We were giving a clinic in Pittsburgh and went running one morning. The race director asked us to stop by and see him in his office in the U.S. Steel building downtown. He assured us that we would be fine in our running clothes. As we went up the escalator, the noon crowd descended for lunch. There we were in our sweaty clothes and running tights, with hundreds of people in suits and professional dress looking at us. "I am comfortable in any social situation," we said to ourselves. We arrived in the office, just in time to be introduced to the TV producer. "You are meeting us at our best!" I said to him, laughing. (No makeup; just sweaty clothes and jet lag.) "I am comfortable in any social situation," my mind was saying. "I belong here." Larry Kuzmanko, the race director, was insistent that we all go to lunch. We protested—"Like this?!" "Sure, you look great! Come on!" Off we went to the Chinese restaurant three blocks away, continuing to create stares of all the business people on the streets in their fine clothes. "They are all noticing what good shape we're in. We have great bodies! We look great in our running tights." And into the restaurant to stand in line to be seated, "I am comfortable in any social situation!" And we were. I could feel my shoulders relax every time I said one of the affirmations to myself. It became more and more true as I talked. It doesn't matter what other people are thinking; the purpose is to put *yourself* at ease and to restore your own self-confidence! Try it; you may be surprised!

Progressive Relaxation

Every athlete knows it is important to be relaxed during competition. Many athletes have trouble knowing the difference between being too relaxed and not relaxed enough. The difference is that the mind must be ready and alert; the body can be relaxed, yet ready to respond quickly in the heat of competition. It is often a difficult balance to find and maintain, especially for young athletes.

It is important to experiment with your own style of being. If you are a quarterback, it is important for you to be calm, cool, and collected, doing your job in an efficient, a fast-moving, and a controlled way. If you are a defensive lineman, you might need to really psych yourself up to be very aggressive, like Mean Joe Green. Your temperament on and off the field might be much different. Some of the discus throwers and shot-putters I have known have been very mild-mannered, quiet fellows on the street, while being extremely aggressive and unfriendly during competition. It is important that you find what style fits your personality and your competitive mental state. The answer is: The right style is the one that feels best and works for *you,* enabling you to perform at your very best.

If you are doing a visualization in the quiet of your room, which we suggest, it is important that you induce your body into a state of quiet relaxation. In *The Mental Athlete,* we recommended the progressive relaxation method, which focuses on the major muscle groups of the body and involves tensing and relaxing each of these groups, one at a time. This is one of the most common forms used before visualizing, and it is very effective in producing a deep relaxed state of both the mind and the body. The two basic forms of progressive relaxation are the long, total body process and the short, immediate form that can be used after you are thoroughly familiar with the long form.

For an athlete with very high intensity energy, and who may have problems with focus, concentration, and visualization, the long form of relaxation may be very helpful in improving concentration and focus, as well as slowing him or her down for better receptivity.

We have been using an even shorter visualization process in our workshops, especially if we have only a few minutes to conduct a visualization process. It is described in chapter 3, Writing and Using Guided Visualizations.

We have also found that during competition it is often important for athletes to relax their bodies. Intensity works well in competition. However, sometimes we get too intense or too tense. Some examples follow.

A tennis player gets more and more tense and tight as he plays. He can simply do a "body check" during his time between games or even walking back to the baseline: relax jaw, drop shoulders, stand up straight with head up, hold racquet head up, three to four deep breaths into the abdomen and belly. These simple physical changes plus a few affirmations can change his mental state quickly.

A runner can do much the same. A quick body check while running a lap: relax jaw, lower shoulders, relax hands and forearms, soften belly and abdomen, breathe deeply into abdomen and belly (when we tire, we often find ourselves breathing into our upper chest), lift knees, lengthen stride if it is beginning to shorten. A runner's affirmations might center around running strong and relaxed, being fit and fast, running smoothly with powerful strides.

A sprinter doesn't have as much time to think as the runner in the previous example. A sprinter's mind often centers around thoughts such as being explosive and fast in the start; leaning and staying low; in the 20 to 35 meters of a 100-meter race, relaxing and focusing straight ahead; in the 35 to 50 meters, accelerating faster and saying, "relax and drive, relax and drive," still focusing straight ahead; in the last 50 meters lengthen and maintain, relax and drive, a very good finish, and a lean at the tape. It is difficult to explain exactly how to relax and drive; the words help induce that physical state in the runner. It is more a kinesthetic response, i.e., a feeling in the body of letting go of tension, while retaining power and strength.

A basketball player often has to switch from high-intensity playing and sprinting to standing still shooting a free throw. A quick relaxation ritual, plus a few deep breaths, can slow the athlete down, so he or she can shoot an accurate free throw. (We have made special guided visualization audiotapes for basketball players who want to be relaxed in their bodies and alert and ready to go in their minds. One of these visualizations is in chapter 5.)

Relaxation before a visualization is important because it creates a receptivity in the mind that enhances the depth of the visualization. If we are relaxed, the visualization goes in deeper and becomes more a part of us. Since visualizations are so powerful, the more relaxed we are, the more the subconscious believes it has experienced the imagined process in reality. What the mind thinks, the body will follow.

Guided Visualization/Imagery

Of the five steps, the visualization/imagery process is probably *the most important.* We have the power to create our own reality with the thoughts and images in our minds. The images, feelings, and sounds we have in our mind's eye have incredible power. Imagining the future, having a dream or vision for the future, greatly increases the possibility of realizing our hopes and dreams. How we imagine ourselves—our abilities, our acceptability, our intelligence, our worth—ultimately determines who we become, what we do, and what we have—our reality.

You have talents and powers that you have not used; all the power that you need. There is nothing greater than the power of the mind.

Paramahansa Yogananda

Our minds are one of our greatest gifts. In the last five years, we have heard some controversy about using visualization processes. We want to assure you that these processes are always under the control of the athlete. Anything that is said in a guided visualization process is in the conscious mind, unless of course, you fall asleep! The athlete always has total control over the visualization process. You are visualizing in the privacy of your own mind, even when following the content of a predesigned visualization process. I think one of the reasons we as westerners are so far behind the Eastern Europeans in mental training is that we in western cultures are very afraid of someone else controlling our minds. We want to assure you that *you* are the one in control of your mind when you use these visualizations—you, and only you.

The reason visualization/imagery works is that when you imagine yourself performing flawlessly and doing exactly what you want, you are physiologically creating neural patterns in your brain, just as if your body had done the activity. These patterns are like small tracks engraved in the brain cells. It has been demonstrated that athletes who have never performed a certain routine or move can after a few weeks of specific visualization practice perform the move. As in physical practice, mental "practice makes perfect" too!

It is still important that we also do the physical training. Mental training and visualization practice are meant to train our minds and create the neural patterns in our brains to help our muscles do exactly what we want them to do—with precision and perfection.

One national-class runner we worked with spent several sessions visualizing an upcoming TAC National Championships' race. He visualized himself staying with the front runners and eventually outkicking them. The pain of such a race is often intolerable, and the winner is the one who is either more fit or more able to tolerate the pain. Often thoughts occur about dropping back to ease the pain. He visualized the race over and over, seeing himself outkicking his opponents. It was such a powerful visualization that in the years following he was able to outkick those opponents in subsequent races, and he dropped all feelings of ever being intimidated by the "big names." In the actual TAC meet, he did not meet his original goal of winning; however, the work he did in the visualization had a long-term effect on his running in later races. Sometimes our physical fitness is not good enough to match our goals and expectations. Sometimes the only difference between athletes is the winner's mental triumph over physical pain and discomfort. On occasion, our time line and the time line of reality are not in sync. The suggestions in chapter 7 for unsetting goals may be helpful in dealing with this issue.

It is very important that the athlete continue to visualize achieving his or her goals and dreams. The positive intent is created; the time line may be off by a year or two; and sometimes we may not get what we *want*, but rather what we *need* for growth. Such times are a reminder to us of letting go with style and grace and going on to pursue new dreams.

My imagination is one of my greatest gifts.

Chapter ■ *Three*

Writing and Using Guided Visualizations

If you can imagine it, you can achieve it. If you can dream it, you can become it.

—William Arthur Ward

We create our own reality by what we think, do, and imagine. We create ideas, and thoughts form in our minds, some of which come into being and some that don't. The whole mental training process is a path of becoming and trusting your inner knowing. Many of us have no idea what our inner knowing is or how to access it. Visualization is the first step in becoming more aware of our intuition and inner knowing.

In the 1990s we will see a growth in the interest of people balancing themselves internally and externally. Creating balance in our lives will begin to nourish us and replenish the energy we expend in our everyday activities. We will begin balancing ourselves in mind, body, and spirit; analytical and intuitive thinking; male and female personality characteristics; physical, mental, emotional, and spiritual aspects of our lives; and career, family, relationship, financial, health, and leisure. When our lives are in balance, there is less stress in our lives. With balance, as athletes or just as persons in the world, we are able to keep up a high level of physical and mental energy; we no longer get burned out.

Have you noticed that after spending time training (being physically active), it is refreshing to physically rest or read a good book, to do something with your mind? Or after working at a computer terminal for two or three hours, to get up and take a run? All this is a matter of balancing and restoring the energy in our physical and mental bodies.

Visualization and imagery help create a story for our physical and mental body to play in and a place to merge. It is the connecting tissue, so to speak, between our minds and our bodies. The mind imagines and the body creates the action to do what is imagined. Positive visualization and imagery help restore balance to our training regimen. Like "all work and no play makes Jack a dull boy," all physical work and no mental play makes Jack a dull athlete. Visualization balances the mind and the body in achieving peak performance.

Types of Visualizations

Visualization and imagery techniques can be used on the field or off the field. Very short, fast mental exercises can be done in the space of a few seconds or minutes, with eyes closed or open, during competition. Longer, specific guided visualizations, usually prerecorded, can be done in the privacy of one's home, office, or bedroom, in peace and quiet, with only a Sony Walkman or a stereo for company. Most of the visualizations in this book are for off the field and are very specifically written for guiding the athlete's mind to excellence and achievement of goals and dreams.

On the Field

During competition, a tennis player may take a few seconds to visualize where he wants to hit the ball on his serve or on his return; a basketball player may visualize just before the free throw, seeing and feeling the ball going perfectly through the hoop; a runner may imagine running quickly past the opponent ahead, feeling powerful and full of energy; a quarterback may imagine the play in his mind, just before calling the play.

When visualizing during competition, the athlete must be careful what he or she is seeing, feeling, and hearing; imagining it accurately; making sure to "stay in the moment" of competition, not spacing off during important plays; and keeping it positive. An effective way of using visualization in practice was described by Ron Finley, the 1984 Olympic Greco-Roman wrestling coach, "In the middle of practice, we would have the wrestlers stop, close their eyes, and imagine what their next move would be; then we would have them start again." This helped wrestlers connect the visualization with the exertion they were feeling in their bodies and brought a physical element to the mental exercise. While this type of visualization is more rare, it can be very useful in the game and during practice.

Many athletes visualize future competitions while riding an exercise bike, rowing on a rowing machine, lifting weights, biking on the road, or racing in practice. The physical exertion with the visualization helps simulate actual competition.

Off the Field/In a Quiet Place

The visualizations in this book are designed to be recorded on audiocassettes and to be used by athletes listening in a quiet room, with few or no distractions. *We do not recommend using them in the car, unless you are not driving and are merely a passenger.* The visualizations are meant to evoke strong images, feelings, and sounds connected to the sport they are describing. For the image to go deeply into the conscious and subconscious mind, it is essential the athlete be in a relaxed and receptive mental and physical state.

We suggest that before a competition you listen to the visualization at least two or three times per week and, preferably, not the day of competition. Most recordings should run about fifteen minutes, including the relaxation segment at the beginning. Such repetitions of listening deepen the neural patterns in the brain, and physical responses become more automatic. Listening to prerecorded visualizations increases mental concentration and focus. The better the concentration while listening, the longer the concentration and focus in the actual event during competition can be maintained.

Visualization Modalities: Visual, Auditory, Kinesthetic

In both *The Mental Athlete* and this book, we have referred to visualization as a generic term for imagery and mental rehearsal. Visualization, in the context of both of our books, refers to any mental imagining, in pictures, words, feelings, or senses in the imaging athlete. Many athletes have said to us, "I don't see anything when I close my eyes." Some of us don't. We may hear the sounds of competition: the footfalls, the yelling of the coach and the crowd, the rhythm of the ball bouncing on the court or hitting the racquet. Some of us may have a feeling deep in our bodies of how it feels to make the perfect shot, basket, tackle, pass. All of these sensory experiences are referred to, in our books, as visualization, even though not all athletes are actually seeing images.

An athlete may experience a visualization in only one modality or way of imagining, or a combination of all three. My own modality is a combination of visual and kinesthetic (feeling it in my body). When I visualize, I can see the court or the track, and I can feel the power in my body of hitting the perfect backhand or running with strength and power.

Any one method or combination of methods is not good or bad. It is merely what is. What is, is. And what is, is worthy of acceptance. It can be helpful to develop another modality of experience, to increase your visual/imagery strength. It is a matter of paying close attention to visual detail, listening more carefully, or becoming more aware of your body sensations. All can be cultivated with practice. In *The Mental Athlete,* you will find a short, ten-item questionnaire in chapter 5 that will help you discover your personal combinations of basic modalities.

Visualization Perspectives

When visualizing, or seeing mental pictures, athletes report either seeing the pictures from within their own bodies, out of their own eyes, or seeing pictures and movies of themselves, as an outside observer or a TV camera, recording the images. Either way of imagining is OK. We have found that for technique sports, such as gymnastics, diving, and field events (discus, hammer, or shot), it is preferable to see yourself and your technique from outside your body. However, we believe it is important to learn to do both, especially if you are only using the outside observation technique. It is important to imagine the experience from within, because that will be the experience you will have when you compete.

One runner we worked with visualized only from outside her body. She was having difficulty pushing herself on the last few laps of a distance run, such as the 3000 meters. When we shifted her visualization techniques to within her body, she was able to overcome the pain and improve her performance. As with other mental training techniques, you as the athlete need to determine what is the best technique for you.

Different Versions Of Progressive Relaxation

It is helpful to relax deeply when we are first learning to use visualization. When our bodies and minds are deeply relaxed and centered, our brain waves slow down, enabling the visualization to go in deeper. When we finally stop our mind chatter, we are able to listen and concentrate at a deeper level. We become receptive and open to our imagination and our inner knowing (our intuition).

Long Version

We have used the long version with athletes new to mental training to help them control and relax the tension in their muscles. The full version of the progressive relaxation can be found in chapter 4 of *The Mental Athlete*. We are assuming that you, as readers, have practiced visualization for sometime and would prefer to use the shorter version. The longer version focuses on major muscle groups of the body and involves tensing and relaxing each of these groups, one at a time. This technique is also helpful in helping athletes learn mental focusing prior to guided visualization. It is a first step for younger athletes, especially, in familiarizing them with focusing and concentration methods.

Short Version

Once you have learned to totally relax physically through the long form, you can do the short form quickly and anywhere you can close your eyes for two or three minutes.

Find a quiet, comfortable place to sit or lie. Close your eyes and center on your breathing . . . breathe in deeply and hold it for a moment, letting go and allowing your mind and body to relax and to become empty and peaceful. Inhale . . . hold . . . and exhale. . . . Each time you inhale, inhale peace and relaxation. Each time you exhale, exhale tension and tightness. Breathe in . . . hold it . . . exhale . . . becoming soft and quiet . . . peaceful and relaxed.

Move your awareness inside and notice if there are any areas of tightness or places where you feel sore or uncomfortable . . . begin on your most dominant side and check in with each muscle group. . . . If you feel some tension or soreness, acknowledge it, send it some energy and peace, and let it go. . . . Move your aware- ness from side to side and from head to foot, acknowledging any tension or tightness and any pain or discomfort . . . sending care and energy and letting go. . . . Return to your breathing anytime you find it difficult to let go or move beyond some pain or tension. . . . breathing into any pain or tension you might feel in your body . . . breathing in, holding, and slowly letting go. . . . Re-center yourself and go back to each area in turn . . . and let it go . . . (a minute of silence) . . . allowing it to relax and become soft. . . . Breathe deeply . . . exhale. . . . Inhale new energy and vitality . . . exhale tiredness and tension.

(When you feel fully relaxed and centered, you are ready to begin your visualiza- tion.)

Grounding and Centering Version

Close your eyes . . . come into yourself and focus on your breathing . . . breath in deeply . . . filling your belly and chest and exhale fully . . . breathe in relaxation and peace . . . exhale tension and worry . . . breathe . . . begin to concentrate on your center . . . the area about two inches below your navel . . . the center of your life force energy . . . connect with this center . . . this power . . . this strength . . . begin to imagine sending down roots deep into the ground . . . down through the base of your spine and out the bottom of your feet . . . down through the floor and deep into the earth . . . strong, sturdy roots deep into the earth . . . spreading . . . connecting you with the earth's powerful and nurturing energy . . . continue to focus on your center, feeling the energy and power in that area two inches below your navel. . . . When you exhale, imagine any tension in your body going deep into the earth through the roots you have established. . . . When you inhale, feel the earth's energy coming up into your body through your spine . . . and up into your heart center . . . just behind your breastbone or sternum. . . . Imagine the earth's energy passing through your heart center and out into the world around you . . . see and feel any uneven, unfocused energy you might have in your body flowing up and out through the top of your head, being dispelled as you exhale . . . see and feel the bright earth's energy flowing upward into your spine and out through your solar plexus (two inches above your navel) into your environment . . . feel the peace, centered connectedness in your body . . . the lightness. Imagine the earth's energy flowing up into your spine and out through your heart center and your solar plexus, focusing you, relaxing you, connecting you . . . the focused awareness connecting you with people and your environment on a deep, confident, and relaxed level. . . . As you feel this new found sense of tranquility and of being centered in your body, notice that your mind is calm and you are in control of your feelings and thoughts . . .

gently breathing in . . . bringing new energy to your body . . . exhaling through your heart center, solar plexus, or the top of your head . . . as the feelings of relaxation, peace, and being centered and focused spread throughout your body . . .

(Insert visualization here or use relaxation alone.)

Imagining Relaxation Spreading

Find a comfortable place to sit or lie; close your eyes; allow yourself to drop down inside; feeling the relaxation in your body and letting go . . . take a deep breath, letting it out with a sigh; feeling peace and relaxation come into your body and mind . . . take another deep breath, and let it go; begin at the top of your head, imagining relaxation flowing from the top of your head; feeling your face relax and soften, feeling the relaxation going behind your eyes, relaxing your jaw, your mouth, letting your tongue rest comfortable inside your mouth; imagine your head emptying of all thoughts . . . draining all concerns and cares away, feeling good; begin to feel the relaxation spreading down into your throat; relaxing your neck, and feeling the warmth of the relaxation going into your shoulders, down into your arms and biceps, into your lower arms, through your wrists, into your hands and fingers; a relaxed feeling, soft and warm; pliable and flexible . . . imagine the relaxation flowing from your shoulders into your upper back and chest . . . going into your sternum and heart center . . . the center of your chest . . . feeling warm and relaxed and open . . . soft . . . down through your solar plexus, relaxing it, feeling at peace in body and in mind . . . feel the warmth of the relaxation spreading down into your belly and your abdomen and your lower back . . . into your hips . . . feeling the muscles relax, down into your legs and thighs, through your knees and calves . . . down into your feet and toes . . . all the tension draining out of your body through your feet into the ground . . . so your body is soft, relaxed, comfortable . . . totally peaceful and in harmony.

(Insert visualization here.)

How To Write Visualizations/Imagery For Sports Performance

Your visualization should start at the beginning of your routine, workout, or competition. Your goals and affirmations should be written and firmly in your mind. Once this has been done, you are ready to write your own visualization. It helps to incorporate as many senses as possible. After your visualization is complete, you can record it in your own voice or have someone else record it for you, so you can listen to it later in a quiet and peaceful place.

Imagine in your mind the whole process and routine of your event in competition in as much detail as possible. Imagine the competition area, the weather or atmosphere of the room, the sounds, the smells, the feelings of your body, before, during, and after your performance.

Imagine your warm-up, your routine, or rituals, before the game, talking to friends or teammates, concentrating—everything you do before competing. Feel and tell yourself how confident, relaxed, and in complete control you are of your body and your mental state. If you are nervous, say a couple of affirmations to yourself—"I am strong and ready," "I am relaxed and ready to compete."

Imagine yourself beginning to compete, going through the entire routine, race, match, or game. For long races or games, pick key points or plays to focus on. Notice everything you do, seeing it exactly the way you want it to be. If you make a mistake, go back, rewind, slow it down, and imagine it correctly. Experience yourself achieving your goal easily and with perfect control and ease. See yourself as successful. Be aware how it feels to succeed, to achieve your goal. Allow yourself to experience achievement and success completely. Remind yourself that you are deserving of achieving your goals and dreams. Remember to include key words, phrases, and affirmations during your competition—hearing them and feeling them in your body.

Imagine your warm-down, feeling your success and achievement, enjoying them. After your visualization is complete, bring your attention back to your breathing and slowly come back to your body and where you are sitting or lying.

Sometimes you may become so involved in your visualization that you will feel tired or will have more energy. Though you competed only in your mind, visualizing can have a powerful effect on your entire body. Your brain's neural patterns are created by both physical and mental acts. If you do feel tired after a visualization, *never* use the visualization the day of your competition. Save your energy for the real thing!

Ten Steps to Writing your Own Visualization

Here is how to create a guided visualization for your own sport:

1. See, hear, and feel yourself performing your event.
2. Write down and dictate into a recorder every detail.
3. Begin with arriving at your competition, going through your warm-up routine.
4. Go into vivid detail, including the weather, the images, the smells, the sounds, and the positive feelings in your body about competing.
5. Imagine yourself being totally relaxed, confident, powerful, and in complete control of your body and mental state. Include your affirmations and key words that will help you during your real performance.
6. Go through your whole event, thinking of each significant point or play. Feel yourself moving smoothly, performing with strength and endurance.
7. After writing your visualization, write statements of relaxation and remind yourself of your confidence, power, and mental toughness.
8. Write everything in a script, rereading it and editing it. Then dictate it yourself or have someone else dictate it for you into your recorder.
9. Listen for flaws, make changes, and then record it again with a relaxation that you like and that relaxes you best.
10. Listen to the finished tape at least once a day or three or four times a week before competition. Pick a quiet time and place where you won't be disturbed. Morning or night are usually good times. Try to stay awake to get the full effect. Sit up if you tend to fall asleep while listening.

Guided Visualizations For Goal Achievement and Power Flow

Visualization for Goal Achievement

(Use a progressive relaxation once you have found a quiet and comfortable space.)

Let go of your body and time completely and begin to think of a time in your life when you knew that you knew . . . a time when you were right on and performed well and at your peak. See yourself at that time . . . notice what you look like, what you are wearing, who is with you, what sounds are around you, where you are. . . . Feel the environment and the energy. Begin to see yourself doing whatever it was you did when you knew you were right on . . . when everything worked perfectly . . . when you were in complete control and at your peak. Watch yourself and feel that feeling . . . connect with all the feelings you experienced as you achieved at your highest level . . . confidently . . . competently . . . exactly the way you wanted to . . . what did it feel like? . . . sound like? . . . look like? Let it all come back to you . . . let it in . . . know it again . . . the joy . . . the power . . . the pride and confidence . . . the completeness . . . the rush of knowing you were performing flawlessly . . . let it become part of you . . . part of your spirit . . . part of your being. Feel fully connected with it all.

Now, while completely involved with this absolute knowing, give yourself a word or short phrase that brings all these feelings, pictures, and sounds sharply into focus . . . a word or phrase that completely connects you with that time and those feelings when you knew that you knew . . . that you felt confident, competent, and right on . . . say the word or words to yourself several times . . . slowly . . . and allow yourself to experience your sense of power and wholeness . . . feel it in your whole body. . . .

Think of your goal . . . what you want to achieve now . . . the importance it has for you . . . remember how it felt to write it down and see it on paper. Begin to see yourself preparing to achieve this goal. Where are you, and what do you look like? Are there other people there? . . . What are they saying? . . . Begin to go for your goal . . . see and feel yourself starting . . . moving toward your personal fulfillment. Give yourself permission to have it just the way you want it to be . . . see it, feel it, hear it perfectly as you move closer and closer to your goal . . . feel that excitement and rush that comes with doing something well, flawlessly, and with control . . . connect with your excellence as you reach and attain this important goal . . . allow yourself to have it, feel it, see it, know it completely . . . say your special word or phrase . . . know those feelings . . . that power, that confidence, that control . . . see your peak performance . . . exactly the way you want it to be.

Know that anytime you need it, you can call up these feelings of peak performance, competence, and power simply by saying your word or phrase . . . simply by reconnecting with your inner knowing and be seeing yourself at the moment of your peak performance.

Experience yourself doing whatever you want to do now that you have reached your goal . . . be aware of how it feels to achieve . . . listen to the congratulations and hear the response of the world around you . . . allow yourself to experience the full impact of the outcome . . . the result of achieving your goal . . . let it in . . .

relish it . . . touch it . . . let it be . . . allow yourself to have it all . . . knowing you are worthy of it and deserve the best.

Begin to let go of the image now . . . see it floating away from you . . . let it go . . . come inside to the peace of knowing and the quiet of your breathing . . . know that you have achieved at your highest level . . . you have succeeded . . . you have done it perfectly, just the way you wanted to . . . and breathe in deeply . . . bringing in new energy and peace . . . and . . . exhale slowly . . . releasing tiredness and tenseness . . . breathe . . . slowly . . . breathe. . . .

Slowly reconnect with the chair you are sitting in or the floor you are lying on . . . move your toes . . . come back to your body . . . move your hands and fingers . . . and . . . quietly and gently open your eyes.

Visualization for Power Flow

(This visualization can be helpful as a focusing visualization for feeling powerful and in control in a general setting and for anticipating short-term goals or activities for the next two weeks.)

Close your eyes, focus deep down inside yourself; feel the relaxation starting at the top of your head; down back behind your eyes, flowing into your throat and neck; relaxing your jaw . . . into your shoulders and upper back . . . into your upper arms, through your elbows, into your lower arms, into your wrists, and through your hands into your fingers . . . feel the warmth of the relaxation in your chest and upper back . . . flowing into your abdomen, stomach, and lower back . . . relaxation flowing down through your hips into your thighs, through your knees, down into your calves . . . through your ankles, into your feet . . . and into your toes . . . feeling your whole body relaxed . . . take a deep breath . . . let it out . . . feel the warmth and relaxation spreading all over your body.

As you are sitting in the chair or lying on the couch . . . imagine roots going from your spine and the soles of your feet deep into the ground through the foundation . . . going deep into the earth and connecting with the earth's energy . . . its strength and its power . . . its nurturing . . . and feel the energy of the earth coming up into your body . . . filling you with power and strength . . . nurturing you, healing you, connecting you.

Begin to turn your mind to a time when you felt powerful and you were in control . . . when you felt you were on . . . take a moment to remember and think of that time . . . that time of inner strength . . . when you felt powerful and in control . . . a time when you were within yourself . . . centered and connected . . . saying what you thought . . . clearly, concisely . . . you were thinking and speaking with your heart . . . let that time come back to you . . . the scene, the words, the feelings . . . when you were connected . . . clear, centered . . . a time of crystal clarity . . . perhaps a time in a meeting . . . being assertive . . . when you were talking with someone . . . when you were presenting an idea . . . maybe simply talking and sharing with a close friend or your partner . . . let the memory of that time come back into your mind . . . and imagine yourself in that situation . . . seeing the environment you were in . . . hearing the sounds . . . feeling the feelings in your body . . . a time of power, strength, flexibility, and clarity . . . allow yourself to relive that moment . . . the feelings, the sounds, the picture . . . with that clarity in mind . . . that centered and focused feeling of power and energy . . . allow yourself to think of a word that represents that state of mind . . . that state of being . . . say the word to yourself . . . feeling the feelings in your body of that experience . . . of clarity and focus and control . . . a state of inner harmony . . . that power, that flexibility.

Imagine seeing that word on a big poster somewhere in your home . . . in any colors you want . . . smiling to yourself . . . knowing when you say that word . . . or hear it . . . or see it . . . you can bring back those images and those feelings of clarity, purpose, and focus. . . . Look at that poster on your wall, say the word to yourself, feeling the feelings in your body . . . and look at your hand in your mind's eye, noticing a small, plastic card in your hand, about the size of a driver's license or credit card . . . it is an exact image of that poster . . . with all the colors and your word printed on it . . . carefully turn it over to see your face on the other side . . . a very good picture of yourself . . . liking what you see . . . and seeing your name embossed underneath your picture . . . liking the picture . . . again turning the card over and seeing your poster on the other side . . . in all the colors, crystal clear.

Take this card and put it in a very safe place . . . knowing you can take it out at any time . . . keeping it in a place where it's safe and secure . . . remembering you have everything within you to be, to do, and to have what you want . . . saying the word to yourself again . . . and feeling the feelings in your body again . . . knowing those positive feelings are always with you.

Slowly begin to let those images fade away . . . and begin to think of what is coming up for you in the next two weeks to a month . . . whatever life events are coming up for you . . . begin to imagine yourself entering into those events and experiences with openness, flexibility, and clarity . . . seeing them as opportunities for growth and change . . . and learning . . . imagine yourself approaching them with excitement and enthusiasm . . . knowing you have your word to help you and to guide you during those times . . . your word . . . . to bring back that state of focus and clarity, of being centered, and of power . . . enabling you to achieve whatever it is you want to achieve . . . see yourself going through the next month, achieving your goal with grace, power, and flexibility . . . being adaptable, open, focused, and clear . . . with style and grace . . . with inner harmony . . . reminding yourself to think with your heart . . . and to come from a place of inner balance and harmony . . . feeling peaceful inside and outside . . . a place of peace, tranquility, and clarity.

Slowly let the image fade, coming back to your body sitting in the chair or lying down . . . feeling yourself connected with the earth . . . with its nurturing and its power . . . . imagining your roots coming back into the bottoms of your feet and the base of your spine . . . still feeling the nurturing power of the earth . . . . connecting you . . . centering you . . . providing you with energy and power . . . when I count to three you can open your eyes, feeling relaxed and energized for the rest of the day or evening . . . one . . . move your hands and your feet . . . stretching . . . taking a deep breath . . . letting it out . . . two . . . move your neck, stretching, breathing . . . and three . . . open your eyes when you are ready . . . feeling relaxed, peaceful, and alert.

©1989 YFM

Chapter ▪ *Four*

Visualizations For Team Sports

In *The Mental Athlete* we described mostly guided visualizations for individual sports. Interestingly, visualizations for team players are sometimes quite similar to those of individual sporting events. Even in a team setting with more variables for change, each team member has a series of tasks to do, as does an athlete in an individual sport. Often it is not the moves the athlete makes but the psychological state of mind that is similar and that the athlete wants to change with the visualization process.

The visualizations in this chapter are aimed specifically at each team sport, with some suggested ideas for particular positions. For more general visualizations about anxiety, nervousness, and other psychological states, refer to chapters 2, 3, 6, and 8. The guided visualizations on goal achievement and power flow in chapter 3 can be helpful as generalized visualization processes.

General Team-Building Visualization

(Use a relaxation sequence from chapter 3 before this visualization.)

Begin to think of a time when you and the team were playing in a big match or in practice . . . when you were all working well together . . . like a well-oiled machine . . . everyone was playing their position with intensity, power, focus . . . playing hard and yet relaxed . . . imagine seeing and hearing your teammates playing, connecting, perfectly in sync . . . you are all superior athletes, contributing to a higher purpose of creating a unity and a team cohesion that is exciting and exhilarating. All of you working hard . . . sharing with each other . . . supreme cooperation and support . . . giving and receiving support and friendship . . . feeling the mutual support of each other's well-being and happiness . . . sharing the pain and hard work as well as the triumphs. . . . You all know each other so well . . . your strengths and weaknesses . . . helping each other improve and be the best you can be . . . feeling your own and your teammates' commitment to excellence, to playing as well as you can in every game . . . all of you easily letting go of the petty anger and resentments that come up when people spend a lot of time together . . . you easily forgive each other for these little arguments or disagreements . . . they mean nothing in the larger scheme of things . . . enjoying your friendships and being buddies . . . allow yourself to enjoy the unity and productivity of your mutual effort . . . being happy when another suc- ceeds . . . being a team player . . . feel the feelings in your own body as you play your position, feeling powerful, in control . . . a valuable and contributing member of this winning machine . . . feel the pride you have in yourself and as part of this team . . . knowing you belong here . . . knowing when one of you wins, you all win . . . being part of a larger and more important whole . . . enjoying these moments of your life . . . moment-by-moment . . . experience-by-experience . . . all creating a more unique and interesting you . . . as a separate and an important being . . . as well as part of the greater whole of this team. . . . Think of the team goals you have written . . . (pause) . . . plus having fun when you play . . . enjoying your interaction with each other . . . believing in each other . . . being proud of your team and what you do . . . working hard together . . . trusting each other . . . enjoy your feelings of unity and being a part of a greater and more powerful whole . . . knowing you can depend on these other people to help you . . . and being willing to let them depend on you . . . for friendship, support, and coming through in the clutch in a big game.

Begin to think of a word that will remind you of these feelings, these images, these sounds of teamwork and mutual commitment to peak performance . . . say the word over to yourself . . . hearing it, seeing it, feeling it in your body . . . and remind yourself that saying this word will bring back this team experience in all its entirety.

Allow yourself to remember all the things your team did in this great game or practice that worked . . . what did you do that worked so well? . . . Begin to list these accomplishments mentally . . . acknowledging your progress and your excel- lence as a team and as an individual player . . . thank your body and mind for their contributions to that peak performance . . . knowing that being part of this team is an honor and privilege for you . . . enjoying your participation, enjoying the process of playing and winning . . . enjoying your learning and accomplishments . . . and thank yourself and your teammates for a job well done. Slowly let the images fade, coming back to your body sitting in the chair or lying down . . . feeling grounded and cen- tered . . . and ready for the rest of the day or evening.

When I count to three, you can open your eyes, feeling alert and refreshed . . . one . . . take a deep breath . . . moving your hands and feet . . . exhaling . . . two . . . stretch your neck and shoulders . . . and three . . . open your eyes when you're ready.

After opening your eyes, write down all the things you and your team did that helped you work well together.

Team-Building Exercise

1. What do I do to help us work well together as a team?

2. What do my teammates do that help us work well together as a team?

3. What are all the things we did in a peak game that helped us work well together?

4. What else could we do to create team unity and cohesiveness that we're not already doing?

5. What do we need to do to improve as a team and to be more successful?

6. What can I do personally to encourage and support my teammates?

7. I think important team goals for our team should be
    a.
    b.
    c.
    d.
    e.

Affirmations For Being A Team Player

(Mark the five that would be most important to you if they were true.)

I enjoy encouraging and supporting my teammates.
I am a good team player.
There is enough glory for all of us.
I assist and help my teammates in any way I can.
When my teammate wins, I win.

I am happy and satisfied with our wins; I trust that I played as well as I could.
I believe in myself and my teammates.
I can count on my teammates to be there when I need them.
We work together well as a team.
We have fun playing together.
We let go of a lost game and look forward with fresh enthusiasm.
We play one game at a time.
We have fun, work hard, and stay loose.
We come through in the crunch.
We believe in each other and support each other.
We are proud of our team.
We are proud and play with intensity and focus.
The pride is back!

Football Visualizations

When deciding what to include in specific football visualizations, it is important to look at some of the most common mental issues that come up for players. Five of the most common issues for football players are

1. injury—coping mentally with injury, healing as fast as possible
2. physical aggressiveness—being aggressive enough on the field
3. mental toughness—dealing with playing intelligently and hard even when in pain and exhausted, dealing with intense pressure from the opposing team or supercritical coaches
4. resiliency—the ability to take physical abuse and go out there and give it 100 percent day after day on a consistent basis
5. giving up—when the mental and physical strain are too much

One team member, a transfer running back with very good speed, came to his new team and dropped pass after pass. He seemed to have "hands of stone." His self-talk was "I got bad hands." The affirmations his coach gave him were

I have great hands!
I catch everything thrown to me.
If I can touch it, I can catch it.
I believe in myself.
I got sticky hands!
I am a "hot" pass receiver!

Another player had trouble after making a mistake and lost confidence, especially in games. When he made a mistake, he would drop his head, walking slowly and dejectedly back to the huddle. The coach had him change that, and when he made a mistake, he would keep his head up, trot back with energy and say to himself

It's OK to make a mistake.
I am confident in myself.
I believe in myself.
I easily let go of a bad play—I let go and go on!

Simple affirmations such as these can change how a player thinks and feels. It is as easy to say something positive, as negative. Simple language changes can make enormous performance changes. Affirmations and visualizations work together to create positive change.

Items to Include for Specific Football Visualizations

With the help of a talented University of Oregon football player, Chris Leupold, we compiled the following list of items to include for writing visualizations for specific football positions.

Offensive Lineman
Mindset/Attitude: mean, aggressive, intense, determined, focused

1. Getting off on the snap count, fast and staying low.
2. Drive blocking situation—coming off the ball hard and low; making contact, sustaining your block, and driving your man downfield.
3. Pass-blocking situation—proper technique; drop back position; butt low, arms straight forward and stiff; make contact and sustain block by moving feet to keep the pass rusher from getting past you.
4. Double-team situation—get your shoulder into defensive lineman's hips; the two of you root him out and push him downfield, not allowing defensive lineman to split the double team.

Backfield—Running Backs (fullback, tailback and halfback)
Mindset/Attitude: intense, aggressive, relaxed and loose, ready for anything, thinking quick and fast

1. Take hand off and hit the hole hard (keeping legs moving, running fast); totally aggressive; keeping feet moving.
2. Take hand off, see the whole field, find your hole and go for it, if designated gap is closed.
3. If a defender comes up to tackle you, run over him aggressively; you juke the defender.
4. After getting by first defenders, you're in the open field; you see the whole field, see your blockers, and make your cuts off your blockers, going all the way—a breakaway for a touchdown!
5. Catching a pass—run your pattern precisely, knowing when the ball is in the air; you watch it coming straight into your hands. Once you've caught it and are holding it safely, turn upfield and run.
6. Blocking—attack defender aggressively, staying low and blocking with good technique and aggression; taking the defender out of the play.

Quarterback

Mindset/Attitude: relaxed, focused, confident, upbeat, team leader

1. See the whole field—all your receivers, the defenders; find your open man and execute a perfect pass; pre-read defense and make sight adjustments.
2. Total confidence in offensive linemen protecting you.
3. Be ready for the unexpected or a situation where your receivers are covered; see your opportunity to run—turning upfield, seeing your offensive linemen going out to block for you, making your cuts off your blockers, and running for the first down.
4. Calm, cool, collected; an alert and a ready mentality.
5. Leadership—you call the plays with authority; remembering you are a leader; being enthusiastic and determined; instilling confidence in other members of the offense.

Receivers

Mindset/Attitude: aggressive, confident, focused, quick in mind and body

1. Running precision patterns—running your pattern with precision and perfection; beating your defender.
2. Watch the ball coming into your hands, catching it, tucking it away, turning upfield, making a quick move to get by your defender and running upfield for a touchdown with power, strength, and speed. (Always lock the ball away *first*.)
3. Catching the ball across the middle—watch the ball all the way into your hands; your concentration totally on the ball; taking your hit and holding on tightly to the ball for a first down.
4. Blocking—seeing your assigned man to block; on the snap of the ball, you attack the defender with power and aggression, taking him out of the play. Knockdowns.

Tight Ends

Use items for both the receivers and offensive line.

Defensive Backs

Mindset/Attitude: focused, relaxed, loose, aggressive, confident, strong belief in self

1. Man-to-man defense—find your man, use perfect technique covering your man; when you can get two hands on the ball, go for it!
2. Zone—see all receivers; when a receiver comes into your zone, you react and cover him with perfection, denying him the pass.
3. A run—react to the run, attacking the running back with aggression and executing a perfect tackle; using proper leverage.
4. Interception—see the ball in the air, react with power and quickness to the ball; watching the ball into your hands, intercepting it and running upfield, using your blockers and going for a touchdown.

Defensive Linebackers

Mindset/Attitude: most aggressive guys on the field; focused, upbeat, fired up, enthusiastic, supportive of teammates

1. A pre-stance read: Run or Pass

    A run—seeing the offensive lineman's blocking scheme, instantly recognizing a run, finding the ball carrier, attacking him with aggression and bringing him down for no gain.
    A pass—recognizing the offensive lineman's scheme, instantly seeing it's a pass, dropping back into your zone; you see all the receivers, and you pick a receiver as he comes into your zone; reacting as the ball is thrown toward him, you intercept it, turn upfield, follow your blockers, and return the ball for a touchdown.

2. Pass rush—a blitz is called; you're designated to rush the passer; on the snap of the ball, you react with quickness; an offensive player attempts to block you; you make a quick pass rush move, getting by him and sack the quarterback.

Defensive Linemen

Mindset/Attitude: tough, aggressive, determined, intense, focused, persistent

1. React aggressively on the snap of the ball; offensive lineman fires out at you; you keep low—pad level; use hands to separate offensive lineman from your body, find the ball carrier; shedding the offensive lineman and make an aggressive tackle for no gain by the running back. *Attack.*
2. React on the snap of the ball, recognizing it's a pass from the offensive line position, use your hands and make a quick pass-rush move on the offensive lineman, getting by him and sacking the quarterback for a loss.
3. React on the snap of the ball, recognizing it's a run, fire into the offensive lineman; you feel and see the double team from another offensive lineman; with aggression and quickness, you drop your body and split the double team, creating a pile at the line of scrimmage.

Kicker

Mindset/Attitude: calm, cool, collected, focused, relaxed, good under pressure

1. Visualization depends on the style of kicking. This visualization should be one of seeing self kicking extra points, punts, etc., both from the outside and from the inside of one's body. Imagining a fairly narrow focus on ball, goal crossbar, and own physical power and accuracy. A kicker should be able to write a specific visualization tailored to his own needs from the suggested steps of writing your own visualization.

Football Visualization for a Defensive

(Precede this visualization with a progressive relaxation.)

It is the beginning of a game . . . you have warmed up . . . stretched . . . listened to final instructions and connected with your inner self . . . you say your word as you move onto the field, taking the correct position for this defensive play . . . you are supremely confident . . . ready and relaxed . . . you are focused . . . you love playing football and turning on your aggressiveness just when you need it. You know you will give it your best and you feel your energy and control. You can get total release and play with complete abandon and skill. You move . . . running . . . hitting hard . . . powerfully . . . you run right through your opponent on your tackles and when taking on blockers . . . experience yourself play after play . . . experience the team completing each play through the first quarter and into the second . . . each time the defense is on the field, you play well . . . powerfully . . . running . . . blocking . . . charging with complete confidence and skill . . . you are relaxed yet powerful . . . you are playing with abandon and control . . . experience it all . . . moving easily . . . powerfully . . . no fear . . . only competence . . . confidence and control.

Now the team is kicking off . . . you are on the special team . . . you love playing on special teams, and you are the best player . . . this gives you energy and confidence . . . you believe in your strength and abilities. Life has been good to you, and you thank your mind, body, and spirit for their health, fitness, and energy. You are totally aggressive when you are on special teams . . . experience yourself playing just the way you want to . . . just the way you know a great player plays . . . you are that great player, and you accept your competence and success . . . play after play you do it correctly . . . powerfully and aggressively.

As the second half begins, you remember your word . . . and notice that you are relaxed and ready . . . feeling confident as you watch the offense . . . learning . . . waiting your turn . . . you imagine watching yourself each time you are on the field . . . moving . . . running . . . hitting . . . tackling . . . being in the right spot at the right time . . . every defense . . . every change of position you handle with confidence and great skill . . . you are a dominant player . . . you are a smart player . . . the best . . . and this is good . . . good for you and good for the team. Into the fourth quarter now . . . playing aggressively . . . meeting your goals . . . allowing yourself to have it all . . . playing with complete skill. You are pleased with your abilities . . . from one end of the field to the other . . . from one defensive player to another, you enjoy being successful . . . you are supreme . . . you are agile . . . quick . . . powerful and strong . . . confident and whole . . . play after play . . . experience it all . . . watch it all . . . you love the feeling of being in the middle of the action, and you trust your body and your mind to be there for you . . . you are whole . . . powerful . . . quick . . . relaxed . . . strong and victorious . . . allow yourself to have it all . . . to experience it . . . allow yourself to hold on to the feelings of success . . . it makes you complete . . . knowing what a powerful player you are . . . what a confident player you are and how important your role is to the team . . . remembering again your word . . . and that you have everything within you to be, to do, and to have what you want . . . you are your own greatest resource.

Let the picture fade . . . knowing you will play well, game after game . . . will always give it your best . . . will run fast and powerfully . . . hit and tackle with complete abandon and control. Let the picture go until your mind is at peace and quiet . . . begin to focus on your breathing . . . you feel relaxed, refreshed . . . strong and confident . . . complete. Begin to reconnect with your body and your present space now . . . breathe deeply . . . exhale . . . breathe.

When I count to three, you may open your eyes . . . one . . . move your fingers and toes . . . reconnecting with your body and the sounds of the room . . . two . . . move your head and shoulders . . . focusing on your breathing . . . feeling refreshed and relaxed . . . three . . . you may open your eyes when you are ready.

Basketball Visualizations

Items to Include for Specific Basketball Visualizations

These items were given to us in an interview with Tori Baker, a shooting guard on the University of Oregon women's basketball team. Tori was an outstanding high school player in Oregon and a starter for the U of O. These items are to be used by the reader in writing a personal visualization for each position. The points for each position apply to either men's or women's basketball.

Point Guard Visualization Items

1. **See the whole court.** Concentrate on peripheral vision as well—**no** tunnel vision. **Dribble with head up.**
2. **Protect the ball.** Have body/arm/hand between the ball and the opposing defensive man.
3. **Play smart.** As point guard, you are team leader and need to be able to exemplify leadership qualities. Don't make mental mistakes. A positive and upbeat attitude helps the team stay motivated.

Shooting Guard Visualization Items

1. **Square up** and be in **triple threat position** when receiving the ball.
2. **Follow your shot!** Keep moving toward the basket—a possible rebound.
3. **V-cut** to get open.
4. **Go toward the pass**—want the ball.

Post/Center Visualization Items

1. **Move a lot** to get good position at all times.
   - To receive the pass
   - To get in rebounding position
   - To remain a threat at all times
2. **Take it up strong**—power lay-up.
   - Be aggressive
   - Be intimidating
   - Be powerful
3. **Pump fake** to get defensive man in the air and off balance. (This move may be appropriate to all positions.)
4. **Hook** the defensive man to get open.

Defense Visualization Items

1. **Be in defensive stance** at all times—stay low, in squatting position with palms up.
2. Have **happy feet**—on tips of toes; be ready.
3. **Respect** the player's **first step**—be wary, ready to react.
4. **Play smart**—no reaching; move to get defensive position, don't reach.
5. **Deny the passing lane.**
6. **Block out the offensive man** after a shot has been put up, and then **go to the boards.**

Guided Visualization for Basketball

Settle down into yourself, putting your focus inside your body . . . having your hands and feet resting comfortably. . . . Begin to exhale and inhale . . . breathing slowly and rhythmically. . . . Breathing in . . . breathing out . . . breathing in relaxation . . . breathing out tension. . . . Focus in on your chest, letting that part in the center of your chest, your heart center, relax . . . allow it to soften and relax . . . feeling safe and comfortable. . . . Feel your shoulders and neck relax . . . feeling a sense of relaxation flowing from the top of your head down into your face and jaw . . . into your neck and throat . . . the relaxation flowing into your shoulders, chest . . . down into your arms and into your hands and fingers . . . the relaxation flowing into your back . . . through your abdomen and stomach . . . into your hips . . . down into your legs . . . all the way down into your feet and toes. . . . Just feel your whole body being relaxed and centered . . . at peace . . . quiet. . . . Feeling comfortable, calm, breathing easily and deeply, getting enough oxygen. . . . Begin to think of a time in your home gym . . . perhaps when you were doing a scrimmage or just playing . . . and begin to remember that old confidence and power you felt in the past . . . when you played really well . . . feeling good, playing hard, but without effort . . . when your playing just flowed . . . easily and without effort . . . playing hard and feeling relaxed and easy in your body. . . . Remember that feeling of control and confidence . . . of being on top of your game . . . see yourself and imagine yourself being the excellent player that you are . . . knowing you belong here . . . feeling good about what you are doing and how you are playing . . . knowing deep down inside that you deserve to be on this team . . . and you are an outstanding player. . . . Feel yourself looking, playing, and feeling confident and relaxed. . . . Imagine the coaches being there, and you're feeling really confident and calm and comfortable being watched. . . you are proud, powerful, and in control.

Imagine yourself shooting with your elbows in and following through the way you want to . . . in good form . . . you are focused and centered on the play, and you know you are paying attention to the action in the game . . . you know what's happening all the time . . . you are aware and alert, ready for anything that happens . . . the crowd's noise is in the background . . . it excites you . . . you take energy from it . . . and you are focused on the game and the action . . . you are playing . . . and you are concentrating well . . . with intensity and power . . . you are enjoying yourself immensely . . . if you make a mistake, you quickly let go of it . . . putting your concentration and focus on the game . . . letting go easily and going on.

You are quick and strong, and you really enjoy being in the game, doing everything the way you want to do it. . . . You are consistent in your shooting . . . shooting strong and accurately . . . seeing the ball go through the hoop . . . you are shooting well and handling the ball well . . . your dribbling is fantastic . . . you have great reaction time . . . and when you get the ball, you take your time, you relax and play with intensity and focus . . . looking around, either shooting or passing it off with power and control.

Feel all those feelings of power, confidence, and control surge through your body . . . playing hard and intensely . . . with a certain relaxation of mind and body . . . flowing with the play . . . think of a word to represent this state of mind and this state of being . . . saying your word to yourself to bring up those feelings of power, accuracy, and confidence . . . remembering that your word connects you with that state of mind and state of being of excellence and peak performance . . . feeling it in your mind and body . . . knowing you have what you need.

In that same gym or any court, imagine yourself now in a big game situation . . . an important game . . . knowing it's OK to feel a little nervous . . . and knowing that it's a natural thing . . . tell yourself, "It's OK that I'm a little nervous . . . it helps me get psyched up . . . I let go of worry easily . . . I'm powerful and aggressive. . . ." See yourself being very intimidating . . . you are intimidating . . . you are big and strong . . . and you are intimidating. . . . Feel yourself being aggressive . . . and know you are making your opponents work hard to keep up with you . . . imagine yourself getting that ball . . . and if you see an opening, then pass it off . . . and if you see an opportunity to shoot, go for it . . . making that commitment to shoot . . . and just do it . . . following through . . . without hesitancy . . . taking your time . . . in an instant, stopping, looking, choosing your move, and committing to an action . . . whatever it is, whether passing the ball off or shooting it yourself, you are doing it right . . . you are in charge . . . you get the ball back . . . and you are in charge . . . you let go of any worry about what people are thinking about you . . . you don't care . . . all you care about is getting the ball and playing with focus and intensity. . . . "I'm focused on the game, and I'm playing for myself, and having fun, and I am enjoying it all. . . . I'm a good player in the crunch . . . and a good team player . . . I support the whole team . . . we all help each other. . . . I get better and better with each game. . . . I am more and more relaxed with each passing day." Allow yourself to experience it fully, knowing you can call up this total experience any time you choose.

Slowly let the images fade . . . and become aware of your body sitting in the chair or lying on the couch. . . . Know that with every scrimmage and game you are going to get stronger and stronger . . . and more confident . . . when I count to three, you may open your eyes . . . feeling relaxed, refreshed, and ready for the rest of the day . . . ready to go out and play . . . one . . . move your hands and feet, taking a deep breath . . . and letting it out with a sigh . . . two . . . move your neck and shoulders, stretching . . . and three . . . open your eyes when you are ready.

Soccer Visualizations

Items to Include for Specific Soccer Visualizations

1. Use good body form—good balance and body position on trapping
2. Keep up intensity (staying awake and alert—no lapses in intensity)
3. Anticipate what is coming your way—keep on toes, be ready for what's happening; this helps you stay involved and alert
4. Take your time shooting—no rushing of shots
5. Be composed and have good form
6. Think about specific moves
   a. Collecting a pass and turning the ball away from a defender
      ■ Advance toward ball
      ■ Make contact with ball
      ■ Turn ball away from defender
   b. Passing to a teammate
      ■ Should become an automatic response
      ■ Develop the ability to recognize how you can help
      ■ Notice who is most likely one to receive the pass
      ■ See where the space is
      ■ Stay in close proximity after passing it off

Guided Visualizations for Soccer

(Use a relaxation sequence from chapter 3.)

Begin to remember the best soccer match you ever played . . . where it was, who was playing with you, all the sights and sounds of it . . . the excitement, the power, the achievement of your peak performance . . . allowing yourself to feel all the feelings from that time . . . . of pride, confidence, achievement, excitement, fun . . . seeing the match . . . hearing all the sounds of your teammates yelling and supporting each other . . . the crowd and its cheering and clapping . . . remember it all . . . and begin to think of a word that represents that state of mind and that state of being . . . to represent all those feelings of confidence, pride, excitement, achievement . . . saying the word over to yourself . . . knowing your word will bring that time back to you whenever you wish . . . that time of peak performance and achievement.

Now begin to think of your next match . . . your goals and what you want to accomplish . . . how you want to play . . . what you want to do . . . knowing about the other team . . . imagining what your strategy will be . . . and what you want to accomplish personally.

Imagine yourself at the soccer field where your next match will be held . . . see yourself and your teammates warming up . . . running, making your moves . . . practicing your shots . . . getting ready for your match . . . feeling the familiar feeling in your stomach . . . excitement . . . anticipation . . . really enjoying the whole process . . . and remembering your word that connects you with your previous peak performance . . . saying it over to yourself . . . bringing up your confidence in yourself and your teammates.

Imagine yourself being as aggressive as you want to be . . . getting the ball . . . looking for a pass . . . breathing deeply, running powerfully, looking, committing yourself to your move . . . being completely relaxed and poised . . . in total control . . . being fast and aggressive . . . confident . . . powerful.

And seeing yourself on the field, focusing on the man you're guarding . . . thinking about what you're going to do next . . . staying alert . . . knowing when to make your move . . . being ready . . . remembering your affirmations.

"I'm strong; I'm fast; I have good concentration and focus; I stay with my man; when the time is right, I go for it!; I'm mentally tough." Knowing that you are intimidating . . . aggressive, powerful . . . making good shots . . . having great endurance and speed . . . using your body well—shielding . . . heading . . . good at getting it, jumping up, and heading . . . having a good shot . . . concentrating really well and focusing on hitting it directly . . . hearing how it sounds when you hit the sweet spot of the ball . . . following through . . . solidly kicked and feeling good . . . seeing your fakes, your moves, your one-on-ones . . . all well done . . . with good intensity and focus . . . anticipating what is coming your way and being ready for it.

Imagine yourself collecting a pass . . . turning the ball away from a defender . . . making good contact with the ball . . . feeling in control and powerful . . . then passing to a teammate . . . seeing who to pass to . . . seeing where the space is . . . staying in close proximity after passing it off.

Know that you have everything you need to play well and at your best . . . you and your teammates play well as a team . . . supporting each other . . . yelling to each other . . . playing together as a well-oiled machine . . . enjoying the team play . . . getting better and better with each game . . . and when you are getting tired . . . reminding yourself that you are strong, powerful, and fast . . . you are as tough as anyone else on the field today . . . believing in yourself and your ability . . . knowing you are a winner.

Slowly allow the images to fade . . . remembering your word . . . your word of power and strength . . . become aware of your body sitting in the chair or lying on the couch . . . when I count to three, you can open your eyes . . . feeling refreshed, relaxed, and ready for the rest of the day or evening . . . one . . . move your hands and feet, taking a deep breath . . . letting it out with a sigh . . . two . . . stretch your neck and shoulders . . . and three . . . open your eyes when you're ready.

Volleyball Visualizations

Major Mental Issues in Volleyball for Visualizations

1. Deal with stress before big matches—want to be relaxed and ready.
2. Get focused before practice—get mentally geared up before practice to get the most out of it.
3. Keep calm and ready to receive the serve.

4. Deal with your "Jekyll-and-Hyde" attitude—being explosive one minute and playing with a soft touch the next.
5. Be flexible with a multitude of different attitudes during the match such as blocking—being intimidating, aggressive, and powerful; and passing and setting—loose and relaxed, narrowly focused.
6. During match, focus on the here and now—be present, let go of missed points.

Items to Include for a Volleyball Visualization

1. Coping with stress before a big match—be relaxed and ready.
2. Being calm and ready to receive serve.
3. Explosive—being forceful and relaxed.
4. Being quick and relaxed.
5. Accelerating through the ball; don't overpower ball.
6. Blocking—fierce power; intimidating.
7. Digging—relax and enjoy it.
8. Fearless and aggressive.
9. Serving—be a gunslinger.

Baseball/Softball Visualizations

Major Mental Issues in Softball or Baseball

1. Pregame nervousness—relaxing, focusing.
2. Hitting—keeping a clear mind, reacting to a pitch versus guessing.
3. Pitching—being aggressive, smart; changing speeds, finesse, right frame of mind; confidence in self; being intimidating; flexibility—changing strategy in the middle of a game; being able to adjust when things go wrong.
4. Double headers/tournament play—keeping energy up; dealing with tiredness and exhaustion; keeping intensity level up during the day; remembering importance of each game—not letting up; each win counts.
5. Defensive—staying alert; being ready for anything; keeping focus and concentration on the game; knowing situation at all times; knowing where the next play is going to happen.

Items for a Hitting Visualization

1. See yourself getting a base hit.
2. Keep short stride.
3. Throw hands at ball.
4. See yourself hitting a line drive.
5. React, don't guess.
6. Keep hips and hands together.

Using the questions at the end of this chapter and the major mental issues in softball or baseball, you can write your own personal visualization.

In our interview with Earl Edwards, a consultant in Phoenix, Arizona, he discussed an interesting technique for dealing with anxiety between pitches. He calls it his prepitch routine. It can also be used for batting. It is especially helpful for players who have a lot of negative self-talk. This routine virtually eliminates negative self-talking by focusing on the patterns between each pitch.

After each pitch, pitcher takes a few deep breaths to restore a semi-relaxed state, says a cue word to himself about relaxation, such as relax, and assumes a relaxed posture; begins to reflect on analyzing his next move or pitch, thinking of strategy; then says a cue word to himself for optimum arousal and peak performance; and pitches. These activities very effectively switch the focus from negativity to relaxation and strategy.

A batter can use the same pattern, relaxing between each pitch and getting ready for the next with good concentration and focus.

Crew Visualizations

In chapter 1 we included part of a letter from Liz Bradley, a member of the 1988 U.S. Olympic rowing team. We interviewed her, and she offered us the use of her goals, affirmations, and visualization she used in preparing for Olympic competition. We believe they are excellent examples for crew competition. As we mentioned in chapter 1, Liz had been rowing for many years and made her first selection camp in 1984. She first competed in 1984 and made the 1986, 1987 and 1988 U.S. teams, placing fourth, fourth, and fifth in the world. She retired after the 1988 Olympics. Her use of mental training techniques was superb. We are grateful for her contribution to this book.

A segment from her letter on why she decided to use mental training techniques: "There were several reasons why I sought out help with the psychological aspects of training. (1) After a few instances of rewards not matching performance, I had a lack of trust in the process. This lack of trust and the attendant fear were sabotaging my performance. (2) I'd always loved practice and been terrified of racing. (3) Much of elite rowing is simply a matter of pain tolerance, which is certainly mind over matter. It made a lot of sense: We train our bodies so hard and carefully; we ought to train our minds as well.

Liz's Goals For Olympic Training In Crew

Goals for every practice:
   Learn as much as I can
   Enjoy it and have fun
   Use every stroke
   No wild mood swings
Technique—finish curve:
   Visualize feet out
   Outside hand/Acceleration/Circle
   Early body angle>no lunge
   Chin over finish

Technique—back support:
  Don't absorb and collapse
  Rigid low back, relaxed shoulders
  This lets the leg drive be awesome!

Technique—arms and shoulders:
  Shoulders relaxed and hanging loose
  Arms extended forward, stretching lats
  Arm lift independent of shoulders
  Gives quick catch

Keep the stroke *forward*:
  Supported, swinging finish
  Early body angle, sit up from low back
  Long arms, up and forward with both shoulders
  Quick catch and legs
  Vision on Cindy's midback, not low back (Cindy rower in front of Liz)

Liz's Affirmations for Competition and Practice

  I attack the margins.
  This is a good row!
  It's easy to row well and hard.
  Every single stroke.
  I am having fun!
  I love to compete and push myself.
  ON DEMAND.
  First stroke and every stroke.
  Visualize the first twenty as the boats start to paddle.
  Here I am again.
  I've learned from the last times and have prepared well, physically and mentally.
  I know that mental power works for me and I know how to summon its effects.
  I am ready.
  I endure more and pull harder than anyone else here.
  I push the other boat back with my oar.

Guided Visualization for a 2000 Meter, Four-Person Crew Olympic Final

See yourself at the village, getting dressed for the race . . . people all around you as you walk to the bus . . . all wearing different colors, different country's uniforms . . . they laugh and talk in foreign languages . . . or are silent in anticipation of competition . . . let their excitement feed your energy, channeling yourself into the tunnel . . . on the bus, notice the athletes around you, then close your eyes and feel yourself in the boat, relaxed and rowing perfectly . . . quick catches . . . long relaxed arms, strong lower back . . . as the bus approaches the course, you look out, checking the wind and the water.

  You feel the familiar grabbing in your belly, which tells you that your body and mind are ready . . . you are well prepared . . . step down out of the bus, conscious of the uniform you wear and what it means to you, and to the world . . . look around and see the colorful uniforms and flags . . . hear the spectators . . . and the public address system, the announcer, the sounds of the races that precede yours . . . feel the breeze in your hair.

Let all these things recede now and center yourself . . . jog down the course to warm up, watching the buoys click by . . . just as they'll click by in an hour or so . . . there's lots to do between now and then . . . none of it to be hurried . . . and all of it important . . . walk down to see Heidi and feel her hands loosen your muscles . . . relax into it, and let her help you . . . stretch out, feeling Cindy, Sarah, Jen, and Kim in the room. You don't need to see each other, to say anything . . . you are linked . . . you know.

Visualize your stroke when you finish stretching . . . quick catches, right with Cindy's quickness . . . midback support in the drive and in the finish . . . feel the unity of the power . . . of the bucket with Sarah . . . swing out of the bow, feeling Jen hold the boat together . . . feel yourself to be calm, confident, relaxed . . . feeling good . . . you are anticipating the race . . . you want it to start . . . you are more than ready for the quick chain of events that leads up to the starting command . . . looking forward to the body of the race . . . have a deep, calm feeling inside . . . knowing you are very well prepared.

Finally, hands on the boat . . . see and feel its smooth, yellow hull . . . and feel the pride of rowing in such a boat with such people . . . Kim walking down beside you, Carol (our coach) alongside . . . Carol doesn't need to make a speech . . . she knows that you're ready . . . walk the boat off and pick it up stern pair . . . immediately falling into sync with Cindy . . . watch her shoulders, her elbows, her slide . . . go into the tunnel together . . . feel the bow pair click in together behind you . . . . through the hull of this fast, responsive boat . . . swing into full slide 80 percent, feeling the synergy building . . . submerge yourself in the boat . . . matching . . . quick catches . . . low back support, confidence . . . long, relaxed, and firm arms and shoulders . . . feeling the heartbeats, bodies, and breathing, all building together . . . taking the first tens . . . you are aggressive from the first stroke to the last . . . just like you use every single stroke of the race . . . start preparing yourself for the speed things move at during the start . . . the thirty gives you time to think, just like the body of the race . . . run down the boat . . . quick catches, perfect sync with Cindy's back . . . swing through with Sarah . . . feeling the unity and power of the bucket . . . . feel Jen put the boat together from the bow . . . start thinking about boat things. . . . We burst off the line . . . we strain at the hands of the stake boat boy . . . we want the race to start . . . on the twenty with the upshift, think about the sprint . . . carrying length and power through the pain and haze of vision . . . keeping eyes open and head up . . . this boat has an awesome sprint.

Down at the starting line, things move quickly . . . the familiar pounding of your heart . . . that familiar excitement that courses through your body before every start . . . loud voices in French over the public address system . . . Romanians pressure breathing next to you . . . Russians a red wall on the other side . . . go into the tunnel . . . Cindy's back, the sole of your feet, and the length through your low back . . . visualize the first twenty strokes . . . anticipate . . . you want the race to start

. . . Jen hand up, Sarah take Jen's oar and scull, hand it back, Sarah dip it, Jen hand down.

We burst off the line . . . soles of your feet, two hands up, one hand up . . . etes vous pres and go! Bodies up and quick . . . lengthen together . . . coxswains screaming all around you . . . go into your boat . . . Kim's voice is excited . . . and yet confident . . . she knows you . . . and you trust her . . . breathe . . . drive the legs . . . keep the arms long . . . now is when you start attacking . . . and you don't let up until you cross the line . . . aggressive on every single stroke . . . when Kim calls the settle, become aware of the pain . . . you are friends with it . . . it has stalked every practice for five years now . . . it means that you're pulling hard enough . . . let it drive you down the course . . . that was a good start . . . now, see the boat from the outside . . . as you power along . . . at a solid thirty-seven . . . see the bodies swing together . . . hear your breathing . . . feel the length of your stroke . . . submerge yourself in the boat . . . and the swing . . . strong finish on the second settle . . . passing through the 500 soon after . . . it's easy to row well and hard, the boat is just sailing along . . . after the 500 comes the body of the race . . . which is your strong point . . . here you start reeling in the boats ahead of you . . . as the 500 marker recedes behind the stern, check in again . . . quick catches with Cindy . . . feel the power and unity of the bucket . . . and Jen in the bow putting the boat together . . . say the affirmations . . . ''I attack the margins . . . I can endure more than anyone else in this race.'' Feel the boat pick up and go as you cross the 750 . . . passing the Chinese four in ten strokes . . . just as Kim called for . . . feel the hull running on top of the water . . . hardly rippling its surface . . . every single stroke . . . think about the seat racing . . . just because you get or lose a margin, doesn't mean you relax or even give up . . . reeling in the Russians . . . a little move just makes you go bananas even more . . . you want it . . . nothing in the world is worth more than the Romanian bowman that Kim is screaming for . . . nothing . . . and you're having fun . . . 1000-meter mark, ten for pry . . . you're in the medals now . . . only the Bulgarians and the Easties (East Germans) ahead . . . you've snapped the Soviets, once you pass them, they break . . . you can endure more . . . you do endure more . . . third 500 sets the stage . . . letting go and pulling so hard that you lose track of where you are in the race . . . the patterns are set . . . like your hand heights . . . Kim will pilot you along them . . . just do what she says . . . collapse your world . . . long arms . . . strong back . . . quick legs . . . feel yourself inching toward the Easties, an inch a stroke . . . every stroke . . . all the other boats far behind . . . fighting for the spot behind you . . . falling back . . . push them back with your oar . . . pulling even with the Bulgarians . . . swinging through and snapping them too . . . you love to compete and push yourself . . . and you're still having fun . . . when you become aware of the fog at the edge of your vision . . . let it push you further . . . every single stroke . . . 750 to go . . . up one with length . . . think of Sarah behind you . . . make it long for her . . . you're enjoying this race . . . you love feeling the boat respond to the bodies . . . feel the whole boat accelerate smoothly together . . . hear the roar of the crowd . . . take their energy . . . make it yours . . . right on to the tip of your oar . . . see yourself as they see you . . . moving up onto the Easties . . . you have overlap and you're moving.

Kim's voice goes up a notch . . . she can smell the gold . . . and she will take you there . . . this four just gets stronger as the race goes on . . . really starting to burn now . . . and it's taking you into the lead . . . each stroke becomes the universe . . . no past, no future . . . rowing on instinct and training . . . and they are good enough to make you win . . . you can't feel the others, only the unit that is the boat . . . submerge yourself . . . give up your identity, your nerves, your muscles to the boat . . . last 500 . . . up again with length, with swing . . . a unit going together towards the finish line . . . support your back . . . drive your legs . . . reeling in the only boat ahead of you in the Olympic games . . . you've never been in a boat that pulled so hard . . . that was so aggressive . . . this boat can reel anybody in . . . pull now for Cindy . . . for Sarah . . . for Jen . . . for Kim . . . let go and go for it! Reach out, long arms . . . think of the 300 meters that remain . . . you need all forty of those strokes to pass the Easties . . . use every single one . . . only half a seat behind now . . . and still moving . . . Kim is screaming now . . . screaming for blood . . . driving you ahead with her emotion and will . . . power ten, a surge of power and speed . . . neck and neck with the Easties . . . battling down the course stroke for stroke . . . a red haze with Cindy's back in the middle of it . . . this race will go to the tougher crew . . . and we are it . . . in two, up two for ten . . . one, two, going bananas and staying long . . . up a seat . . . crowd screaming . . . willing the boat forward . . . you're pulling harder than you ever knew you could . . . building for the last ten . . . one, two, on this one . . . your world converges to your catch and your length . . . you can't even think any more . . . you're just going for it . . . hear the finish line horn . . . know that you have won!!!

Now you can give in . . . let the pain take you . . . let your oar drop . . . let your body bend over . . . as your breathing slows, a feeling of elation and euphoria washes over your body . . . thank your body, your training, your boatmates for this win . . . you hear familiar voices of parents and friends as you turn and row past the stands . . . you row up, turn again and get into lane one, pull up to the dock . . . knowing the taste of victory . . . savor the feelings washing through your body . . . as you stand in the sun . . . with your arms around Cindy and Sarah . . . take the flowers . . . bend your head for the medal . . . feel its weight against your chest . . . turn toward the flag . . . and let the emotions go as the anthem plays . . . as it ends, more cheers erupt . . . you all hold each other, then get in the boat and row away . . . as always, on demand . . . the boat sets up and runs like a dream.

Allow yourself to let go of the image and the feeling now . . . and slowly begin to reenter your present space . . . reconnect with your physical world . . . the feel of the chair . . . the relaxation and heaviness of your arms and legs . . . gently move your toes, and then your fingers . . . becoming aware of your breathing . . . inhale deeply, hold . . . and exhale . . . you feel relaxed and filled with new, quiet energy . . . when you are ready . . . open your eyes.

Liz and her boat, a four with coxswain crew team, finished fifth in the 1988 Olympics. East Germany won, followed by China, Romania, Bulgaria, the U.S., and Great Britain. Liz and her teammates beat the Russians in the last heat to make the Olympic final. "The level to which I raised goal setting, using your techniques, got me to and through the Olympics. Like the level of physical training needed to be in Olympic shape, it was not sustainable (by the very definition of 'peaking'). I've had to learn to stop driving myself, physically and mentally.''

Many elite athletes, after a big competition, experience a huge letdown and, often, depression. As a result of our conversations with Liz, we included the unsetting of goals in chapter 7, to assist athletes in coping with the after effects of setting high-level goals and the end of important competitions.

Writing Your Own Visualization for a Specific Team-Sport Position

If your team sport is not included in this section, or if you wish to write a visualization for your particular position, complete the following questions:

1. Five issues/items to include in a visualization for my position are

    a. _____

    b. _____

    c. _____

    d. _____

    e. _____

2. What do I need to do to improve my playing? (technique and form)

    a. _____

    b. _____

    c. _____

    d. _____

    e. _____

3. What do I need to do to improve my mental game?

a. _____

b. _____

c. _____

d. _____

e. _____

4. What affirmations do I want to include in my visualization?

a. _____

b. _____

c. _____

d. _____

e. _____

5. What strengths of mine do I want to include in my visualization?

a. _____

b. _____

c. _____

d. _____

e. _____

Taking this list, refer back to one of the visualizations in this chapter or in chapter 3, and write your own visualization. After reading it and making corrections, read it slowly into your Walkman in your own voice, or have a friend record it for you. Listen to it for speed and pace. If it is too slow or too fast, record it again and listen again. Keep redoing it until you feel it is the right one for you. When you get the recording you want, listen to it as often as you wish, focusing on your words, actions, and images, knowing that this personal visualization will improve your concentration and focus and will assist you in positive mental preparation.

Chapter Five

Visualizations for Individual Sports

Ingrid Kristiansen

In 1989, Ingrid Kristiansen held the world records in the Women's marathon (2:21:06), half marathon (1:06:40), and 10,000 meters (30:13 track/30:39 road), and 5,000 meters (14:37). She has been the top woman in women's long-distance running for five years. No runner has ever held such a diversity of world records for such a long time.

We were interested in talking with Ingrid because she has long been an advocate of mental training and has used sport psychology in her training regimen since 1983, beginning with learning relaxation training to supplement her lack of sleep after her son was born. She was one of the first world-class athletes to openly discuss her mental preparation strategies. She began working with Norwegian sport psychologist Willi Railo in 1984, learning to use visualization processes before and during competition. Ingrid's mental attitude about racing, world-class competition, and her own mental preparation is one that is worthy of thoughtful consideration by any athlete, regardless of their sport.

Before a race, how often do you do a visualization?

Before big races like Bislett, Olympics, and one marathon, I would visualize that particular race five to six weeks before . . . and all the things I hoped would happen in the race . . . I do the training almost everyday . . . it's the same with the mental training as it is with your fitness . . . if you feel you are tired, you take a day off . . . this is very important so you don't get over trained . . . also mentally.

When I don't want to do the mental training, I take one or two days off . . . normally I do the training once a day the last four weeks before a big competition.

Do you do the mental training on the day of the race?

If the race is in the evening, yes. But not if the race is in the morning.

Does your heart rate go up?

No. I think it would be very low . . . I am very relaxed . . . I can be coming directly from training, and feel really fresh, come down to Willi, and we start to work, and he can have me almost asleep after five minutes.

Do you always do the visualizations with Willi, or do you use audiotapes?

No, not always . . . I have tapes. . . . If we are closer to a big competition, we see each other more often. Normally, we're together only once a month . . . before a big competition, we may be together four to five times a month.

Also, when I am training hard, I see myself in the race.

So when you are doing your training, you think of the race, and if you're tired, say on the last lap of an interval, you think of the race and push harder.

Yes . . . and I had some tapes some years ago, telling me I was ahead of the big names like Mary (Slaney), Zola (Budd), and all these others . . . so it has helped me . . . I think more people need to start training mentally, instead of training only the rest of the body . . . there are so many people training hard and all, and they ignore the mental . . . I think it's from the neck up that's important.

What kind of tapes might you listen to before a big race?

Before a marathon . . . it is often two and one-half hours . . . it is a really long race, and you have to concentrate for so long . . . in the tape, we don't start the competition (mentally) when we start the race . . . I don't start my competition then . . . if I started concentrating then, I'd be too tired . . . so we start the race with me feeling relaxed, having fun, keep on going . . . feeling nice . . . thinking, "I am well trained . . ." and I do this until about halfway . . . and still think this until about 30K . . . and then when it starts hurting, I say, "I am so well trained . . . this is easy." I get much more aggressive in my thinking, . . . "I am much better trained than Joanie . . . and I have to beat her . . . I am in really good shape . . . and this is easy . . . I have been training for so many hours, and we only have one hour left . . . " and I do this almost until the finish.

What do you say to yourself at the beginning of a race?

I go into myself and say, "This is my race, I do my own race, and I will beat them." Normally, I don't look at the list before a race. I don't care about who is running. I know I have to run my own race . . . so I see them and I say, "Good, it will be a good race." I never ask about who is in the race. I know the good ones will push me.

When do you start your kick?

About 30K. I'm not sure about the pace . . . but I start using my head about 30K. I am the kind of person who starts a little too hard in most of the races, so I try to not start so fast.

How do you relieve the pressure before a big race?

I was really relaxed before the Olympics. I saw all the other girls before the race, and most of them were really nervous. I thought, "Oh, that's good. They're more nervous than me. So this will be fun." When I'm going to a race, I try to say to myself, "This is fun." It's really important to have fun. If you don't have fun anymore, you can't do a good race.

It's very important for me . . . I have a coach that thinks like me . . . he likes it because it's fun . . . and in a training, if I say, "I am tired today, I can't do this," he says, "It's OK; you're the only person who knows your body. So take the day off, and maybe you can do this training tomorrow."

How long did it take you to get over the disappointment from the 1988 Olympics? (She was injured after leading the 10K race and dropped out.)

Maybe one week . . . when we were finished with the race, I was really disappointed . . . when we came back to the hotel, Arve (my husband) said to me, "This is history . . . that's it . . ." I had planned to take a rest this year because I was a little bit tired of training and racing on a high level . . . I want to be in the Olympics in 1992 . . . and I think to be in shape and be one of the best in 1992, you have to take years off where you don't push yourself too much . . . Arve said, "I think you need to go one more year and to prove you're still one of the best," so I decided to race this year (1989).

What was the lesson that you learned in the 1984 Olympics? (Grete Waitz and Ingrid were running in the pack with Joan Benoit Samuelson, and Joan ran off and left them, never to be seen again until the finish line, where she won the gold medal.)

I didn't run my own race; I ran Grete Waitz' race. She is the type of runner who doesn't want to take a chance. She ran conservative and safe, and I did just the same. I can't believe I did that. I am more a person like Joanie . . . try something and if I do it, fine. If I don't get it, I have at least tried.

How long did it take you to get over that?

We came back to the hotel room, Gaute (my son) was standing in the room laughing to me, I said, "OK, I was training for this gold medal, this is my gold and that's it." It took me a day or two. I always try to look to the next time. If I'm winning, if I'm doing a great race, I'm still looking this way (gestures ahead of her) . . . never looking back . . . only forward.

You were talking about the Russian long-distance runners. What have you noticed about their team?

I like the Russians. They are really nice . . . I am good friends with them. One thing I see in the Russian team is that they support each other . . . if there are three or four girls going into the same competition, they say, "If I don't win, it's good that one of the others wins. Maybe next time will be mine." They were supporting each other in the 1986 European championships and the World Championships and in the Olympics. They all took their turns . . . they are like in a team . . . I think it's good . . . I think we have something to learn in this part of the world . . . to help each other. I think that the Russians can more easily live together as competitors. It's more relaxed.

You know you are going to a competition and you want to be the best . . . for sure . . . but the week before, if you're lying around a campus, it's nice to have a nice team around you, instead of fighting each other the week before . . . then you are tired (mentally) before the competition starts.

How do you get that support for yourself?

I feel that I do my best races if I have may family with me, because then I can life as normal as possible. If I stay too long in hotels by myself, I feel that I miss something. I like to live, I call it "normal." Because most of my friends in Norway are people with two or three kids, housewives, or people working as teachers or dentists or doctors . . . for me it's really important to be with people who talk about other things than diet and training.

What advice would you give to young runners coming up?

It's always been better for me to be myself and to feel that I'm doing the right thing. I like to be with people, and it's important for me to be myself, instead of being what someone else thinks I should be. Somebody may like me and somebody may not . . . that's OK . . . I will be myself and that's it.

So (1) be yourself; (2) have balance in your life (running is not the only thing); (3) don't train too hard; (4) don't read about yourself in the newspapers before things happen . . . read after it is over . . . if you read before, you feel the pressure . . . don't use your energy reading it before it happens.

Is there anything else you want to say/advice, etc.?

There are so many women in Norway who want to be the best long-distance runner . . . and they don't think they can do more than the training; can't go to school, can't work, can't have friends, so they think, "I want to be the best, and I have to train twice a day; I can't eat this stuff, and I can't eat that stuff, and I have to go to bed at nine," and they have so much stuff that they "have to" . . . that's their problem . . . it's no fun anymore.

I think the answer is to try to live as "normal" as possible . . . you have to train hard to be one of the best . . . but you don't have to give up everything to be the best . . . it's fine if you are good and you have given things up, but if something happens, you have nothing else. You can't train more than three hours a day . . . and what are you doing the rest of the day? Worrying about the next training? There should be more in life than just racing.

In *The Mental Athlete,* we talked of the seven traits of champions. Ingrid Kristiansen exemplifies these and adds three more. The original seven traits of elite athletes are

1. **Total belief in self** and abilities
2. **Competing to win,** not to place second
3. **Absolute and total concentration and focus** during competition
4. **Practicing visualization and affirmations** for at least a month before a big competition
5. **Analyzing any losses for learning** to improve future performances
6. **Letting go of defeats easily** and **looking ahead** to the future
7. **Never seeing self as a loser** even when one loses

Ingrid's important additional suggestions are

1. **Have fun** in training and competition
2. **Encourage and support your teammates**
3. **Have balance in your life**—have a full and varied life, don't have all your focus on your sport.

Guided Visualizations for Individual Sports Events

All the visualizations in this chapter should be preceded by some type of relaxation process from chapter 3. Any version of relaxation may be used. It is important that the listener be in a very relaxed and receptive state of mind and body as he or she listens to the visualization on audiotape.

At the end of the visualization, readers may want to add the words: Slowly allow the images and feelings to fade . . . coming back to your body sitting in the chair (or lying on the floor/bed, etc.) . . . when I count to three, you may open your eyes, feeling relaxed, awake, and ready for the rest of the day (or evening) . . . one . . . move your feet and hands . . . taking a deep breath . . . letting it out with a sigh . . . two . . . move your neck and shoulders, breathing deeply into your abdomen . . . slowly exhaling . . . feeling relaxed, and awake . . . three . . . open your eyes when you are ready.

Track

Running is 80 percent mental.

Joan Benoit Samuelson
1984 Olympic Gold Medalist
Women's Marathon

Choking in Competition

A number of coaches have approached us with this problem, especially in young, inexperienced runners. The typical statement from the coach is something like, "Bob

---

is outstanding in practice. He runs hard and works hard. Then he gets in a race and freaks out, often losing to runners who have slower PRs than he does. What can I do about it?

Usually when an athlete chokes in competition, he or she is self-sabotaging by worrying about

1. expectations of others and their approval
2. disappointing others by a poor performance
3. all the attention they have received from others—the attention is embarrassing to them (They usually do very well as underdogs.)
4. forgetting the fun they used to have running and racing

If you are an athlete with this problem, you can begin with

1. learning to enjoy competition again and run for the fun of it
2. relaxing your upper body during your race
3. doing body checks to relax tense areas as you run
4. lengthening your stride when you are tiring
5. learning strategies of racing: when to pass, when to surge, when to kick, how to respond to other's advances and passes
6. keeping your mind on the race, your form, your body, and keeping your mind off "how I look," or "what people will think if . . ."
7. keeping contact with the pack or a passer
8. using positive self-talk
9. writing a visualization for yourself for bringing enjoyment back to your running and racing

Are You a Type A Runner?

(This questionnaire, designed by us, was originally printed in an article, "Futile Attraction," by Marlene Cimons in the July, 1988, issue of *Runner's World.*) For those of us who are compulsive and are exercise addicts, it may offer a bit of insight into learning how to relax and enjoy ourselves more.

_____ Are you frequently injured?
_____ Are you frequently burned-out? Do you get sick and tired of training?
_____ Do you feel that you have to run a PR in every race?
_____ Are you disappointed when you run slower than you think you should?
_____ Are you frustrated when you don't meet your goals? Do you then push yourself even harder?
_____ When you do achieve your goals, are you still not satisfied?
_____ Do you run most of your training runs like a race?
_____ If you miss a day of training or don't run twice a day, do you feel as if you're going to lose your edge or that you've somehow "failed"?
_____ Are you running and competing to please or to gain the acceptance of others besides yourself?
_____ Do you eat, breathe, and sleep running?

If you answered yes to four or more of these questions and want to enjoy your training more, try this advice to cope with Type A behavior:

- **Make training fun.** Put some variety into your workouts. Notice and enjoy the weather, the scenery, your breathing—the total experience.
- **Give yourself permission to take a day off.** Sleep in, read the paper, spend time with your friends and family.
- **Run with friends who are not Type A.** Make that workout fun and relaxing.
- **Learn to breathe properly.** Breathing exercises will calm you down and teach you how to be rather than do.
- **Go to races and watch without competing.** Instead, support a friend who is racing.
- **Listen when your coach** and, more importantly, your body tells you to stop, slow down, or reduce your mileage.
- **Allow yourself to rest.** Get at least seven to eight hours of sleep four to five times a week, especially during heavy training periods.
- **Keep sugar and caffeine intake to a minimum,** particularly during heavy training.
- **Stay focused in the present.** Don't dwell on past defeats or obsess about the future.
- **Make sure your life is balanced.** It is important to make time for family, friends, your primary relationship, career, and training—without allowing any one of them to get out of control or be neglected. All parts nourish you and make you a whole person.

Sprints

In writing the visualizations for the sprints and relays, we talked with George Walcott, an assistant coach at the University of Oregon and a former Pac-10 championship sprinter in the 200. George competed for Jamaica in two Pan-Am Games, one World Championship, and numerous international competitions. His help was invaluable in the design of these sprint visualizations.

Guided Visualizations for the 100 Meters

Begin to turn your mind to a time . . . to a race . . . the best race of your life when you felt powerful, and you were in control . . . absolutely right on . . . that time of inner strength . . . running totally within yourself . . . centered and connected . . . running with your heart and soul . . . when your mind and body were totally and fully connected and worked as one . . . let that time come back to you . . . the scene, the sounds, and the feelings . . . when you were clear, centered, and powerful . . . remember the feelings in your body . . . the race . . . let the whole memory come back to you . . . imagine yourself in that scene . . . those powerful feelings of strength, flexibility, clarity . . . running fast and without any apparent effort . . . relive that moment . . . the pride, the confidence, the power . . . allow yourself to think of a word that represents that state of mind, that state of being . . . say that word to yourself . . . feeling the feelings of inner harmony, power, and strength . . .

imagine seeing that word on a big poster in your home . . . in whatever colors you want . . . knowing when you say that word or hear it or see it that all those images and feelings will come back to you . . . of focus, concentration, power, and speed . . . in your mind's eye, look down at your hand and notice that you have a small plastic card about the size of your driver's license in your hand . . . it's an exact image of that poster . . . turning it over and seeing a very good picture of yourself . . . liking what you see . . . with your name embossed under your picture . . . knowing you are fast and powerful and strong in this race . . . turning it again to see the image of the poster, in all the colors . . . imagine taking this card and putting it in a very safe place . . . knowing you can take it out at any time and look at it again to remind you of your greatest performance . . . keeping it in a place where it's safe and secure . . . remembering you have everything within you that you need to be, to do, and to have what you want . . . saying the word to yourself . . . feeling the feelings.

Slowly let those images begin to fade . . . and think of the next race you will be running . . . the next 100-meter race . . . imagine yourself entering into that race with openness, flexibility, and clarity . . . seeing it as an opportunity for growth and change and learning . . . imagine yourself approaching it with excitement and enthusiasm . . . knowing you have what it takes to perform well . . . enabling you to achieve what you want to achieve.

See yourself arriving at the track . . . jogging, warming up, concentrating on being on your toes, lifting your knees high . . . doing your stretching . . . doing your pre-race warm-up . . . your drills, your wind sprints . . . getting excited, psyching yourself up, and maintaining a calm feeling inside . . . excited, yet calm and in control . . . a contained energy . . . getting psyched . . . ready to explode out of the blocks and down the track . . . feeling your energy contained and ready for the race . . . feeling good, feeling psyched up and confident . . . see yourself taking off your warm-ups, doing your last stretches and strides . . . going to the line . . . to the blocks . . . hearing the instructions from the starter . . . getting in your blocks . . . saying your word to yourself . . . feeling the power and strength go through your body . . . waiting for the sound of the gun.

Being ready and alert . . . hearing the gun go off . . . responding instantly to it . . . exploding out of the blocks . . . concentrating, driving, exploding out of the blocks . . . pushing hard and fast . . . totally focused, staying low and driving hard and fast . . . remembering you're a great starter . . . an awesome sprinter.

Feeling good, taking off . . . getting an explosive start in the first ten yards . . . being where you want to be . . . and in the next twenty to thirty meters, relaxing and being totally focused straight ahead . . . feeling good . . . thirty-five to fifty yards, accelerating fast . . . relaxing and driving . . . relax and drive . . . relax and drive . . . focused straight ahead . . . knowing the very best part is coming up . . . you're a great finisher . . . you relax, you drive . . . relax and drive, focusing on the finish line . . . reaching the finish, you lean . . . running through the finish . . . you win!!! . . . slowing down now . . . catching your breath . . . thanking your body for a great job . . . well-done . . . you feel strong, powerful . . . invincible . . . you are very pleased with yourself . . . happy . . . you're exactly where you want to be . . . you've done what you wanted to do . . . thanking your body for all that it gives you . . . its power, strength, and flexibility . . . and you thank your mind for its focus and concentration . . . feeling good about this season, knowing you will make PRs . . . that you will reach your goals.

Slowly let the images fade . . . coming back to your body sitting or lying . . . focusing on your breathing, taking a deep breath . . . letting it out with a sigh . . . remembering your word . . . seeing and feeling yourself as a great sprinter . . . knowing you have what it takes to make it . . . the ability, the mind, the heart to run your best.

When I count to three, you can open your eyes, feeling relaxed, refreshed, and ready for the rest of the day or evening . . . one . . . take a deep breath, moving your hands and feet . . . two . . . stretching your neck and shoulders, taking a deep breath . . . letting it out . . . and three . . . opening your eyes when you're ready.

Guided Visualization for the 200 Meters

(Reader should insert the first paragraph from the 100-meter visualization here.)

Begin to think of the next 200-meter race you will be running . . . being at the track . . . beginning your preparations for the 200 . . . warming up, stretching . . . your usual prerace routine . . . jogging . . . stretches . . . strides . . . concentrating on your form . . . staying up on your toes . . . high knee lift . . . remembering for a moment your strengths . . . your power . . . . speed, your excellent technique . . . efficiency in form . . . your fast finish.

Remind yourself of your affirmations for the start of any of your races . . . "I am alert and ready . . . I have great concentration . . . I have great reaction speed . . . I explode out of the blocks . . . staying low . . . driving powerfully and hard . . . I am a great starter . . . I am an awesome sprinter. . . . My starts are great this season."

Imagine yourself having completed your warm-ups . . . hearing the call for the 200 meters . . . going over to the start . . . taking your sweats off . . . getting in your lane . . . adjusting your blocks . . . everything ready . . . feeling that excitement, that energy . . . that contained energy . . . knowing you are keeping it for the start to transform it into an exploding energy out of the blocks and in the race . . . you're looking forward to this race a lot . . . knowing how good you are in the 200 . . . hearing the instructions from the starter . . . see yourself, feel yourself getting in your blocks . . . getting ready . . . waiting for the sound of the gun . . . when you hear it, you explode and drive out of the blocks . . . staying low . . . driving hard and powerfully . . . feeling good . . . concentrating . . . totally focused . . . loving to run the curve . . . knowing you are a great curve runner . . . concentrating, feeling great . . . propelling off the curve, feeling relaxed, and running hard . . . relaxing and driving, relaxing and driving . . . focusing straight ahead, running your own race . . . great form, high knees, focusing straight down the track . . . feeling good, accelerating faster, relaxing and driving . . . focusing on the finish line . . . leaning forward . . . having a great finish . . . feeling great . . . knowing you've run your best . . . so pleased, so happy, so powerful . . . knowing how much you love running this event . . . thanking your body for what it gives you . . . thanking your mind for its clarity and focus.

See yourself warming down . . . feeling really good . . . satisfied . . . elated . . . ecstatic . . . allow yourself to enjoy that feeling of exhilaration and joy . . . knowing you have done your best and achieved your goal . . . remembering your word . . . and knowing deep inside you have everything you need to be, to do, and to have what you want . . . in your sport . . . in your life . . . having the best races of your life this year . . . continuing to have great starts and great finishes . . . and running well in between . . . thanking your body again for its power, speed, and strength . . . for its good health . . . continuing to take good care of your body and giving it what it wants . . . knowing you are one of the best, if not the best sprinter . . . knowing that you belong here . . . on the teams of your choosing . . . you deserve to be here . . . you are good enough.

Allow the images and feelings to fade . . . knowing you can bring them back at any time . . . when I count to three you can open your eyes, feeling relaxed, refreshed, and ready for the rest of the day or evening . . . one.

400 Meters

The keys to running a fast 400 are to maintain good form and technique and to run with a relaxed body and mind. The 400 is most frequently broken down into four phases, each of 100 meters. In the first 100, the top priority is to get out of the blocks as fast as possible, driving hard from the blocks; the second 100, in the backstretch, is fast and steady, maintaining relaxation of body and mind. The third 100 requires mental toughness, intense relaxation, maintaining of speed around the curve, feeling powerful and comfortable on the curve, accelerating and floating around the curve. The fourth 100 requires the most mental toughness of any of the parts—digging down deep for the extra reserve inside; having strength, power, and determination, an iron will to win and conquer; maintaining form, with knees high, more drive, more power, more relaxation, with superior arm action; being totally relaxed in body and mind, relaxing and driving, focusing on the finish, while accelerating with power and grace.

Guided Visualization for the 400 Meters

(Use the first paragraph of the 100-meters visualization.)

Begin to think of the next 400-meter race you will be running . . . being at the track . . . beginning your preparations for the 400 . . . warming up, stretching . . . your usual prerace routine . . . jogging . . . stretches . . . strides . . . concentrating on your form . . . staying up on your toes . . . high knee lift . . . . remembering for a moment your strengths . . . your power . . . your speed . . . your excellent technique . . . efficiency in form . . . your fast finish.

Remind yourself of your affirmations for the start of any of your races . . . "I am alert and ready . . . I have great concentration . . . I have great reaction speed . . . I explode out of the blocks . . . staying low . . . driving powerfully and hard . . . I am a great starter . . . I am awesome in the 400 meters. . . . My starts are great this season."

Imagine yourself having completed your warm-ups . . . hearing the call for the 400 meters . . . going over to the start . . . taking your sweats off . . . getting in your lane . . . adjusting your blocks . . . everything ready . . . feeling that excitement, that energy . . . that contained energy . . . knowing you are keeping it for the start to transform it into an exploding energy out of the blocks and in the race . . . you're looking forward to this race a lot . . . knowing how good you are in the 400 . . . hearing the instructions from the starter . . . see yourself, feel yourself getting in your blocks . . . getting ready . . . waiting for the sound of the gun . . . when you hear it, you explode and drive out of the blocks . . . staying low . . . driving hard and power-fully . . . feeling good . . . concentrating . . . totally focused . . . loving to run that first curve . . . knowing you are a great curve runner . . . concentrating, feeling strong and powerful . . . propelling off the curve, feeling relaxed, and running hard as you run down the backstretch . . . fully relaxed in body and mind . . . relaxing and driving, relaxing and driving . . . focusing straight ahead, approaching the curve, maintaining your speed . . . loving this particular part of the race . . . feeling yourself propelling around the turn . . . focused and powerful, floating and accelerating . . . running your own race . . . great form, high knees, powerful arm action . . . focusing straight down the track for the last 100 . . . knowing you are almost at the finish . . . digging down deep inside for that extra reserve you know is there for you . . . feel-ing good, accelerating faster, relaxing and driving . . . relaxing your entire body as you run faster and faster . . . a relaxed jaw . . . low shoulders . . . arms and chest relaxed . . . knees high . . . driving and powerful . . . arms pumping hard . . . focusing on the finish line . . . running through the finish . . . leaning forward . . . having a great finish . . . feeling great . . . knowing you've run your best . . . so pleased, so happy, so powerful . . . knowing how much you love running this event.

Thanking your body for what it gives you . . . thanking your mind for its clarity and focus . . . see yourself warming down . . . feeling really good . . . satisfied . . . elated . . . ecstatic . . . allowing yourself to enjoy that feeling of exhilaration and joy . . . knowing you have done your best and achieved your goal . . . remembering your word . . . and knowing deep inside you have everything that you need to be, to do, and to have what you want . . . in your sport . . . in your life . . . having the best races of your life this year . . . continuing to have great starts and great finishes . . . and running well in between . . . thanking your body again for its power, speed, and strength . . . for its good health . . . continuing to take good care of your body and giving it what it wants and needs . . . knowing you are one of the best, if not the best 400-meter runner . . . knowing you belong here . . . on the teams of your choos-ing . . . you deserve to be here . . . you are good enough.

Allow the images and feelings to fade . . . knowing you can bring them back at any time . . . when I count to three, you can open your eyes, feeling relaxed, re-freshed, and ready for the rest of the day or evening . . . one . . . etc. . . .

Relays

The key to successful relays is to get the stick around safely and as efficiently as possible. Three important points in any relay are concentration, the makeup of each relay leg, and the team members being in sync with each other and functioning as a smoothly working and communicating team.

1. Concentration is especially important at two points.
   a. Receiving the baton.
      ■ Stay on your side of the lane.
      ■ Take off when the man is on the check-off marker.
      ■ Receiving arm is away from body and parallel to the ground, with good separation between thumb and forefinger, palm spread as wide as possible to make a good target.
      ■ Listen for the "cue word" from the approaching runner and keeping your hand up in the receiving position until you receive the stick.
   b. Handing off the baton.
      ■ If the receiving runner takes off too soon, tell him or her to slow down so you're still within the zone in handoff.
      ■ Maintain proper arm's length distance between incoming and outgoing runner, so the end of the baton is placed exactly at the top of the outgoing runner's hand.
      ■ After incoming runner hands off, he/she needs to stay in their lane *until all* other runners on opposing teams have safely made their exchanges. This insures no disqualifications occur due to lane infractions.
2. On each leg of the relay, the following are good combinations:
   a. First leg: Usually is the best starter; fastest out of the blocks, powerful, explosive, and a good curve runner.
   b. Second leg: Runner has good speed endurance, powerful, able to handle the stick well; is a good receiver and a good passer; good mental and physical strength; a pure, natural sprinter.
   c. Third leg: Is the best curve runner; fast, smooth, good receiver and passer.
   d. Fourth leg: May be the slowest runner, or maybe not; might be the least effective in handing off the baton; gets the stick and runs; much burden on this leg—should have great concentration, focus, determination, and motivation.
3. All four members must be in sync with each other, concentration and goal wise. The team must be of "one accord" and believe in each other; important to practice together as a team; to support each other; build a "chemistry" together; good rapport and a common focus; a well-oiled machine.

Guided Visualization for a Relay Team's Second and Third Members

Imagine yourself getting ready to run the relay with your team . . . you have already run your own events . . . you feel good today . . . you are warmed up and ready to go for it . . . imagine yourself doing your warm-up routine . . . your stretches, strides . . . practicing the handoffs with your team members . . . all of you in sync with each other . . . all with a common goal . . . you trust each other and feel confidence in your abilities . . . you are the "well-oiled machine" . . . all superb athletes . . . strong, powerful, and fast.

Begin to imagine your leg of the relay . . . concentrating on staying on your side of the lane . . . seeing your team member approach . . . taking off when he or she is on the checkoff marker . . . your arm in perfect position to receive the stick . . . you listen for the cue word and keep your hand up as a perfect target . . . you get the stick, and you are already nearing your top speed . . . loving the feeling of this event . . . so free . . . so fast . . . flying . . . you approach your team member for the handoff . . . he or she sees you approaching . . . you yell the cue word . . . he or she takes off . . . again with hand in perfect position to receive . . . you hand off, perfectly placing the baton in the waiting hand . . . watching your team member begin his or her leg.

Cheering for your buddy . . . seeing him or her hand off, again a perfect execution of the move . . . and your last member flying to the finish . . . winning in record time . . . your concentration, determination, and speed have been outstanding . . . you all jog off together . . . slapping each other on the back . . . enjoying your victory . . . feeling great . . . a real team . . . knowing what it is like to work together to achieve a mutual dream.

Guided Visualization for 800 Meters

See yourself arriving at the track where you will be competing, wearing your uniform and your sweats. As you get out of the car, your mind is on the race. Notice the environment . . . what the weather is like . . . the sun, the clouds . . . whatever you can see. Notice the other runners and feel yourself to be calm, confident, and relaxed . . . really feeling good. You are anticipating running . . . looking forward to your race . . . having a deep, calm feeling inside, knowing that you are very well prepared . . . you have been doing your training and you are ready.

See yourself doing your normal warm-up routine . . . imaging yourself doing your stretches and your warm-up sequence that gets you ready for your race . . . stretches, strides, warm-up jogs. Visualize yourself going through all the motions of your warm-up routine. After you have completed your warm-ups, see yourself taking your sweats off, doing your final stretches . . . your final strides . . . and lining up at the starting line for the 800-meter race you are about to run. Hear the starter giving you the instructions . . . you notice your opponents and you recognize some of them . . . you know their strengths and weaknesses . . . feel yourself to be very relaxed, yet excited and anticipating this race. You can feel the adrenaline flowing in your body, and you are relaxed . . . your muscles are ready to go. You are calm and alert, knowing you will be ready to take off when you hear the gun and you are ready for this race. You have been looking forward to it for a long time.

As you stand at the starting line, you can feel the familiar pounding of your heart . . . that familiar excitement that courses through your body before any race. Know that you are there to run and that you will run very well. You have been anticipating this race and looking forward to it, and you will enjoy it thoroughly. The gun sounds and you take off . . . everyone is racing and jockeying for position . . . the pack settles into a fast comfortable pace, and you have a good position in the pack. Make sure to take your time . . . keeping relaxed and fluid . . . fast and relaxed . . . stay with the people you want to stay with . . . be in the position you want to be in at the beginning of the race. You are watching the other people around you out of the corner of your eye . . . keeping track of where they are . . . knowing you are running a strong, controlled race. Your stride is smooth . . . you are centered and balanced, and you feel comfortable . . . you are enjoying this race very much. You love the feeling of competition . . . coming around the curve . . . you love to lean into the curves . . . feel that power and energy surging through your body.

You are finishing the first lap. You know your strategy . . . you continue to implement this strategy . . . you start surging, moving ahead, passing people . . . you start your kick. It feels as if you're going into overdrive . . . you are picking it up. You feel the intensity in the race . . . you feel the excitement . . . you feel the power in your body . . . you feel the control in your body . . . you are running and running. You are concentrating on this third 200 meters. You relax and run hard, mentally preparing for the final 200 of the race. You get in position . . . this last stretch is important. You are ready and confident. You stride out, passing the 600-meter point. You start the final 200 meters, go into the curve, running fast and relaxed . . . striding, arms pumping powerfully . . . blasting off the final curve into the home stretch. You're a sprinter now . . . moving powerfully down the straight away. You have good form, and your are keeping that form . . . you feel like you're floating . . . very fast . . . you are just flying along, and you are passing the people you want to pass. You can feel the energy surging through your body . . . feel the control and feel the power . . . your legs and your arms are pumping and moving, and you feel good.

You're coming down the final 50 meters, picking it up even more now, and you and your competitor are shoulder to shoulder. You dig deep inside yourself for that extra reserve you have been saving and turn it on. You surge by this last competitor. You maintain your speed and form . . . taking strong, powerful strides, always smooth and confident. You feel your body in perfect control and perfect form striding out and moving away. You look up and see the finish line and tape. You fly toward the line, and you feel the tape hit your chest and know you have won.

A feeling of euphoria and elation passes through your body. You know you have done what you have wanted to do. You know how strong you are, and you have the joy of achieving your goal . . . the satisfaction and the completion of a job well-done . . . you know you are strong mentally and physically, and you have the physical and psychological edge over your opponents. You have done your physical training and mental training, and it has all paid off.

You come to a stand still . . . your sides are heaving . . . you are getting your breath. You have a feeling of complete satisfaction and joy. People are coming up to you and shaking your hand, slapping your back, and they're happy for you too. Hear their voices full of excitement and listen to what they are saying. Having caught your breath, you jog slowly, knowing the taste of victory and savoring it in this special moment of your life . . . this total moment of satisfaction when you have done your best. You thank your body . . . your legs, your lungs, and all your body parts for the excellent way they have helped you and served you. You jog around the track on your victory lap to the applause of your friends and people you don't even know, who've enjoyed watching you race. You have achieved your goal.

Guided Visualization for 1500 Meters

Imagine yourself at the track where you will be competing, wearing your uniform and your sweats. Your mind is on the 1500-meter race. Notice the environment, the weather, the sun, the clouds . . . whatever you can see and feel . . . notice the other runners and feel yourself to be calm, confident, and relaxed . . . feeling great . . . looking forward to running . . . running your best . . . feeling fit and fast . . . loving the feeling of competing and running hard . . . starting well . . . running a good race . . . you are looking forward to your race and have a deep, calm feeling inside, knowing you are very well prepared . . . you have been training hard, and you are ready.

See yourself doing your normal warm-up routine . . . doing your stretches and strides . . . your whole warm-up sequence . . . after completing your warm-up, imagine taking off your sweats, doing your final stretches and strides and lining up at the start . . . hear the starter giving you the instructions . . . you notice your opponents . . . feeling excited, exhilarated, yet calm in your mind . . . ready to run. You feel the adrenaline flowing in your body, and you are relaxed and ready . . . your muscles are ready to go.

You stand at the starting line, feeling the familiar excitement that you feel before every race . . . the gun sounds and you take off . . . running and jostling for position . . . the pack continues to change and move as you run . . . You take your time, staying relaxed and fluid . . . getting in position . . . staying with the people you want to stay with . . . being in the position you want to be in at the beginning of the race . . . someone may bump your shoulder . . . you keep your form and balance . . . watching the other people around you out of the corner of your eye . . . keeping track of where they are.

Your stride is smooth . . . you are centered and balanced and feel comfortable . . . you are enjoying this race very much . . . you love the feeling of competition and feel the power and energy surging through your body as you lean into the curve. On this first lap, you feel yourself floating along easily in complete control, running hard and fast.

You finish the first lap cruising through and feeling very good. Starting on the second lap, you go down the backstretch, knowing your legs are strong . . . you feel their power, striding smoothly . . . you may feel the wind a bit; if you do, you may tuck in behind someone, feeling perfectly comfortable and at ease within your body . . . cruising . . . maintaining a steady, fast pace . . . going around each curve smoothly . . . hearing your time for the 800 you have run so far . . . feeling good about the time . . . if it's fast . . . telling yourself how strong you are and how well you're doing . . . if it's slow . . . picking up your pace and starting to move up . . . encouraging yourself.

On the third lap, you begin to concentrate fully, focusing your mind and taking long, powerful, and smooth strides . . . doing a body check . . . jaw relaxed, neck and shoulders relaxed and low, arms pumping smoothly, hands and forearms relaxed . . . belly and abdomen, expanding easily, flexible in their breathing . . . legs . . . stride length long and powerful, knees coming up as they should . . . perfect form . . . you begin to push the pace . . . digging down inside a little, enjoying this third lap immensely; knowing how to push yourself and to feel good about it . . . knowing running a little faster helps you get another burst of energy. Knowing that other runners are getting tired, you tell yourself you are strong, tough, in control . . . your form is good . . . you are hungry for this race and this win . . . pick it up again, passing, blowing by someone, jockeying for another position in the pack or beginning to make your move if you're ready.

Notice the people around you, making sure you are in the right position that you want to be in, hearing the bell or gun sound for the last lap . . . you shift into another gear . . . accelerating around the curve and into the backstretch . . . flying off the curve . . . pumping, running fast and relaxed . . . coming up on the 200 point, accelerating around the last curve, full steam and power ahead . . . feeling your momentum building . . . into your fastest kick ever . . . you are running in yet another gear, flying along . . . fast, powerful, in control . . . and feeling incredible . . . your body loves the feeling of your arms and legs pumping . . . your lungs pulling in new energy and oxygen to fill your body . . . your body responding to the renewed energy . . . your body working at its best.

Passing the others . . . surging . . . passing whomever you want to pass . . . attacking the final sixty meters . . . feeling yourself sprinting away from them all . . . you are running as fast as you've ever run . . . feeling the energy surging in your body . . . feel the tape on your chest as you burst across the finish line . . . enjoying that inner euphoria of having done your best . . . of feeling good . . . of being in control of your race . . . of winning . . . of a PR.

Stopping . . . breathing heavily . . . catching your breath . . . feeling great as people congratulate you . . . having people pat you on the back, shaking your hand . . . the exhilaration, the relief, the joy you feel when it's over. Slowly again you start to jog, to warm down, to go around the track on your victory lap . . . slowly jogging, feeling a tremendous sense of accomplishment and completion. Listen to the applause . . . wave to your friends and know that you have run one of the best races of your life . . . allowing your body to be flooded with the joy and excitement of the moment . . . knowing you were physically and psychologically prepared. Thank your body . . . your legs, lungs, and all your body parts . . . for the excellent way each helped you and served you. You have achieved your goal.

Let go of the image and feeling now . . . slowly begin to re-enter your present space. Reconnect with your physical world . . . the feel of the chair . . . the relaxation in your body . . . slowly move your toes and fingers . . . become aware of your breathing . . . inhaling deeply . . . exhaling deeply. You feel relaxed and filled with new energy. When you are ready, open your eyes . . . remembering you have inside what you need to be, do and have in your racing and your life.

Guided Visualization for 3000 Meters

It is the day of the race . . . you feel good and are excited about the race . . . you have prepared well . . . taken in a lot of fluids and you feel ready and fit . . . you begin your warm-up routine . . . moving from exercise to exercise . . . stretching . . . moving . . . striding . . . running on the inside of the field . . . feeling good . . . relaxed and confident . . . you are aware of the crowd and the weather, and you are focused on warming your body, concentrating your energy on the race and your strategy . . . allow yourself to move freely . . . feeling your body stretching . . . putting your excitement into energy . . . "I feel good during the race. I feel strong and relaxed. I am confident about my fitness."

You take off your sweats and move toward the start . . . you notice your competition . . . some are familiar . . . you know that you are as good as anyone else racing today . . . you feel confident in your body and in your mind to perform for you . . . you listen to the instructions and find your favorite spot on the line . . . you take a deep breath . . . concentrating . . . focusing . . . relaxing . . . "I believe in myself. I trust my body and my endurance. I am fast and fit." . . . you say your word . . . waiting. . . . The gun sounds and you start out strong . . . energy focused . . . you are ready for this race . . . you feel the other runners around you . . . you know you are strong and fit . . . you run the first lap, feeling strong, powerful, fluid . . . your stride is long and smooth . . . your breathing is easy, and you are aware of your strength . . . you hear your time . . . right on schedule . . . you run the second lap . . . effortless . . . and the third . . . you run lightly . . . smoothly . . . confidently . . . you love to run like this and you feel good . . . you finish the fourth lap . . . you begin to dig deeper into your reserve of energy . . . you are staying with your competition . . . you are right next to them . . . you are focused . . . settling into the smoothness of your stride . . . you pass a few . . . using your power and endurance . . . you begin your mental training now . . . telling yourself of your ability and your training . . . these next two laps are important . . . lap five . . . you are powerful, in control . . . you surge, push . . . running harder, lengthening your stride . . . relaxing your shoulders . . . doing a body check to relax your upper body . . . you go into the sixth lap . . . knowing you are strong . . . and powerful . . . what great endurance you have as you begin to pass others . . . you maintain your pace . . . passing . . . surging . . . you are strong in this sixth lap . . . it is your best one . . . you are mentally tough . . . you have a deep reserve of energy and strength.

You have everything you need . . . you have prepared well . . . physically and mentally . . . you can hear the other runners' heavy breathing . . . they are tired . . . you are powerful . . . you concentrate on your stride . . . racing in control with confidence . . . you begin the seventh lap. . . . You are relaxed and focused . . . feeling good . . . running powerfully . . . getting ready . . . for your kick . . . you are right with the leader . . . concentrating on your breathing and your smooth, easy stride . . . you have plenty of strength left . . . you have prepared well for this race . . . rested well . . . eaten well . . . and you are ready for the last 600 meters . . . you begin to pick it up . . . feeling your power . . . leaning into the curve . . . feeling good . . . running easy . . . lengthening your stride into the last 400 meters . . . hearing the bell or the gun . . . you can feel your opponent getting tired . . . you enjoy racing like this . . . you make your move . . . speeding up . . . passing . . . feeling in control and strong . . . kicking hard . . . you feel the power in your kick as you come into the last turn . . . into yet another gear . . . your body strong . . . arms pumping . . . legs moving smoothly . . . powerfully . . . you widen the distance between you and the competition as you run as fast as you can . . . pushing . . .

sprinting . . . relaxing your upper body . . . relaxing and driving like a sprinter . . . flying down the last 100 meters . . . in front of the crowd on their feet . . . you cross the finish line feeling the joy of winning . . . hearing the cheering of the crowd . . . knowing that you have run one of the best races of your life . . . feeling excitement and exhilaration.

You slow . . . catching your breath . . . easing into a walk . . . allowing yourself to feel all the enthusiasm and pleasure of your success . . . you have reached your goal for this race and you are happy.

You jog to where you left your sweats and put them on . . . thanking your body . . . thanking your legs for their strength and power . . . thanking your lungs . . . thanking your mind for its support and positive focus . . . you smile . . . you feel great . . . you join your teammates . . . relaxed and pleased knowing you have done your best . . . allow yourself to hear their comments and notice what they have to say to say to you and how pleased they are for you . . . enjoy their congratulations . . . you begin your victory lap, waving to your friends . . . you are a winner . . . you have accomplished what you set out to do. . . . Slowly let the picture fade now . . . beginning to float away . . . you come back to your easy, even breathing becoming aware of your present space and the peace of your mind and body . . . feel the room around you and the sounds of your breathing . . . remembering . . . "I am fast and fit. I enjoy racing and pushing my body. I believe in myself. I relax and surrender to the process."

Guided Visualization for 5000 Meters

(This visualization can be used for track or cross-country. If used for 5000 meters on the track, the reader should insert various lap numbers within the text of this visualization. Of the twelve-lap sequence, readers should break the laps down into sections and put some affirmations into each section. For some, the "eight laps and four laps to go" signs might be depressing, and you may need encouragement at those points. Put affirmations and power statements within these sections, plus adding your own affirmations to the strategy and kicking sections.)

Imagine yourself at the track or course where you will be competing, wearing your uniform and your sweats. Your mind is on the 5000-meter race. Notice the environment, the weather, the sun, the clouds . . . whatever you can see and feel . . . notice the other runners and feel yourself to be calm, confident, and relaxed . . . feeling great . . . looking forward to running . . . running your best . . . feeling fit and fast . . . loving the feeling of competing and running hard . . . starting well . . . running a good race . . . you are looking forward to your race and have a deep, calm feeling inside, knowing you are very well prepared . . . you have been training hard, and you are ready.

See yourself doing your normal warm-up routine . . . doing your stretches and strides . . . your whole warm-up sequence . . . after completing your warm-up, imagine taking off your sweats, doing your final stretches and strides and lining up at the start . . . hear the starter giving you the instructions . . . you notice your opponents . . . feeling excited, exhilarated, yet calm in your mind . . . ready to run. You feel the adrenaline flowing in your body, and you are relaxed and ready . . . your muscles are ready to go.

You stand at the starting line, feeling the familiar excitement that you feel before every race . . . the gun sounds, and you take off . . . running and jostling for position . . . the pack continues to change and move as you run on. . . . You take your time, staying relaxed and fluid . . . getting in position . . . staying with the people you want to stay with . . . being in the position you want to be in at the beginning of the race . . . someone may bump your shoulder . . . you keep your form and balance . . . watching the other people around you out of the corner of your eye . . . keeping track of where they are.

Your stride is smooth . . . you are centered and balanced and feel comfortable . . . you are enjoying this race very much . . . you love the feeling of competition, and you feel the power and energy surging through your body as you continue to run effortlessly . . . you feel yourself floating along easily in complete control.

Your mind is on your race . . . your form . . . the runners around you . . . you speed along, feeling strong and powerful, enjoying the race, approaching the first mile, you hear your first mile time . . . so quickly the miles come up . . . you are right on schedule . . . you begin to push a littler harder . . . knowing this second mile is important . . . focusing on your form, your technique, your breathing . . . you begin to surge . . . passing a few people, getting into better position . . . surging, passing, keeping in contact with the pack, if there is one.

You pass the two-mile mark . . . hearing your time . . . you adjust accordingly . . . according to your plan and strategy . . . you feel your legs under you pumping powerfully, using your arms down as you pump and begin to slowly pick up your pace . . . knowing this is an important mile . . . keeping your focus and concentration . . . surging, passing . . . thanking your body for its strength, power, and ability . . . thanking your lungs for feeding your arms and legs with oxygen . . . you run on . . . enjoying and savoring this part of the race . . . enjoying the competition . . . relaxing your jaw and your upper body . . . breathing deeply into your abdomen . . . your stride is long and sure . . . you begin to pick it up again, the last 800 . . . reaching down deep inside yourself for the rest of your reserve . . . into another gear . . . you are to the last 400, and you really begin to kick hard . . . telling yourself what a great kick you have . . . passing more people . . . kicking . . . relaxing . . . driving to the finish . . . you sprint through the finish line . . . hearing the cheers of the crowd . . . feeling the joy and exhilaration of winning . . . of running a PR . . . you slow, catching your breath, your sides heaving . . . aah . . . air . . . oxygen . . . you begin to jog slowly . . . hearing the congratulations of your teammates and your friends . . . you thank your body for everything it has given you . . . promising to be nice to it and to let it rest soon . . . you have achieved your goal.

Slowly let the images fade . . . coming back to your body sitting in the chair, etc.

Guided Visualization for the 10K (Road Race or Cross-Country)

See yourself arriving at the race area. See the starting line. . . . Notice the crowds of people and hear them talking among themselves . . . seeing and hearing all the sights and sounds of a festive 10K race . . . the colorful T-shirts, the fun runners, the serious competitors. Feel the nervousness in your gut . . . that old familiar feeling . . . and know that it is your normal preoccupation with a race . . . remembering that the minute you start, all the feelings of nervousness disappear. It is all part of the prerace psyching you do for yourself while standing in the line for your last pit stop.

As you start your warm-up routine . . . your stretching . . . whatever routine you do to warm up, take pleasure in those moments in your life that you enjoy and remember with fondness . . . all the times you reached your goal and did your best. . . . Imagine yourself doing your strides . . . the strong, powerful movements of your legs stretching out . . . your body feels good . . . it feels strong; both your mind and body are anticipating this race . . . you are looking forward to it. Even though you get nervous, you know how good it feels to run hard and how good you feel at the end . . . that sense of euphoria and feeling of accomplishment . . . you know that it is always worth it . . . the nervousness is just part of the game and part of the way you play . . . you acknowledge it and let it go . . . slide away.

You are in your favorite running clothes, taking off your warm-ups; getting ready to start the race . . . you are completely focused within now, and you are taking your last few strides . . . stretching out . . . feeling your muscles warm and supple in your body. Take your place at the starting line . . . hear the instructions from the starter . . . hear the sound of the gun.

You take off. You are familiar with the course . . . you have seen the course before . . . feel all the people around you . . . bumping, breathing, some still talking . . . you know some of them . . . you have your eye out for certain runners . . . you know who they are . . . you know what your strategy is . . . feel your body moving easily. Your body is like something that has been cooped up in a cage and is now being let free . . . your body is free to run.

The first mile always feels so good . . . the adrenaline is pumping . . . you have been looking forward to this race . . . you have trained hard . . . you are in great physical shape . . . you are ready. Imagine yourself on the course . . . focusing on your form, your body, your competitors . . . you are in perfect rhythm and sync with your environment . . . feel the sun or the wind, or perhaps, a little rain on your body . . . the physical sensations of the weather on your body feel good and safe . . . feel the breeze on your face . . . feel your body working, holding its form, running strong . . . and say a few of your affirmations to yourself . . . "I feel good; I am strong; I am relaxed; I am on pace; I am running very well and within myself."

When you reach the first mile mark and hear the time, what is it? Are you on pace? Are you a little fast? What are you telling yourself? . . . Imagine yourself running the goal pace you have set for yourself . . . feeling comfortable . . . you can feel the pavement under your feet, the wind in your face . . . your body is warmed up now and feels good. You are maintaining a very comfortable pace. You notice the people around you; you then focus on your form and your breathing . . . steady, rhythmic . . . feeling in complete control of yourself . . . notice where you are in the course . . . you know this course well. Feel yourself running powerfully and in control.

You reach the two-mile mark . . . you check your time . . . right on schedule . . . your pace is good and you keep it up, faintly noticing familiar parts of the course going by . . . you know where you are . . . the three-mile mark is coming up soon. You pass it, hearing your time again . . . check your pace and how you are doing . . . do you need to pick it up? You know that when you change the pace, you feel better . . . it gives you a renewed burst of energy . . . as fartlek always does. You surge and stabilize, surge and stabilize. . . . You notice that the four-mile mark is just ahead . . . that was quick . . . thank your body for the fine job it is doing . . . your body is in good shape and it serves you well.

Four miles is where the race begins for you . . . it is where you start using your strategy. See yourself passing the four-mile mark; you hear your time read, and you make adjustments accordingly. If you are off your pace and slow, you start to pick it up . . . you know your body is ready . . . if there is pain from exertion, you welcome that pain like an old friend . . . it is all part of the game. If you start any negative self-talk, merely say, " Aah, hello . . . here we go again . . . I hear you so you can go away now . . . this is a special race for me and I am going to dig deep down inside myself and push myself hard . . . I am doing well and I will run the race I want to run. I will give you what you want later . . . later you can relax and take some time off . . . if you come through for me now, I promise you, I will reward you later . . . water . . . a coke . . . a soak in the hot tub . . . a massage . . . anything you want . . . come through for me now . . . and thank you." You pick up the pace . . . if you feel a little tiredness in your body, acknowledge it and turn your concentration to your breathing. You might say to your body, "I know you're feeling some of this . . . and I know you are strong, well-conditioned, and you have been training very well . . . I know you will come through for me." Reassure your body and bring your focus back to your form and your breathing.

Imagine energy breathed in and tiredness breathed out. On the inhale, feel the energy coming into your body; on the exhale, feel the tiredness leaving your body. All that new oxygen is going to your muscles to provide them with strength and new energy . . . "I am strong; I am running well; I am running in complete control and within myself; My body is well-conditioned; I feel good." Say your affirmations to yourself.

Your shoulders are relaxed; your body is centered; your legs are lifting with your knees high; your form is good.

Some runners are moving up on you. If they begin to pass you, pick it up and stay with them . . . you don't let them get by . . . you know they will eventually tire . . . you know you are playing a waiting game . . . a psyching game . . . you know you are just as strong as they are. When they least expect it . . . you pull ahead . . . you surge for maybe sixty yards, not looking back, just surging ahead . . . you know you can leave them far behind . . . you have broken their concentration and focus. They will not pass you again. You feel the renewal of energy and exhilaration.

You see another runner ahead of you . . . you quietly move up . . . then put on another surge . . . passing him or her so quickly he or she is taken by surprise . . . you know that you will stay ahead of him or her also. After the surging, you feel your body relax again . . . you hear the five-mile time . . . another quick mile. Your time is good and you know there is only a little over a mile to go.

You feel the excitement in your body . . . another rush of adrenaline . . . this is it
. . . you do a body check, relaxing your upper body . . . pick up the pace again . . .
notice your breathing . . . relax your shoulders . . . lengthening your stride . . .
another runner ahead. You surge again . . . maintaining a strong pace . . . passing
and going ahead. You know there are only couple of minutes left, and you begin
your kick . . . you see the finish line . . . you begin to hear the crowd . . . you are
surging, kicking . . . in perfect control . . . you see the last opponent in front of you
. . . you surge again . . . just as you pass your opponent, you cross the finish line
. . . you have succeeded . . . you hear your time . . . you know you have achieved
your goal . . . you have run one of the best races of your life!

You feel euphoric, happy, tired, and content. You have done your best . . . hands
on your hips . . . gasping for breath . . . breathing hard, you tell yourself . . . "You
did it!!! . . . thank you, legs, lungs, arms . . . thank you . . . thank you, mind." You
walk . . . start jogging for your warm-down . . . feeling happy, knowing that you
have run your best . . . a feeling of accomplishment and completion . . . all the
mental and physical training you have done has culminated in this moment . . .
knowing you have done your best . . . thanking yourself and your body . . . knowing
you can do it again, both physically and mentally, anytime you wish.

Guided Visualization for a Marathon

It is the beginning of a marathon. There are balloons and banners, colors and noise.
You are standing in a crowd of runners. You can hear them talking to each other,
and you can smell their presence and excitement. Some people are yelling, smiling,
talking, and some are silent. You stretch, feeling the strength, the readiness in your
muscles. It is a cloudy day, cool with a slight breeze that moves your hair and makes
a noise in the trees by the side of the road. You feel the excitement in your stomach.
You take several deep breaths and look down at your feet. It is quiet for a moment
. . . the gun goes off . . . and everyone starts moving.

Your feet begin feeling the hardness of the pavement as they strike, and someone
bumps you as they pass by. Be aware of your feelings as two or three more runners
pass you, finding their own pace. You know you have twenty-six miles to go, and
you are aware of your goal. Notice how your body feels and what your words are to
yourself as you pass the one-mile mark and become aware of your time. Are you on
schedule? Have you gone out too fast?

You can feel the wind against your chest as you find your rhythm and begin to
move out of the crowd. It is cooling, or is it pushing at you, slowing you down? You
pass someone and then another as you reach six miles. Be aware of your breathing.
Are you sweating yet? How do your legs feel? Just notice and then let go of your
thoughts. Come back to your breathing as you continue along the road as it turns and
becomes rougher. There are trees all along the sides of the road now, their branches
mingling over your head. Feel the pebbles of the rough road under your feet.

You are running alone now, for the moment no one is next to you . . . mile after
mile, the world is yours . . . you feel strong and in control, and you notice there is
no breeze now . . . just a stillness and peace as you move smoothly along nearing the

ten-mile mark. You run on . . . your body running on its own . . . you pass thirteen miles, then fifteen . . . the time and the miles are flying by.

The road turns again and your body leans. How does it feel? You can hear footsteps behind you and voices in the quiet. What are they saying . . . what are you saying to yourself as runners begin to catch you? Is there a tightness or fatigue anywhere? Begin to say your affirmations slowly and in rhythm with your stride and breathing . . . "I am strong. I feel good." You pass the eighteen-mile mark, thinking of all the training runs you have done of eighteen miles . . . a piece of cake . . . you are strong and feeling good . . . just another two miles and the real race will begin.

You run up a small incline, out of the trees and onto a blacktop road feeling stronger and keeping your form. The wind is at your back, and the sun has briefly broken through the clouds. Notice your response to the warmth on your shoulders and the glare from the road. Your legs are still moving smoothly, powerfully . . . thank them . . . thank them for the work they are doing . . . thank them for their strength. You are so well-conditioned and trained.

Your breathing is even as you approach the final six miles and the twenty-mile mark. . . . This is the most challenging part of the race . . . the last 10K . . . focus on your form. Notice how strong you are and how your body feels. Say your affirmations again . . . knowing you are close to the end. Only a 10K to go . . . you focus on your form . . . thanking your body for what it is giving you . . . promising it whatever it wants after the race . . . water . . . a massage . . . a soak in the hot tub . . . thanking it for its strength and fitness . . . for all the miles of training . . . "I am mentally tough . . . I am doing well . . . I have trained hard for this race . . . I am enjoying myself . . . Good job!" . . . twenty-two miles . . . you push on, relaxing your jaw, lowering your shoulders . . . breathing deeply into your belly . . . imagining energy coming into your legs from the earth . . . golden energy to lift your body and spirits . . . your knees lifting . . . being lifted by wires held by some giant puppeteer . . . relaxing your upper body . . . chest . . . neck . . . lengthening your stride . . . twenty-four miles . . . not far to go now . . . you will make it and run well . . . "I am doing great . . . I use the energy of the crowd to push me along" . . . you see a giant hand pushing you from behind . . . great energy . . . power.

The crowds along the course are bigger now . . . there is music. . . . Are you smiling? The sweat rolls slowly from your eyebrow as you lengthen your stride, passing three runners . . . twenty-five miles . . . you begin your kick . . . passing people . . . "a half mile to go" someone shouts . . . you kick harder . . . digging deep inside yourself for the reserve you know is there . . . you can see the finish line banner now as your shoulders relax and you become comfortable with your powerful, striding form. Your breath is coming faster, and you hear people laughing and shouting. Your feet reach the end . . . you fly over the finish line . . . seeing the finish line under your shoes . . . you push the button on your watch and slow your steps with a deep sigh . . . you catch your breath.

You feel fantastic, euphoric . . . you are floating . . . your legs feel that wonderful tiredness of a good, hard effort . . . you are smiling . . . you breathe deeply as you walk slowly through the chute feeling exhilaration and relief . . . hands on your hips. . . . It was a good run . . . a good race . . . you were strong. You remember your affirmations and relax. Someone speaks to you . . . you smile. . . . Notice the peace surrounding you and your sense of accomplishment. Listen to the music and the announcer as more runners cross the finish line.

The crowds begin to spread out, taking their colors, smells, and sounds with them. You are cooling down . . . your legs relaxing . . . breathing becomes normal. . . . What are you saying to yourself? . . . You ran well . . . and you finished well . . . thank your body and your mind for being there for you . . . a job well-done. . . . Thank your body for its strength and power, its speed and its health. Give yourself permission to rest, knowing that anytime you aim at a goal, you can feel it, see it in your mind's eye, and eventually, have it in reality.

Guided Visualization for the Steeplechase (3000 meters)

(This visualization was written with helpful hints from Mike Manley, a coach and former Olympian in the steeplechase from Eugene, Oregon.)

Imagine yourself arriving at the track to run your race. You begin to do your warm-up routine, jogging, stretching, drills—whatever you do to physically prepare yourself for your race. You finish your warm-up and hear the announcer call for the steeplechase. You report to the start, do any additional stretches and strides and take off your sweats, getting ready for the race. You hear the instructions of the starter and line up. In those last thirty seconds or so, you feel excited and determined . . . you take two or three deep abdominal breaths to relax and calm yourself and to reoxygenate your body . . . feeling ready for this race.

You line up, get ready, set, and the gun goes off . . . you feel good, and you concentrate on staying clear of the other runners, staying to the side or back, concentrating on your form, clearly seeing each hurdle as you approach it, getting a good foot plant, clearing the barriers with efficiency, getting a leg down underneath your center of gravity . . . feeling yourself coming off each barrier, running smoothly . . . on each barrier, you approach, clear easily and with good form, and come off running.

On the water jump, you come down having your trail leg coming through, just another running motion . . . a continuation of the running motion and momentum you are building . . . feeling like one large step . . . jumping across the puddle.

On a hurdle, if your form somehow fails, or is not perfect, you get right back in it . . . you may sink a little, but you recover quickly to pick up the pace again . . . running tall . . . putting any small error quickly behind you . . . accepting any obstacle and letting go of it to recover your form and your enthusiasm . . . you are ready and able to easily overcome any mistake in technique that you might make . . . always returning to running tall.

Each lap of the seven and one-half laps just ticks by; for the first 3 to 4 laps, you run easily, relaxed, and comfortable . . . finding your stride and your own rhythm . . . enjoying the race . . . on lap five and six you begin to push, asking your body to be there for you . . . knowing you have the mental strength and toughness to stay with it . . . you are easily able to stay in the race at all times . . . if you need to gut it out, you do it with power and grace.

On each lap you stay mentally in the present . . . telling yourself you are strong, powerful, and centered . . . mentally and physically tough . . . that you have great concentration on barriers and you come off each hurdle really well.

When the time comes to make your move . . . you stay in the present, relaxing, making a strong move . . . running within yourself . . . running tall . . . running fast . . . taking each hurdle smoothly, your hips underneath you . . . with 500 to go, you know you're competitive . . . you stay in contact with the group and the leaders . . . and coming off the last water jump, you are strong, running well, pumping your arms powerfully . . . flying off the curve . . . approaching the final hurdle, your momentum building . . . you are sprinting as hard as you can, eyeballing the hurdle and flying over it smoothly with grace and power, running in complete strides as you land with perfect form past the hurdle . . . you sprint to the finish, picking off people . . . knowing no one can catch you . . . you go through the finish, feeling the excitement and power of a great race . . . slowing down, beginning to catch your breath . . . thanking your body for its gifts and its performance . . . thanking your mind for its toughness.

Slowly begin to let go of the images and feelings; coming back to your body sitting in the chair . . . when I count to three, you may open your eyes, feeling refreshed, relaxed, and ready for the rest of the day or evening . . . one . . .

Guided Visualization for 400 Intermediate Hurdles

After arriving at the track and doing your warm-up routine, imagine yourself standing at your blocks, listening to the instructions of the starter . . . you are excited, yet relaxed . . . feeling the familiar feelings of nervousness that are really excitement and exhilaration . . . you take two or three deep abdominal breaths, relaxing yourself, and getting you ready . . . oxygenating your blood and your lungs . . . you do your familiar routine of getting in your blocks, taking your time . . . savoring the moment . . . you are in position . . . hearing the instructions, waiting for the sound of the gun, your mind a blank.

The gun roars and you take off . . . you feel good, you've had a good start . . . you approach the first hurdle in perfect position, your lead leg going over smoothly, powerfully, your steps perfect . . . you love running the curve . . . you soar over the next hurdle . . . feeling at ease and in perfect harmony with your environment . . . your steps again perfect . . . the third hurdle is also easy . . . all so easy . . . so fast . . . so enjoyable . . . you are running in great form, very relaxed, smooth, and powerful . . . the fourth and the fifth feel great . . . again you notice how much you enjoy running the curves in this event . . . the sixth hurdle you clear, digging down deep into yourself for that extra power.

Your steps still perfect, your form flawless . . . you're over the hump now . . . a piece of cake . . . your focus still on the approaching hurdle . . . the seventh hurdle on the curve, beautifully cleared . . . the eighth hurdle is your best one . . . you are really flying now . . . you are fast and pushing off perfectly . . . the ninth is easy, pushing off, keeping your speed . . . the tenth, and your stride is smooth and powerful . . . you sprint to the finish . . . passing people . . . relaxed, fast, smooth . . . leaning at the finish for your finest race ever . . . thanking your body for its power, grace, and speed . . . you lean over catching your breath . . . slowly beginning to jog, feeling the excitement, exhilaration, and joy of doing your best.

Slowly begin to let the images and feelings fade, coming back to your body sitting in the chair . . . when I count to three, you may open your eyes, feeling relaxed, refreshed, and ready for the rest of the day . . . one . . .

110 High Hurdles

Items to include in a 110 high hurdles race visualization:

1. Strong, powerful, fast start from the blocks.
2. Consistent number of steps to the first hurdle.
3. Driving arms forward.
4. Same lead leg over each hurdle.
5. Attack the hurdles.
6. Keep upper body down over each hurdle.
7. Strong sprint at the finish.
8. Leaning hard over the line.

Race Walking

Items to include in a race walk visualization are:

1. Keep shoulders low.
2. Get a powering force from arms.
3. Pump arms powerfully.
4. Extend form from back . . . push off from back toe.
5. For a longer and powerful stride . . . be fluid in hip movement, without jerking.
6. Keep head upright.
7. Elbows graze top of hips—"keep elbows down."
8. Fast turnover and longest stride you can get.
9. "I am fit, fast, and fluid."

In race walking, the same psychological factors are present as in long-distance running. Goal times, endurance, and muscle tiredness may be addressed. Race walkers can take the 5,000 and 10,000 meter running visualizations and adapt them to walking, using the language of race walking and specific affirmations relevant to their needs. Both form and psychological factors should be included.

Field Events

Guided Visualization for the High Jump

(This visualization was written by one of our clients. It is here as a sample of what might be written for a high jumper. For each jumper, the number of steps and push off foot will differ. The reader can use this as an example and adapt it for personal use.)

You have been warming up . . . doing your entire warm-up routine . . . you are getting ready for the competition . . . you have stood where your approach is, seeing yourself in slow motion going over the bar as you wish . . . you feel easy and light . . . you imagine yourself beginning your approach . . . letting your body do it . . . letting your mind go.

You enjoy this mental preparation of seeing it all happen in your mind before you jump . . . you are lost in the reverie of perfect jumping . . . feeling the adrenaline surge . . . focusing the energy into your legs . . . into your jump . . . internally focused on your event.

You hear your name called . . . it is time for you to jump . . . you walk up to the bar slowly . . . you take your body through in slow motion what you want to do in your jump . . . planting your foot in the take-off area . . . bringing your arms through . . . with the right higher than the left . . . driving your knee up as high as you can . . . feeling your body rising up, head vertical, back straight . . . right knee high . . . left leg extending and carrying up . . . visualizing the feeling of being airborne . . . traveling upward . . . reaching the peak . . . your head back . . . hips high.

As you drop your knee . . . slapping your right leg with your hand . . . you slowly walk back tracing your approach to the starting point.

You take off your T-shirt . . . turn around, standing at the first step of your approach . . . telling your body . . . ''These are the things I want you to do . . . it is easy to do.'' . . . and you picture your entire sequence from start to finish.

Then you begin your approach . . . three steps backward with right foot . . . two-step jog into your approach . . . take a minute to relax . . . bring up your concentration . . . blocking out everything else but the runway . . . focusing internally . . . weight on the right foot, left foot slightly in front . . . weight on left foot . . . right foot back . . . rock back . . . two-step jog in . . . setting your rhythm . . . feeling the rhythm of the approach in your body . . . on your fifth step, landing with your right foot . . . feeling the initiation of your turn . . . easy, relaxed . . . legs and arms moving quickly . . . floating . . . moving through the turn, beginning to accelerate . . . lean inward toward the left . . . fluid . . . easy . . . on the eleventh step on right . . . right arm is back . . . left forward . . . accelerate into the plant . . . hips forward, feeling very dynamic . . . plant left foot . . . right arm is low . . . right leg pushes off . . . both arms rise up . . . right arm nearly fully extended . . . your head vertical . . . your back straight . . . right knee driving very high . . . left leg fully extended . . . rising upward . . . feeling your head and back rising . . . your eyes picking up the sight of the bar as it moves down and you move up . . . you are relaxed and very aware . . . you reach the top of the jump . . . your head lays back easily . . . hips continue to rise . . . knee stays high . . . both legs bent . . . feel yourself soaring . . . your hips cross over the bar . . . you sense the bar nearing the calves of your legs . . . your hips drop, your legs extend . . . you somersault . . . you made it!!!!

You feel good . . . you raise your arms in a victory *V* . . . thanking your body and your mind for working together . . . your focus and awareness have been internal and perfect . . . you love the feeling of flying through the air . . . the feeling of freedom . . . lightness . . . soaring . . . the exhilaration of flying . . .

Guided Visualization for the Long Jump/Triple Jump

(This visualization was written from the suggestions and comments of Randy Huntington, coach of 1988 Olympic silver medalist Mike Powell. The visualization can be used for both the long jump and the triple jump. The only difference is on the last three steps . . . for the long jump, the sequence is "push, pull, plant," while in the triple jump, the sequence is merely "plant.")

Imagine yourself arriving at the track for your competition. You have been warming up . . . doing your entire warm-up routine . . . you are getting ready for the competition . . . you have stood where your approach is, seeing yourself in slow motion going through all the motions exactly as you want them to be . . . you feel easy and light . . . you imagine yourself beginning your approach . . . letting your body do it . . . letting your mind go.

You enjoy this mental preparation of seeing it all happen in your mind before you jump . . . you are lost in the reverie of perfect jumping . . . feeling the adrenaline surge . . . focusing the energy into your legs . . . into your jump . . . internally focused on your event.

You hear your name called . . . it is time for you to jump . . . you walk up to the runway slowly . . . you take your body through in slow motion what you want to do in your jump . . . all in your mind.

You arrive at the runway . . . as you focus down the runway, you imagine you are now on stage, doing your walk, jog . . . the only thing that exists in your awareness is the runway . . . like running down a tunnel with tunnel vision. . . . You begin your approach . . . you start slowly, accelerating . . . building your acceleration as you go . . . with the body lean . . . your head in line with your body . . . your eyes focusing fifteen feet ahead of you on the runway . . . running fast.

Slowly, you begin to bring your head up, body up, approximating an upright position . . . your focal point slowly rising . . . you are close now to the top speed you will have on the runway . . . and you begin thinking about your thigh drive downward . . . your foot dorsiflexed at the top of its movement . . . and an active foot plant.

About five to seven strides out, you look at the board and visually adjust . . . your thigh drives and plantar flexions are very aggressive now . . . you maintain the range of motion in your stride, while you are driving downward hard with the thigh.

In the last three steps, you push, pull, plant . . . (or drive, pull, plant/pull, pull, plant) . . . you have very aggressive knee and arm drive . . . you feel the explosion of the take-off leg and . . .

Suddenly, you are airborne . . . you soar through the air . . . hanging as long as possible . . . fully extended . . . flying . . . you love this part the best . . . the hanging in the air . . . holding that position as long as you can . . . holding, holding, holding . . . now your knees come to your chest in preparation for landing . . . you extend your legs and your arms move forward . . . your arms overhead, your upper body and knees meeting . . . arms driving down to keep your legs up, you begin to land . . .

letting the pit come to you . . . your momentum carries you forward, and you land in the pit . . . knowing you have jumped farther than ever before . . . the crowd is on its feet, cheering for you . . . for they know what you have done . . . and you know also.

Allow yourself to experience and savor this moment of history . . . this power and grace . . . the excitement in your body and the joy in your soul . . . a truly magnificent accomplishment . . . thanking your body for all it has given you . . . and your mind for helping you to achieve your greatest goal.

Pole Vault

In 1988 and 1989, the top American vaulter was Kory Tarpenning. In an interview with the *Eugene Register Guard* on June 15, 1989, he discussed his attitude about competing. In 1988 in the USA/Mobil National Track and Field Championships, not all the top U.S. vaulters showed up. "I got there and I thought, 'Well, nobody's here; I could win this.' And I started thinking that way, and then I did win."

"I think I learned how to win last year. There's a difference in going out there to compete to be one of the top two or three athletes in the competition, meet after meet, and there's a difference in going out there and winning."

"I think that's the biggest difference I have now as opposed to two years ago. I'm not so intimidated by the bigger name athletes who have reached that level before me. I used to have the attitude that I wanted to compete well and be up there, but until last year, I didn't have the attitude that I wanted to go into those big competitions and *win*."

"The biggest factor is believing that you can do it. Before I always wanted to be in the top three or four, and I believed I had the ability to do that, and that's where I always ended up. I was one of the top guys, but never the winner. It was like going on to the next step of confidence and belief in yourself, and that's the attitude I have nowadays."

We believe that too many of our American competitors want to be in the top three of their event—and they don't make that leap of faith and belief in themselves that will put them in the number one position. Kory's story is a good one for aspiring athletes to remember when setting their goals—go for the win instead of settling for second or third.

Guided Visualization for the Pole Vault

(This visualization was written with the help of Jay Davis, an excellent vaulter from the University of Oregon.)

Imagine yourself at the end of the runway . . . you have done all your warm-up stretches, your warm-up routine, and jumps . . . this is your first scoring jump of the competition . . . let your mind relax . . . focusing within your body . . . and on the runway . . . narrowing your concentration and your focus . . . focusing on yourself . . . your body, the pole, the runway . . . doing your routine for starting . . . being centered, focused . . . begin your sprint with an intention of gaining speed . . . with quick and powerful strides . . . feeling the rhythmic buildup . . . going faster and faster . . . dynamic . . . fast . . . powerful strides . . . your run is controlled and fast moving . . . faster and faster . . . then transferring the speed, power, and velocity gained into the proper and perfect pole plant . . . and positioning the pole for takeoff . . . feeling the pattern . . . feeling the timing . . . knowing the pole has stored all the energy from your powerful approach . . . feeling your shoulders square, hips square at takeoff . . . feeling the transfer of the energy propelling you . . . the pole driving up and out in front of you, keeping a high, tall plant . . . extending your top arm to its maximum length . . . using your other arm as a stabilizer to keep your body in line . . . feeling the lift . . . your chest feeling the compelling, driving force . . . getting full extension out of your hips and legs . . . gaining maximum power at take-off . . . lifting off your toes . . . allowing the energy to lift you powerfully off the ground.

You feel your arms moving back into the correct position, maintaining the force of your top arm . . . feeling the minute hesitation and pushing the pole out in front of you, using the pivotal points through your shoulders . . . you feel and enjoy the elating sensation of moving forward and up . . . feeling the pole store all of your energy now . . . your force allowing the knee drive to complement to pole . . . moving forward, putting your body into a position of parallel closeness, the pole rolling forward . . . your arms moving to your legs . . . trusting your body to become as close and as one with the pole . . . beginning by extending the feet backward over the runway, feeling the pole begin to lift, creating the sensation of your feet moving forward and up, your hips moving in next to the pole, hands near your knees, top arm still straight; bottom arm, allowing the closeness, guiding you with the pole . . . your hips extend into your hands . . . your shoulders dropping . . . chest and hips rotating around the pole . . . the excitement and power of allowing yourself to surrender and become one with the pole . . . letting go of any fear . . . feeling safe and secure . . . trusting your body totally and completely.

Feeling the familiar stiffening of your legs, your buttocks tight, and the positioning of your body and the pole as one . . . your torso controlled and rigid, the feeling of becoming a human projectile off of the pole's energy with your arms guiding your body . . . feeling the power that the energy from the pole has given you and allowing your arms to maintain the speed, power, and rhythm you need for maximum height.

Feel yourself drifting through the air, over the bar, curving your body at the pinnacle of height, around the bar . . . allowing your chest and arms to roll over the bar . . . your body moving freely and safely away from the bar as you begin your gradual descent into the pit.

Feel your body hitting the firmness of the pads . . . experiencing the elation of a great jump . . . feeling happy and excited with your effort . . . hearing the crowd cheering and clapping . . . allow yourself to think of a word that will represent this feeling of power and control . . . this excellent jump . . . and say it over to yourself . . . knowing you can recall it at any time to bring back these powerful images and feelings.

Thank your body for its power and grace . . . and it health and fitness . . . knowing that you will take care of it and nourish it.

Guided Visualization for the Javelin

(This visualization was written with the help of Sally Harmon, a former NCAA Champion, three-time All American, and the women's throw coach at the University of Oregon. She is also the TAC National Women's Javelin Coordinator.)

Allow the pictures, feelings, and sounds to come as you begin to experience yourself on the field . . . you are beginning your warm-up routine . . . as you stretch and move, be aware of the environment . . . the weather . . . the colors . . . the sounds of the crowd . . . feel the grass soft under your shoes . . . feel your body readying itself for your big performance . . . you feel good . . . relaxed . . . easy . . . ready . . . go through your whole warm-up routine . . . stretching . . . bending . . . moving . . . staying centered and focused . . . you know you are strong and powerful . . . you know you are ready for this competition . . . you have worked hard . . . trained hard . . . and you are the best . . . you know you can win.

You take off your sweats . . . feeling good and centered . . . you are focused and relaxed as you move toward the runway . . . you pick up your javelin . . . you feel the javelin in your hand . . . an extension of yourself . . . you feel good about today . . . you take a few practice jogs . . . getting ready . . . you take your place on the runway . . . beginning your run . . . feeling your body relaxed . . . fluid . . . well synchronized . . . you run with your javelin by your ear . . . with a low center of gravity . . . linear steps . . . progressively faster and faster . . . controlled and building up power . . . focusing forward . . . beginning the first of your crossovers . . . drawing the javelin back as you move into your first crossover . . . the tip of the javelin by your eye . . . your throwing arm extended behind you, with your palm facing upward above the should level . . . your other arm, rhythmically balancing in coordination with your cross-step, stabilizing your upper body in a relaxed and fluid movement . . . the javelin feels like part of your body.

You and the javelin are connected like a long and powerful whip . . . you are going through your crossovers on a straight-line path with a smooth and horizontal movement . . . your throwing arm is extended behind you and your feet are grabbing and driving from the ground like a powerful, galloping gazelle . . . strong and graceful . . . you are reaching the block . . . your whole body is collecting an explosive energy like a slingshot . . . you are stretching your body to its limits to capture the power you are generating . . . on your last crossover to your block, your body becomes a catapult releasing the javelin with a powerful, reflexive snap . . . you let go and hurl the javelin like an arrow from your body . . . like the cracking of a whip . . . you watch the javelin as it pierces through the sky, its tail waving goodbye . . . disappearing and becoming a small point in the distance.

You walk away from the runway . . . feeling good, powerful, and in control . . . you have thrown well . . . you thank your body and all its parts for working together in such a well-synchronized precision . . . all flowing together for an outstanding throw . . . you hear the cheers of the crowd, acknowledging your achievement . . . you smile and wave . . . feeling good . . . knowing you have achieved your goal and can do so again.

Guided Visualization for the Discus

(This visualization was written with the help of Kevin Carr, an outstanding All-American thrower from the University of Oregon.)

You are completely relaxed and at peace . . . it is the day of a competition and you are ready . . . your mind is quiet and focused on the competition ahead . . . you feel fit and ready . . . you are healthy and relaxed and confident in your ability to win . . . you are a superior athlete . . . the toughest thrower in the world . . . you have more experience, wisdom, and finesse than anyone on the field this day . . . you feel the control and readiness within your body, and you are connected with your power and strength . . . you are the best . . . the supreme athlete. You are warmed up and ready . . . you think for a moment of your affirmations . . . "I am the best. I am the supreme athlete in the ring. I am low, centered, and powerful when I throw."

You have been announced and are moving toward the ring now . . . you feel confident and know that you can trust your body and mind to do what you ask . . . you think of your special word and feel yourself centering . . . you are tall . . . strong . . . in control . . . powerful and at peace . . . there is silence . . . you are in the ring now . . . you focus and center yourself . . . the disk feels light . . . the turn begins to happen inside your body . . . effortlessly . . . smoothly . . . your body, resting low on your legs with just the right separation creating a strong base, begins to respond . . . moving low . . . centered . . . powerful . . . relaxed and balanced . . . your right leg swings hard across the circle . . . your timing is just right and smooth . . . you turn . . . then the experience of release . . . like an explosion you fling the disk way out in front of you like a huge, expanding catapult . . . arm fully extended . . . reaching . . . flinging . . . It is that moment of "out-of-control" power . . . long and smooth . . . your body moves powerfully from its solid base . . . with perfect timing and finesse . . . you recover well within the ring . . . balanced and in control again as you watch the disk sail . . . cruising through the air . . . floating . . . moving . . . sailing . . . and finally coming down well past the 200' mark . . . it is a PR.

You stand for a moment . . . knowing that you have done it perfectly . . . and remembering your affirmations . . . "I am the toughest thrower in the world. I have superior feel for the throw. I finesse the discus with awesome power. I throw a big PR anytime I choose. I am the best. I am the supreme artist in the ring."

You feel safe and confident back on your island for the moment as you allow yourself to experience the joy and exhilaration of having done your very best . . . being the very best. . . . You begin to relax into the peace and tiredness of having completed your competition . . . you have won . . . you have handled everything that might have distracted you . . . you are pleased . . . you are the best and it was fun; you feel great.

Reconnect with your space now . . . returning to your breathing . . . the rhythm and warmth of your body . . . hear the sounds around you and become aware of the smells . . . you feel relaxed and refreshed . . . say your special word again . . . connecting with those feelings . . . that knowledge of confidence . . . perfection . . . strength . . . you are a beautiful . . . powerful . . . supreme athlete.

Guided Visualization for the Shot

Allow the picture, feelings, and sounds to come as you begin to experience yourself on the field . . . you are beginning your warm-up routine . . . as you stretch and move, be aware of the environment . . . the weather . . . the colors . . . the sounds of the crowd . . . feel the grass soft under your shoes . . . feel your body readying itself for your big performance . . . you feel good . . . relaxed . . . easy . . . ready . . . go through your whole routine . . . stretching . . . bending . . . moving . . . stay centered and focused . . . you know you are strong and powerful . . . you know you are ready for this competition . . . you have worked hard . . . trained hard . . . and you are the best . . . you know you can win.

You take off your sweats . . . feeling good and centered . . . you are focused and relaxed as you move toward the ring . . . you pick up the shot . . . it feels smooth . . . round . . . and light . . . it is familiar . . . it is a friend . . . it knows you and you know it . . . you feel powerful as you move into the ring . . . this too is familiar . . . it is a friendly place . . . you are comfortable here . . . you are strong here . . . you look out across the lines to the spot where you are going to throw . . . you know you can do it . . . you concentrate and get your body into position . . . the shot feels light and easy in your hand . . . close to your neck . . . you are relaxing . . . moving . . . easy . . . ready . . . balanced . . . confident . . . you go low and smooth out of the back . . . your body fluid . . . strong . . . smooth . . . you get the right leg under and stay closed as you turn and explode . . . you are quick and powerful . . . keeping your left leg bent as you go out and up . . . exploding . . . feeling aggressive . . . strong . . . quick and powerful . . . you watch the shot move through the air . . . out over the lines . . . you have thrown far . . . it finally lands out well past the sixty-foot mark . . . you have been successful . . . you are the winner . . . you are pleased . . . you knew you could do it . . . you knew you could do it . . . and it felt good . . . you were smooth and strong . . . you were focused and powerful . . . you were in control all way, and you were successful.

Be aware of the feelings and the roar of the crowd as you leave the ring . . . let in all in . . . allow yourself to know the feelings of success and winning . . . know that you have done your best . . . remember how it felt to be in that ring . . . moving relaxed . . . moving with power . . . knowing exactly what to do and trusting your body to do what you asked of it . . . as you put your sweats back on . . . thank your body for its strength and health . . . thank it for coming through for you . . . allow yourself to rest now and to know the pride of achieving well.

Guided Visualization for the Hammer

(This is a very short, modified statement that can help the thrower with his mental images and state—more technique can be added by the athlete to suit his individual needs.)

It is easy for me to use the ball . . . it orbits like a planet . . . perfectly round . . . there is no tension or tightness in my body . . . my body is loose and relaxed . . . my arms are hanging . . . just going for the ride like a piece of the wire . . . just part of the hammer . . . I have perfect efficiency . . . and economy of motion.

The ball almost takes me around without any effort on my part. . . . My legs are bent . . . shoulders round . . . foot coming down at 180 . . . my hands hanging with the ball . . . just letting it hang out. . . . The radius is long and my head is right on the ball . . . it never moves away . . . my mind is at ease . . . no tension upstairs, just clarity and focus . . . my foot is on the ground a long time . . . I am back . . . way back, and the left side of my body is in control . . . I'm moving with great speed, and my release is a natural thing . . . it just snaps out . . . I let it go . . . letting go with power, strength, and grace . . . watching it fly through the air in a perfect trajectory . . . going as far and farther than I have ever thrown it . . . it sails with a mind of its own, lifting and flying away from me . . . my body knows how it feels to throw this way . . . with grace and perfection . . . with economy and tremendous power . . . it is easy for me to re-create this motion and feeling again and again . . . my heart soars with the ball . . . in a feeling of elation, power, and excitement . . . mind, body, and hammer working as one powerful and explosive unit.

Tennis

Some items to include in a tennis visualization are

1. Concentrate and be focused.
2. Keep temper under control—if point is lost, let it go; focus on the next point.
3. If in the lead, keep playing and play aggressively to close out the point; keep thinking positively.
4. See self hitting all shots well and powerfully.
5. Say affirmations to self in the visualization—"I am mentally tough," "I am aggressive in closing out a game, point, set, match."
6. Between points, let go of lost points and think about strategy—get ready for next shot; if serving, think about serve and where to place it.
7. Play with relaxed intensity.
8. If behind, play with aggressiveness also.
9. Think of your best match and what you did in it; imagine doing that in your upcoming match.

Some strategies for dealing with stress on the court are to

1. Breathe deeply into abdomen.
2. Play a lot of matches so you're used to competing.
3. Talk positively to self; reassure self; encourage and support self.
4. Think of past successes when facing a similar situation.
5. Remind yourself it's only a game.
6. "Lighten up and have fun."
7. Sit down between games, breathe, focus, and relax your mind and body.
8. Drink plenty of water.
9. Let go of missed points easily.
10. Stay in the present moment; let go of past; forget the future.
11. Be committed once you hit a shot.
12. Anticipate returns and be alert.

A Guided Visualization for Tennis

Imagine yourself as you arrive at the tennis courts . . . see people playing . . . feel the air, the environment . . . hear the sounds of balls and racquets . . . feel the weather on your body . . . enjoy anticipating the match . . . experience the feeling in your stomach and in your body . . . you are a little nervous but very ready . . . remembering that these are common feelings before you play a match.

You begin to hit on the court . . . hitting with long, powerful strokes . . . hitting smoothly . . . rapidly . . . accurately . . . feeling relaxed and confident . . . remembering some of your affirmations as you are warming up . . . "I encourage myself after a good shot. I am a positive person. I turn negative experiences into positive ones. I support myself. I am a confident player. I believe in myself and my abilities. I play each shot in the moment and I am very focused as I play. I am in control of my temper and am free of anger and resentment. I am confident, relaxed, and play with good form."

Experience yourself and the energy as you now ready yourself for the start of your match . . . you feel good and strong . . . you focus your energy and power and stand poised . . . ready for the match to begin.

The match starts . . . you are moving well . . . you are light and quick . . . you are focused . . . as the ball comes to you on each shot, you concentrate on the ball, and you begin to establish a rhythm of bounce, hit, bounce, hit . . . hitting with power, strength, and accuracy . . . as you hit each ball, you see it going over the net exactly where you want it to go . . . you feel the perfection in your body as you hit the shot . . . you hear the sound of the ball hitting your racquet in the right spot . . . notice yourself enjoying the match immensely . . . you are glad to be out on this day playing . . . and playing well . . . you feel relaxed . . . loose . . . you are breathing out as you hit each ball . . . your forehand is powerful, strong . . . accurate . . . you feel light on your feet, and you are ready for each shot when it comes to you . . . you easily place the shot wherever you want it to go . . . with accuracy and ease.

See and feel yourself getting into position . . . the ball coming to your forehand, you are in the perfect position to hit it . . . you hit it and watch it go straight to the place on the court where you want it to go . . . you hit a forehand crosscourt, placing it well . . . the ball returns . . . you hit a backhand crosscourt . . . a forehand straight down the line . . . deep in the corner . . . you win the point and feel good about your game. . . . A serve comes to your backhand, you stroke perfectly, hitting it down the line . . . another winner . . . another serve to you, coming to your forehand; you put a nice drop shot just over the net . . . your opponent scrambles to get it and hits a high lob . . . you settle into position and quickly execute an overhead smash . . . you receive another serve . . . to your backhand and execute a deep backhand crosscourt shot, you feel powerful and controlled . . . you win the game . . . a service break . . . you know you are good at playing aggressively and closing out points and games . . . experience your body sensations . . . determination, relaxation, control, quickness . . . knowing you are right on . . . if your opponent calls a shot out that you are sure is in or if he (she) accuses you of cheating, experience yourself remaining calm and centered . . . you focus your aggression and feelings into powerful and expert playing. . . . You are sure of your own competence and ability to overcome any negative energy . . . you have a high level of confidence and composure . . . you are mentally tough and overcome any obstacles that confront you.

You breathe deeply and continue to focus on the ball . . . you hit each stroke with power, accuracy, and control . . . if you miss a shot, you notice what you did in error, make the necessary adjustments, and let it go . . . letting go easily of any negativity you might feel . . . always coming back to the present moment for the next point . . . alert and ready for whatever shot comes to you . . . all that exists in your focus is one shot at a time . . . one point at a time . . . you are living and playing in the moment . . . moment-to-moment.

©1989 YFM

energy . . . you have a high level of confidence and composure . . . you are mentally tough and overcome any obstacles that confront you.

You breathe deeply and continue to focus on the ball . . . you hit each stroke with power, accuracy, and control . . . if you miss a shot, you notice what you did in error, make the necessary adjustments, and let it go . . . letting go easily of any negativity you might feel . . . always coming back to the present moment for the next point . . . alert and ready for whatever shot comes to you . . . all that exists in your focus is one shot at a time . . . one point at a time . . . you are living and playing in the moment . . . moment-to-moment.

Experience your body enjoying the sensations of play and competition . . . enjoying your aggressiveness . . . playing well . . . centered and focused . . . point-by-point . . . being alert and ready at the line . . . rushing the net with confidence . . . experiencing the feeling of confidence in your body and mind . . . telling yourself that you are an excellent player.

Experience the power you feel each time you serve . . . you are an excellent server and in control of your body and its strength and accuracy . . . imagine yourself poised to serve . . . centered . . . confident . . . powerful . . . connect with every movement . . . the height of the ball . . . the swing of your arm . . . the sound as you hit the ball in the perfect spot and send it over the net exactly where you want it to go . . . like a bullet . . . notice how your opponent has to scramble to return your serve . . . you are powerful and in control of this game and match. . . .

During the minute-and-one-half changeover, you sit relaxed . . . breathing deeply. You think of your affirmations. . . . "I am in control and have superior skills. I am focused and powerful." You are enjoying the challenge of this match . . . You know you can win . . . you are in command. You feel strong and confident as you begin to play again . . . experience yourself again as an aggressive and controlled player . . . you move with ease to the net . . . your backhand is accurate and your serve is unbreakable.

Imagine the entire game . . . each point . . . every movement that is important to your success and the achievement of your goals . . . you trust your body and your abilities . . . and you are having fun.

Continually experience yourself as a good and competent player . . . a player who wins . . . a player who gives everything and plays the best he (she) knows how . . . you have achieved your goals . . . you have played well and feel proud, complete . . . allow yourself to enjoy it all as you remind yourself that you have everything within you to be, to do, and to have what you want on the court.

Golf

(This visualization was written in the first person, "I", to give the reader an example of a first-person visualization. The reader can change it to the third person if it feels more appropriate to do so. It was also written from the perspective of a player on the professional golf tour.)

I am in my car on my way to the golf course. . . . I feel and look good. . . . I am aware of the day around me . . . the weather . . . and the sounds as I drive to the gate of the course. . . . I drive in and park . . . it is a good day. . . . I know I am ready for this tournament. . . . I have practiced hard. . . . I have done my mental workout, and I feel strong and prepared. . . . I really enjoy all the special treatment I receive when I play . . . and I know that I am special and that I deserve it. . . . I have worked hard and am ready to succeed.

I grab a sweater from the car and walk slowly . . . with confidence across the warm parking lot. . . . I am aware of the colors and smells of the cars as I pass and head for the locker room. . . . I enjoy saying hello to some of the attendants. . . . I know that I am in control and will play well today. . . . I notice the smell of the locker room and how I feel when I reach my locker, open it, and throw my sweater in . . . there are other sweaters in there, and I feel confident that I am prepared for anything. . . . I feel the bench beneath me as I sit down and take a deep breath. . . . I am beginning to center myself and focus on the round ahead of me.

Slowly I begin to stretch my muscles . . . they feel relaxed and ready . . . they feel strong, and I let my strength reach every fiber of my muscles. . . . I know that I am powerful and well trained . . . this is my sport and I can feel the excitement and challenge that helps me perform. . . . I untie my sneaks and take them off . . . lean over to my locker and pull out my polished golf shoes. . . . I throw my sneaks into the bottom of the locker and listen for the sound . . . this makes me feel good. . . . I slip my feet into my golf shoes tying the laces. . . . I think of my affirmations and the key thoughts for this tournament. . . . I breathe. . . . I feel confident, prepared, and focused as I put on my visor.

As I walk out onto the putting green, I am aware of the feel of the grass under my shoes and the smell in the air. . . . I notice the breeze on my skin and the warmth that seems to surround me . . . it is a good day and I am glad that I am in this tournament. . . . I connect with my caddy . . . he is my friend and I trust that he supports me and my playing. . . . I know that he is there for me and I am happy for the help . . . together we head to the range. . . . I begin to think of my goal as I stretch with my club . . . moving my body gently . . . stretching and swinging without a ball. . . . I feel solid and centered. . . . I know that my body works together like a well-oiled machine . . . it is smooth and powerful . . . it is well trained and flexible. . . . I begin to hit a few balls, connecting with the feeling and the movement . . . bringing myself within. . . . I back off and let a few good swings and solid hits go through my mind . . . remembering my key word and affirmations. . . . "I belong here . . . this is my game . . . my course. . . . I have trained enough. . . . I deserve to win. . . . I am confident in my game and my abilities." . . . I step back up and hit a few more . . . they feel good. . . . I am comfortable taking my time . . . breathing before each shot. . . . I know this helps me settle into a good tempo. . . . I go through the clubs . . . gaining confidence and strength with each swing . . . as I return to the putting green, I carry a solid feeling with me . . . my short game is good . . . I stroke a few and the roll has good overspin. . . . I smile to myself. . . . I feel ready and my looking forward to this round.

I go back to the locker room and think of my key word, my goals, and my affir-mations once more . . . carefully taking myself through a visualization of the course and then stretch and focus inward . . . this is my time. . . . I relax and focus . . . emptying my mind of all other thoughts but the round ahead. . . . I breathe . . . center and breathe again. . . . I am ready.

As I walk to the first tee and wait for the group in front of me, I notice the people who came to watch . . . some of them came to see me . . . others just came to watch. . . . I walk over to them . . . get a few hugs for energy and support and hear them wish me good luck. . . . I return to myself and the round ahead. . . . I know how to focus and center on my next move. . . . I give my caddy a smile as I get my balls. . . . I like the feel of them and I know that they are my friends. . . . they are on my side. . . . I hear my name and my list. . . . I feel good about my accomplish-ments. . . . I know I will add to my list this year and that excites me. . . . I am totally focused now and set into my routine . . . slow . . . gently . . . feeling sure and solid. . . . I know I am in control of the course. . . . I have done clear mental work on each hole . . . this round is mine . . . my swing is powerful and smooth. . . . I have great confidence in my swing . . . it feels good and I watch as it sailed away from me, heading right where I wanted it to go. . . . I am pleased and I smile. . . . I know I will play the course the best way for me and that is good enough.

As we walk from hole to hole we talk. . . . I stay focused on the game . . . we discuss what I am doing well and where I might improve . . . we laugh and support each other . . . this helps ease the tension for me . . . this is part of the fun. . . . I can hear the sound of the clubs in the bag and an occasional burst of applause in the distance . . . at each hole my swings are smooth, solid, and strong. . . . I stop and breathe and think each shot through, making good, clear decisions . . . taking my time . . . giving it my best effort. . . . I am a professional. . . . I am a strong player. . . . I can feel it in my walk and the time I take for each shot. . . . I am concentrating and making each shot with my best effort. . . . I am into it 100 percent, and it feels good. . . . I let myself indulge in *my* game. . . . I am worth it and it feels right.

I feel the pressure with just a few holes left. . . . I breathe deeply and remember my strategy. . . . I love this challenge. . . . I know that pressure is my friend and that I rise to the occasion. . . . I stay focused and relaxed . . . saying my affirmations and continuing to take my time . . . centering myself. . . . I am playing golf now . . . watching each putt fall . . . each shot land where I want it . . . I continue my routine . . . smooth . . . centered . . . solid. . . . I am great. Each time I make a good shot the crowd cheers. . . . I let its energy wash over me. . . . I am proud of myself. . . . I am doing it my way and it feels good.

After the last putt, everyone cheers. . . . I accept the praise. . . . I have earned it. . . . I have played the best I knew how, and it was good enough to reach my goal. . . . I let the good feelings flow through my body. . . . I worked hard, and now I let myself feel this easy sensation. . . . I let the success in. . . . I am excited. . . . I did it . . . and it was good enough. . . . I walk off the green enjoying being finished . . . in the press tent, or if I am stopped by the press, I feel confident and pleased with myself . . . the reporters like me and are interested in me. . . . I enjoy telling them about me. . . . I expand on questions and give them insight about who I am and what my game is all about. . . . I love the attention and the feeling of success. . . . I leave knowing it is *me*. . . . I did it and I *am* that good. . . . I belong here and I am great and enough. . . . I know that I have everything within me to be, to do and to have what I want.

Swimming

(This is a guided visualization for a 100-meter freestyle; the form can be adapted to other distances and styles as needed.)

As you focus on your breathing, become aware of the warmth of the room and the smell of the water as you enter the pool area. It is a very familiar smell and feel to your skin. Notice the sounds of the room . . . the echo . . . the water moving . . . the voices . . . you feel right at home and very comfortable. Imagine yourself as you dress down to your suit and begin to stretch and prepare your body to compete. You know this pool . . . it is pretty much like any other pool . . . you move your body . . . stretching . . . bending . . . waiting your turn . . . your name. . . . Be aware of your energy . . . you are well prepared for this race . . . it is your favorite, and you are fast and strong . . . you are ready.

You dive into the pool, feeling the water on your skin and hearing the splash as you enter . . . you surface and stroke smoothly to the end of the lane. You have always enjoyed warming up . . . moving powerfully and smoothly from one end of the pool to the other . . . gauging your kick turn just right . . . pushing off powerfully and in complete control. You do one more lap and pull yourself up out of the water just as they announce the final call for the 100-meter freestyle. You take your towel . . . drying off just the spots you always dry and walk to the waiting area . . . you are relaxed and ready . . . you are calm and warm and confident as you walk with the other competitors and stand in front of the block at your designated lane . . . you like this lane.

Become aware of your thoughts and inner focus now as you quiet your body . . . remember your affirmations . . . and that special word or words that connect you with your strength and success. . . . "I am strong and powerful."

"I am smooth and fast . . . I am as good as any other swimmer in the race today . . . " You step on the blocks . . . arms easy at your sides . . . breathing deep and full . . . you are ready . . . completely focused and centered . . . you take your mark . . . set . . . and hear the gun.

Your body stretches is full length as you propel yourself off the blocks . . . every muscle extended . . . reaching . . . you feel yourself enter the water . . . cool against your skin . . . you flutter to get as much distance as you can before you surface and begin to stroke . . . you are powerful and in complete control. You are swimming now . . . stroking easily . . . pulling with great strength and confidence . . . stroke . . . stroke . . . your breathing even and deep . . . every movement efficient and perfect. You are aware that there is someone near you in the next lane . . . you can feel their stroking and hear their splash as you near the end of the pool and ready for your kick turn . . . you put them out of your mind and center yourself for the turn . . . the kick turn is one of your strengths and you lower your head, raising yourself . . . flipping . . . legs over . . . feet against the wall . . . pushing hard . . . in complete control . . . arms outstretched . . . body lengthening . . . reaching . . . cutting smoothly through the water . . . a little flutter and you begin to stroke again.

You feel alone in the pool as you head toward the finish . . . focused completely on your stroking and your breathing . . . you are swimming perfectly . . . doing everything just as it should be done . . . pulling with great force and power . . . kicking perfectly and effectively. As you stroke into the final twenty-five meters, you sense the swimmer in the next lane again . . . he/she is pushing for the lead . . . you concentrate on your power and dig even deeper with each stroke . . . pulling . . . kicking . . . lowering your head . . . fewer breaths now . . . stroking powerfully . . . reaching . . . pulling, . . . surging ahead . . . knowing you can outkick anyone . . . you are strong and powerful . . . reaching . . . pulling . . . propelling yourself forward . . . you touch the wall.

You outtouched the next lane . . . you look up at your time . . . it is your best time ever . . . you look down the wall in both directions to see if you have won . . . you have succeeded, and you begin to focus on your breathing. . . . Slowly, you become aware of the noises . . . the colors of the blocks and the timer's clothing . . . the crowd and other swimmers milling around on the deck above you . . . you have won . . . you have reached your goal . . . you lift yourself out of the pool and stand, reaching for your towel . . . slowing your breath and relaxing into the feelings of excitement and accomplishment. . . . The feelings rise inside you . . . the pride of succeeding . . . having given it your best . . . winning.

Allow yourself to experience it all . . . the congratulations . . . the euphoria . . . the tiredness . . . the joy . . . as you dry off . . . heading for the area of the room where you left your sweats . . . you feel good . . . it was a good race, and you know you did your best . . . you think of your special word again . . . you smile.

Begin to come back into your physical space now . . . becoming aware of your breathing . . . deep into your belly . . . exhaling slowly. . . . Reconnect with your body and the feel of the chair or the floor beneath you. Move your feet and hands . . . reconnect . . . you are relaxed and rested . . . you are full of new energy and confidence . . . breathe . . . and slowly, when you are ready, open your eyes . . . breathing deeply . . . reconnecting . . . trusting . . . believing in your ability and your strength . . . you are a great swimmer.

Springboard Diving

The following information was furnished by Keith Ranney, an NCAA All-American, three meter, from 1974–1977 at Southern Methodist University and an Olympic diving trials competitor in 1976 and 1980.

The most common issues of divers that come up in mental training are

1. Setting aside all distractions, focusing on self, the water, and the diving board.
2. Relaxing and going for it.

3. Trusting body and getting to the end of the board correctly.
4. Developing an attitude of letting go of a past negative dive and focusing ahead on the next dive.
5. Dealing with the time between dives.

Guided Visualization for a Dive (Reverse Two and One-Half Somersault in the Tuck Position)

Imagine yourself at the pool for the competition . . . you have warmed up . . . practicing your dives . . . feeling the air, the water . . . hearing the familiar sounds of competition . . . in the ten to fifteen minutes before your next dive, imagine yourself reviewing what you will do . . . concentrate on the stretch . . . stay centered . . . drink plenty of water . . . and go through your dryland mental rehearsal. . . . You begin to see yourself. . . . Composure: posture, centering, rhythm, approach (heel, toe), and hurdle (fast/straight arms, high knee, step down). . . . Stretch arms up further still while descending to the board for press . . . then straight-arm press, head position (stationary, eyes focused on water as arms drive through bottom of press), follow-through press to powerful arm reach straight overhead. . . . Drive knees to chest. . . . Squeeze tuck position with hands on ankles. . . . Knees/legs together (no split tuck), spot (see) the water, looking straight over the top of the knees . . . once, spot twice. . . . Kick to full body extension (arms preextension set position, head stationary, stomach tight) . . . Reach with arms to water entry location. . . . Tighten body, grab hands for lineup, punch through the water surface . . . stretch to pool bottom.

You see it all and feel it all with precision . . . doing it all correctly in your mind. . . . You hear your name called . . . it is only a minute or two before. . . . you start bouncing . . . get yourself pumped up . . . warming up your body . . . looking forward to your turn on the board . . . you love this competing . . . it is so exhilarating . . . you hear the sounds of the water being sprayed onto the pool surface . . . you know the feeling of the grip of the diving board surface . . . your concentration goes to your body . . . focusing inward . . . you stand at the beginning of your approach, and your mind is empty . . . you focus on your body . . . you trust your body to do this dive that you have done dozens of times . . . you begin your approach . . . your body moving perfectly and with precision . . . you are centered, rhythmic . . . you get to the end of the board and do your hurdle on the end of the board . . . perfectly timed . . . perfectly placed . . . your body begins its upward movement and you enjoy the sensation of being in the air . . . seeing, spotting, everything moving perfectly . . . your body goes through all the movements automatically and with precision . . . you are stretching and pushing through the water surface . . . hearing the "rip" entry . . . no pressure either on the front or the back of your legs . . . the pool bottom coming to you very quickly . . . you know you have done very well . . . you feel the excitement in your body.

You come to the surface, hearing the cheering of the crowd . . . seeing your coach smiling happily . . . knowing already that you have done an outstanding dive . . . hearing the scores echoing throughout the natatorium . . . and seeing them on the scoreboards . . . allow yourself to enjoy the feelings of elation and exhilaration . . .

you have performed very well . . . you are an outstanding diver . . . you have achieved your goal.

Some Affirmations for Diving

These affirmations may be applied to any dive by any level of diver. They are helpful reminders of positive thinking.

I stay committed to the dive all the way through.
I concentrate and focus on every part of the dive.
I have good concentration and focus.
It is easy for me to let go of mistakes and go on.
I dive well regardless of my warm-ups.
I easily let go of worry and come back to the present.
I set aside all distractions and focus on my dive.
I trust my body.
I relax and go for it!

Cycling/Biking

It is the day before the race, and you leave in plenty of time to get where you are going early and rested . . . it is a relaxed drive . . . you stop and walk around whenever you want . . . keeping your body relaxed and loose . . . you are excited about the race tomorrow . . . you know you are ready and strong . . . it is clear in your mind that you are a dominant factor in this race . . . you feel the confidence rising in you, and you begin to think of your goals for this race . . . you also remember how much fun it is to race . . . the speed . . . the power . . . the control . . . and the feeling of success and satisfaction . . . you are ready . . . relaxed and anticipating the race . . . you have a good dinner . . . you check all your gear . . . your bike . . . your equipment . . . if this is a long race, you check your food and water supply for the feed zone . . . making sure everything is ready and in good shape . . . you are a professional . . . you are in control and you know how to prepare yourself and your equipment so you will race at your best . . . now you allow your body and mind to rest . . . to sleep . . . to be centered in knowing you are well prepared . . . ready . . . trained and confident.

Waking on the morning of the race, you feel refreshed after a good night's sleep . . . you are excited . . . you know this is your race and you will succeed . . . you have your favorite breakfast . . . fueling the body for the race ahead . . . you think of your goals and some of your affirmations . . . fueling the mind. . . . "I am safe! . . . I am healthy and strong! . . . I have great endurance. . . . I am a strong and dominant hill climber. . . . I am a quick and powerful sprinter. . . . I enjoy pushing hard all the way across the line!"

You load the car and leave for the race and find a good place to park . . . no hassle . . . no rush . . . feeling relaxed and ready . . . you begin your warm-up . . . riding by yourself . . . going over everything that is important to you . . . extra

wheels . . . someone to take care of you before and after the race . . . you feel good
and eager . . . calm and in control . . . ready and focused . . . you ride fast . . .
getting in touch with the feel again . . . being sure everything works . . . then a few
jumps . . . sprints . . . feeling your body responding . . . knowing the bike . . . the
movements . . . the feel . . . you slow and get off your bike . . . it is time to relax
and focus your energy before a race, and you smile to yourself . . . sometimes the
other racers talk and laugh about the race or past crashes . . . you think to yourself
how silly they are as you sit down and close your eyes . . . you breathe and focus
within . . . centering and remembering that you are in control and well trained for
this race . . . you focus your energy now on the race . . . only the race . . . remembering the course . . . remembering your strategy . . . remembering your goals . . .
you breathe again . . . deeply . . . then you open your eyes and move to the start.

You stand quietly for a moment . . . and the race begins . . . you get a good start
. . . strong and in the front . . . you position yourself well in the front pack . . . this
is your spot . . . this is where you belong . . . you dominate from this position . . .
always in the top five to ten riders . . . this is your power spot . . . you are comfortable here . . . you begin to establish your rhythm . . . it feels good to be racing . . .
you are totally committed to this race . . . to your goals . . . to yourself . . . and you
feel powerful and in control . . . you take each mile as it come . . . as you come to
hills you take them as challenges and an opportunity to use your strength and body
in a different way . . . you stay in the front . . . trusting your food will be there when
you need it . . . knowing you have all the strength you need to conquer each hill . . .
the hills are your friends . . . they remind you of your fitness and power . . . as you
crest each hill, you are in the front . . . you are the conqueror . . . the king . . . you
focus this power and commit yourself to the rest of the race . . . every turn reminds
you of how much fun racing and riding is . . . it feels wonderful to lean around the
corners . . . to be in the front pack . . . to be so connected and in such control . . .
there is almost a sense of flying in unison . . . if it is wet, you know you have the
control and training to handle it . . . it is merely a part of racing . . . you pedal on
. . . in front controlling the race . . . controlling your body . . . controlling your mind
. . . feeling fast and smooth . . . feeling strong and focused . . . you are ready for
each downhill that comes your way . . . getting on the drops . . . staying in front . . .
dominating the race and the strategy . . . you ride easily over any gravel knowing
you have the power . . . knowing you are safe . . . on you ride . . . coming closer and
closer to the line . . . eating and drinking when you need it . . . trusting your endurance and toughness . . . you are totally devoted to the race now . . . you are racing
smart . . . knowing when to make a move and when not to . . . staying in front . . .
controlling and committed . . . you are sprinting now . . . there is no one and nothing
between you and victory . . . heading for the line . . . after all . . . what's a line
for . . . you dig deep . . . totally focused . . . pushing all out now . . . flying . . .
crossing the line . . . you have reached your goal! . . . you have dominated the race
and finished well in the top three . . . you are a winner.

You slow . . . and ride easy now . . . allowing your body to rest . . . to cool down
. . . thinking a little about the race and what you did well . . . what you learned . . .
all the things that worked for you . . . you are pleased . . . you are proud of yourself

for your commitment and focus and strength . . . you allow the sense of success to fill your mind and body and know the joy and peace of achievement . . . you feel calm and centered . . . tired and well spent . . . you feel full . . . you look forward to a long Jacuzzi or shower and rest . . . you thank your body and mind for being there for you and for giving all . . . you are a powerful and successful cyclist.

Fencing

Six top mental/psychological issues and concerns of fencers are

1. Learning to **relax body,** yet being **ready and aggressive. Breathing deeply** abdominally for two or three breaths before the first round begins to oxygenate the body and calm the nerves.
2. Dealing with nervousness at the beginning of the first round. Being **centered and focused** on the match.
3. Frustration with the inaccuracy of directors when you think you deserve the point and don't get it. (**Letting go of anger** at unjust/unfair calls.)
4. Losing confidence in certain moves that are usually your good ones. While you are fencing in a match and you are hit, **combating the self-doubt** that arises.
5. **Flexibility** of being able to change strategy in the middle of a match—important to change it, so you aren't stuck in a negative mental groove.
6. Dealing with impatience. Developing **patience** to draw your opponent out. Stop rushing moves.

States of mind and being that are helpful to cultivate:

1. Complete confidence—feel it and show it.
2. Perfectly in control.
3. No anxiety about your capabilities, trusting yourself.
4. If you get bad calls, focus it into your match and be more aggressive.
5. A very slight arrogance might be helpful. (Arrogance to some may be confidence to others!)

Our thanks to Angie Herbert-Hodges, a former British fencer who now lives in Virginia. She was most helpful with her comments and information.

All-Around Gymnastics

Imagine yourself entering the gym . . . marching proudly with confidence in line with your team . . . you are aware of the usual slight nervousness and you know how to turn it into energy . . . you are ready and in control . . . experience the sounds and colors of the room . . . the layout of the equipment . . . the smell of the chalk . . . the lights are bright, and you feel warm and relaxed . . . you have gone through your warm-ups . . . perfectly . . . just the way you always do them . . . easy . . . smooth

. . . light . . . you did your whole warm-up routine and allowed yourself to feel confident and graceful . . . relaxed yet ready . . . now you notice the judges and smile . . . they are your friends.

It is time to begin . . . it is quiet in the room . . . you stand at the end of the runway . . . centering . . . relaxing . . . getting ready for your vault . . . you take a deep breath . . . look at the horse one more time and explode into a sprint down the runway . . . you are powerful . . . you are fast . . . you are in control as you jump, hands outstretched, reaching . . . placing perfectly . . . legs moving smoothly through the air . . . you turn . . . beautifully . . . and land solidly on the mat . . . feel the joy and energy as you listen to the reaction of the crowd and see the faces of the judges . . . it was perfect . . . flawless . . . you feel beautiful . . . you feel great.

You move to the bars . . . there is no fear . . . your body is relaxed . . . it knows each swing . . . each dip . . . just exactly where to put your hands and how to control your power . . . you stand quiet . . . another deep breath . . . and you mount through the air to the bars . . . you feel that sense of freedom your body knows so well when working the bars . . . watch each movement . . . each swing . . . each change as you move smoothly and powerfully through your routine . . . this is fun . . . you are good . . . it is like flying and you are in complete control . . . see it all perfectly . . . the way you want it to be . . . you feel strong and light as you turn . . . gracefully into the air and stick your dismount . . . you smile . . . you are pleased.

Watch as you reconnect with your team and move to the next two events . . . your scores have been good and you know you are doing well . . . you rest . . . preparing yourself for the beam and the floor . . . rest.

You stand in front of the beam . . . calm and centered . . . you take a deep breath as you focus your energy inward and prepare to mount . . . up you go with complete control and grace . . . feel your control as you complete each trick . . . smoothly . . . easily . . . you are the master of your body . . . and it moves for you, through your dance . . . gracefully . . . just the way you want it to . . . see your whole beam routine perfectly . . . to the dismount . . . you arch your back . . . arms in the air . . . you did it and the judges are pleased.

You walk confidently to the large mat . . . it is your last event . . . it is your best routine and you feel strong and light as you stand, ready, waiting for the judges signal . . . you smile, making eye contact with the judge and the crowd beyond . . . it is important to play to the crowd, and you become playful and full of spirit as you start with your tumbling pass . . . over the mat you move . . . like a feather . . . a snowflake . . . you dance, listening to the music . . . concentrating on the rhythm . . . full of joy and energy . . . you are having fun, and you can feel the excitement of the crowd . . . they are your friends, and you take strength from them as you dance . . . it is your final pass and the familiar ending of the music . . . your body stops . . . quiets . . . rests . . . you were perfection . . . you stand . . . smiling . . . letting it all come in . . . the pride . . . the joy . . . the feelings of success . . . you were beautiful.

You form the line with your team members and march triumphantly out of the room . . . everyone did well . . . your scores were your best ever . . . the team won, and you are very happy and tired from a job well-done . . . thank your body and your mind for the willingness to be in support of you and for their strength and control . . . you are happy.

Wrestling

Ron Finley, the coach of the 1984 U.S. Olympic Greco-Roman wrestling team, and the wrestling coach for the University of Oregon, has used mental training with his athletes for a number of years. His pointers were invaluable in the design of this visualization. Coach Finley also recommends that the wrestler take a rest period about three hours before competition, where he rests and relaxes. The warm-up starts about an hour before the match.

A Guided Visualization for Wrestling

Imagine yourself at the competition . . . you begin your warm-up, going through your moves, wrestling with your teammates, practicing technique . . . stretching, rolling, working up a good sweat . . . getting your body warm and ready for your match . . . you take some time to see yourself doing each move, reacting, working on speed . . . practicing your favorite moves . . . seeing and feeling yourself to be mentally tough, aggressive, intense, fast, and explosive . . . saying some of your affirmations to yourself . . . "I've got great reaction time," "I am strong and powerful." Imagine yourself wrestling, stopping an attack . . . countering an attack . . . being aggressive . . . feeling the moves in your muscles . . . being tough and smashing . . . imagine getting hit . . . and it doesn't hurt . . . nothing stops you . . . you feel no pain . . . you are tough and powerful.

In the time before the match, imagine yourself resting briefly . . . and right before the match begins, you take two or three deep abdominal breaths, letting all your muscles relax . . . then get your heart rate up and get your adrenaline flowing . . . your match is announced . . . you line up and shake hands with your partner.

You go out, shake hands, step back . . . the referee blows the whistle, and you are on your way . . . you take the first step . . . being aggressive and powerful . . . you are thinking positively . . . you know you can beat him . . . you are starting hard . . . very aggressively . . . you wrestle with intensity and focus . . . he attacks, you stop the attack and counter it . . . you love this . . . you are quick in your moves . . . tough . . . intense . . . your reaction time is fast and you are explosive . . . he can't keep you down.

It is nearing the end of the match now . . . you feel him tiring . . . you remember to make him more tired than yourself . . . you keep thinking . . . "I'll make him quit; I'll make him quit; he'll quit; he's getting tired; I can feel him letting up; he's running out of energy; he's quitting." . . . and you explode in a final series of moves, totally overwhelming him. . . . You are concentrating well . . . you are error free . . . no mistakes . . . you keep your intensity up throughout the entire match . . . you stay aggressive . . . you are an incredibly intense wrestler . . . the buzzer sounds . . . and you know you have won . . . you shake hands, see your score, and the referee holds your hand up in victory. . . . You have won!!

You feel the exhilaration of the best performance of your life . . . you allow your-self to savor the victory . . . feeling the excitement, pride, and happiness of win-ning . . . you have achieved your goal! . . . and you thank your body for everything it has given you . . . making sure you will take care of it soon . . . with food, drink, and rest . . . a job well-done.

Triathlon

See yourself arriving for the start of the swim . . . notice the people, the environment . . . listen to the sounds and be aware of the colors . . . notice how your body feels . . . you are in your suit and goggles . . . number written on your leg or arm . . . other swimmers are milling around, engrossed in their own thoughts . . . listen to the sounds and feel the energy around you and within you. You begin your warm-up routine . . . loosening up . . . beginning to focus . . . concentrating on your goal . . . the bike is ready, the running shoes are waiting . . . you are confident that all is well, and you let them go from your mind and focus just on the swim . . . the energy in your body and your breathing . . . you begin to say your swimming affirmations to yourself . . . "I am comfortable swimming as hard as I can," "I am free of fear while swimming." You relax . . . remembering your goals . . . knowing you are well prepared for this event and feeling ready and strong.

You line up . . . feeling the excitement in your body . . . hearing the instructions . . . watching the water . . . waiting . . . the gun goes off. You run to the water and charge in feeling the coldness on your skin . . . people are all around you . . . you remain calm as you throw your body into the water . . . stretching . . . swimming with your arms pulling hard toward you . . . you remind yourself to keep pushing . . . you focus on your form and your stroke . . . moving for a good position out of the crowd . . . picking up your pace as you go and checking your focus point to make sure you're going in a straight line . . . stroking powerfully . . . feeling relaxed and ready . . . arms moving evenly and in control . . . every movement pulling you closer to the finish. . . . "I am a strong, smooth, and powerful swimmer." You make the halfway point . . . swimming hard, fast, powerfully through the water . . . seeing the shore . . . feeling yourself slicing through the water smoothly . . . every move-ment . . . every stroke feels right and strong—your body knows its strength and power as you move closer and closer . . . you can hear your rhythmic splashing as your arms move powerfully . . . stroking . . . pulling . . . you focus on your breathing and how smooth you are in the water . . . you swim harder, knowing you are almost finished . . . you will soon be out of the water . . . you feel good . . . you are aware of your energy and how ready you are for the whole event . . . it feels good to push hard all the way.

You reach the shore and feel the ground beneath your feet as you run to the change area and get into your clothes . . . you have practiced this change over and over . . . you feel the pull of the material on your wet skin . . . you are an expert at this . . . you change with great speed and with a minimum of effort . . . very quickly and efficiently . . . you are focused and in control as you jump on your bicycle and take off . . . spinning easily and establishing good speed. . . . "That was fast . . . great job . . . got that done perfectly" . . . you think as you focus on your breathing and settle into the bicycle rhythm, pedaling smoothly . . . your hands and feet begin to warm up slowly . . . you are feeling better all the time . . . strong and in control . . . fast and smooth . . . you spin powerfully with your legs . . . pedaling hard . . . relaxing your body . . . stretching your neck . . . shifting your body on the bicycle to a comfortable position . . . riding confidently next to another biker. You begin to talk . . . nice way to keep yourself going . . . you feel light . . . controlled . . . your cadence is good, just where you want it to be . . . you spin powerfully, maintaining approximately ninety turns per minute . . . your wheels are spinning faster . . . easier gears . . . you feel good . . . leaning into the hills . . . using control on the downgrade . . . eating some bananas, drinking water, refreshing yourself with some needed carbos . . . feeling a little tiredness and feeling good at the same time . . . you are aware of the feel of the air on your face and the sounds of the wind as it flies past your ears . . . there is a sense of freedom and lightness as you push your legs powerfully . . . passing others . . . spinning . . . flying.

You remember your affirmations and goals for this biking section" . . . spinning smooth and fast . . . working hard . . . feeling good . . . almost finished." The ground seems to be flying beneath you as the miles go by and you focus on your rhythm . . . you are leaving it all behind you as you come closer and closer to the finish . . . thoughts of running begin to enter your mind . . . you notice them and then let them go as you focus on your breathing and a hard sprint to the finish . . . you become aware of the crowd and allow them to give you energy.

You ride over to your assigned spot, put your bike in its proper place, and quickly put on your running shoes . . . lacing each with speed and control . . . you take off running . . . great change and fast again . . . no wasted effort . . . , your legs feel good, this is a different feeling . . . they are loose and warm and ready to go . . . you begin to loosen up all over . . . warming up . . . breathing evenly and deeply . . . your body begins to settle into its rhythm . . . you feel very good . . . this is the easy part for you . . . become aware of the pavement under your feet and the sound your strides make. . . . "I am a powerful runner," "This is my strongest event," "I run hard and with ease for the next few miles."

You begin to push yourself after three miles . . . picking up the pace . . . noticing the sounds around you and how the ground changes as you race above it . . . you push hard on miles four and five, knowing the end of the race is near . . . the miles pass beneath you . . . you are light and strong . . . you say your affirmations. . . . "I easily push through the tiredness." "I am a strong and fast runner," Focus on your arms feeling powerful and relaxed . . . you see the six-mile mark ahead . . . you are passing some other runners now . . . in complete control . . . you push . . . surging . . . passing . . . accelerating . . . beginning to sprint the last 400 meters . . . passing more runners . . . taking them all by surprise . . . your legs seem to be moving by themselves . . . lifting . . . stretching . . . reaching . . . you cross the finish line . . . you gasp for breath . . . slowing to a walk . . . sides heaving . . . breathing hard . . . tired . . . exhilarated . . . excited . . . joyful . . . pleased.

You hear the crowd now and become aware of the colors of the finish line area . . . you can feel the euphoria rising in your body . . . the happiness, the contentment . . . you know you have won . . . you have done your best . . . you have reached your goals . . . experience it . . . let your accomplishment in . . . thank your body for all it has given you today . . . let it all flow through your entire body . . . in every blood vessel and every cell . . . feel the pride, the confidence, the sense of accomplishment . . . hear the crowd . . . see your friends and their joy for you . . . experience it all . . . and let yourself rest . . . reward yourself for your fine effort . . . experience again the feelings of completion, happiness, and contentment for doing your best and finishing this triathlon . . . allow yourself to rest now . . . enjoying the tiredness and focusing on your breathing, knowing you have everything you need to be, to do, and to have what you want in your triathlon competitions.

Skiing Nordic

(The following visualization for a Nordic 10K race was designed for an Olympic skier we worked with before the 1988 Olympics. The visualization follows a specific course; it may be modified for other courses.)

Imagine yourself at the ski area . . . you are warming up by yourself . . . skiing part of the course . . . checking it out . . . testing waxes . . . you look for rest areas on the course where you can let up a little . . . making your plans for the race as you go . . . looking at the best line on the downhills.

You go back to your room . . . changing your shirt . . . drinking some liquids . . . then you go out to the stadium . . . getting your skis, warming up, and doing sprints . . . you watch people go out and remind yourself that you are good . . . you're confident . . . you can do the same or better . . . you feel the excitement rising in your body . . . you know you can do well.

You get in the pen and stretch . . . you warm your hands, getting ready . . . reminding yourself of your affirmations: "I am strong; I am prepared; I am the best; I am confident and ready; I trust myself and my body." You are good and you belong here.

You are in the gate . . . there is the 10-second warning . . . countdown from five . . . go anytime . . . three . . . you push hard . . . you go really hard, double poling . . . the pace is set . . . you are sprinting to the woods . . . on the flat for 200 yards . . . you begin to start up the hills . . . you are long, stretched out, and powerful . . . your tempo is quick . . . you concentrate on powerful skiing with excellent technique . . . you hear your time at 1K . . . at the top of a steep rise . . . you adapt your pace accordingly . . . if it's slow, you pick up the pace, telling yourself that it's OK . . . if it's fast, then that's OK too . . . you are strong and powerful.

You start down the hill . . . you ski aggressively; you are relaxed and centered . . . breathing deeply . . . you let go, you relax, you let your skis run fast . . . "I'm safe and staying light; I am loose and relaxed. . . ." After 5K the course turns a sharp corner and heads up the hills again . . . you ski aggressively up the hills, pushing hard, keeping a quick tempo . . . you are so strong . . . and you are making good time . . . you hear your times and they are good . . . you are pleased . . . at 7K you hear your time . . . if it's good, you keep it up . . . if it's a little slow, you remind yourself of Judi Brown King in the 1984 Olympic final 400-meter hurdles, saying, "I've come too far to let it go here at the Olympics." and you push harder and more aggressively . . . you are tough. . . . "Be tough; I do well; I'll make it."

You are aggressive, quick . . . and fast downhill . . . you center yourself, breathing deeply, relaxing your shoulders . . . skiing light and loose . . . going for it . . . lots of corners now . . . fast, fast downhills . . . think smart . . . they're easy . . . "I stay loose and relaxed; I anticipate and control." You see yourself as a downhill skier, graceful and aggressive . . . smooth, powerful, and in control.

At 9K you hear your time . . . it is good . . . and another uphill approaches . . . you are really excited now . . . you increase the tempo . . . knowing you're almost finished . . . remembering good road races where you pushed yourself . . . knowing how strong and fast you are . . . every second counts in the long run . . . there is a steep and short uphill . . . you do an aggressive herringbone . . . quick, quick, quick . . . the momentum carries you over the top . . . you turn through the woods and go into the flat and out into the stadium . . . you hear the cheering and yelling of the crowds and the announcer's voice . . . you are skiing hard . . . sprinting these last 200 to 300 meters in the open . . . mostly flat with a little hill . . . you go around the last corner . . . 100 meters to the finish . . . you are double poling . . . sprinting for all you are worth . . . with good form . . . and you cross the finish line . . . smiling, laughing, hearing the announcer . . . knowing you have skied the best race of your life . . . you catch your breath . . . feeling the excitement of a good race and of the Olympics . . . knowing you deserve to be here . . . knowing you are the best . . . you hear the announcer say, "The time to beat is . . ." and it is your time . . . this is your year.

Alpine/Downhill

Mental Preparation of an Alpine Skier

You are standing at the top of a steep, beautiful, snow-covered hill; gazing down at the slope. Feel the feelings in your body . . . what are your thoughts about your upcoming run down the mountain . . . if you feel any tension in your body, focus your thoughts to relax those body parts . . . feeling yourself to be centered, with your body's center focused two inches below your navel . . . feeling your center of gravity over your skis . . . feeling the power and flexibility in your knees and legs . . . you follow the course with your eyes, imagining yourself skiing down the slope with power, flexibility, and grace . . . the moguls disappearing under your expert skiing . . . your upper body is relaxed . . . your body totally in rhythm with your turns . . . taking a deep breath, you push off powerfully, remembering your affirmations, "I am powerful, strong and graceful. I am balanced, skiing with good rhythm." You ski the hill, making powerful and graceful turns, feeling the skiis under your feet, turning effortlessly . . . you feel excited, exuberant, and powerful. You are skiing fast and under control . . . you are skiing the best run of your life . . . you reach the bottom of the hill, happy and exhilarated. . . . You have skied your dream.

Taking a deep breath, thanking your body for its performance and all it has given
to you, you come back to your body sitting in the chair in your living room . . .
counting to three, you take a deep breath, stretching your arms and legs, stretching
your neck and back, and opening your eyes when you are ready.

Relaxation and imagery are important in the mental preparation of any sport, and
skiing is no exception. A skier can improve his or her performance by taking as few
as fifteen minutes a day to relax and visualize skiing down their favorite mountain.
In the fall of 1987, we were contacted by Brent Haverkamp, a member of the University of Oregon ski team. We worked with Brent over a period of five months,
working to improve his performance in the slalom and giant slalom. His original
goals were to improve his concentration and focus; to ski injury free during the season; to be more relaxed during competition; and to make the team and be in the top
seven. He also wanted to enter the season with a higher level of explosive power, for
example, quicker and more powerful turns.

He achieved all of these goals for his 1988 skiing season. His best race was eighteen of 130, and he was fourth in his age group of nineteen and over. I interviewed
him to learn how the mental training program worked for him; what he did differently as a result of the training; and how his performance was improved. His answers
should help both recreational and competitive skiers.

Which mental training techniques did you use the most?

I used the affirmations a lot. They literally changed the way I think before and
during a race. I also used the guided visualization tapes the night before my race. I
wrote five important affirmations and read them twice a day—at night and when I
woke up in the morning. I put them all over the house so I would see them. They
really helped me change my attitude about myself.

What did you learn?

I learned how important it is to be mentally and physically prepared. I began
thinking, "Hey, I can do this!" instead of thinking or saying that I can't. I really
succeeded in getting the "I can't" business out of my mind.

Goals are a step-by-step process. I had a few setbacks, but I kept moving forward.
I had obstacles, but I overcame them.

What helped the most?

The visualizations and affirmations. I used the tapes every other night at the beginning of the season (November), and then I started to do it on my own during the
season. I would listen to them once a week, or so, after I had started competition.
The affirmations helped me stay positive and motivated. I stopped worrying about
things. Even in a race when I raced in the last position, where the course was terrible
and rutted out, I went for it and finished eighteenth. I was very pleased and happy.

During the summer I was training at Timberline (Oregon), and I would think,
"Oh, I can do this," and I would correct my form, and tell myself I could do anything I wanted to—it was within my capability to do it. And I would do it. I would
watch the really good racers and imagine myself being that fluid and powerful.

How was your performance different?

I've improved a lot. My points went down. One of my goals is to qualify for the Northwest Cup. It is a series of races where you have to have 182 points for slalom and 167 for giant slalom. I'm a much faster skier now, and I don't worry as much as I used to. I feel much more confident—in racing and training, in myself, in my competitions. I learned not to put myself below anybody. You just have to *believe* that you are one of the best, or *the* best.

The other benefits I've noticed were that this filtered into my social life and when I was out with friends. I am more relaxed and confident. It's helped with my studying and in my schoolwork. I am doing well in my sport and I feel good about myself in general. This makes you a happier person—just saying positive things to yourself.

I even used it for a job interview. I prepared myself just like for competition. I psyched myself up; I thought about the questions they might ask. I felt good about myself and my abilities. The interview went very well and I got the job.

In competition, what do you do mentally?

In competition, I inspect the course before the race, memorizing each gate. Then I take some time and visualize myself racing the course, making each turn smoothly, flawlessly, and as fast as possible. Then during the actual competition, I just go for it.

When I am just free skiing, and not in competition, I concentrate on relaxing my upper body more—after four or five turns, I feel more relaxed. I do a body check— from the top of my head down to my feet; head, jaw, and neck relaxed, upper body relaxed, arms relaxed; I check to see that I'm breathing well; I check my form for my legs, knees, and feet.

In the gates, I am doing what I've been rehearsing. I'm always looking for the fastest turn. Before the race I warm up for two or three runs, and then I slip the course. This is the most important, so I can inspect and look at the course itself. I think about my strategy and how I am going to run it.

I used to look at the other racers and freak myself out. Now I look at them; I watch them and learn from them. I imagine myself in their place as I watch them. That's me doing that superfast run down the slope. I am not worried about them any more. I stopped comparing myself to them. It's helped a lot to stop doing that.

Do you have any suggestions for recreational skiers?

Go out there and just have fun! Don't worry about what you look like. Go up and have fun skiing. That's what it's all about. Don't try too hard.

What about skiing a scary slope?

Just tell yourself "I can do this! I believe in myself. Go do it!"

Some of Brent's affirmations were

I am one of the top five members of the ski team.
I own a top five spot on the ski team.
I am quick and powerful in the turns.

I am explosive.
I am stronger than I have ever been.
I am physically and mentally tough.
I enjoy shinning the rapid gates.
The rapid gates are my friends.
It is easy for me to shin the gates.
I am strong and explosive.
I am just as tough as my competition.
I am fast, quick, and accurate.
I am fearless in competition.
I accelerate out of my turns.
I believe in myself.
I hold the key!
I am on the team!

Brent achieved all his goals for the 1988 season and was happy with the changes mental preparation made in his life. As with physical training, mental training must be practiced over time, weekly and daily. What your mind imagines, your body performs.

Slalom

Become aware that you are riding in the van . . . you can hear the voices and laughter of your teammates, and you notice the feel of the wheels, and they move beneath you on the road and snow . . . you are beginning to focus on the race ahead of you today . . . you know you have trained well and you are ready and well prepared for this race . . . you talk to some of the guys . . . you feel good and strong . . . you are comfortable with this team . . . they are friends and you know they support you . . . you breathe deeply and bring your focus back to the mountain and the lodge as the van stops. You go inside with the team and find a place where everyone can put their stuff . . . and you check in and get your bib . . . you begin to put your gear on . . . pulling on your sweater . . . sliding your feet into your boots . . . you think about your affirmations and your goals for this race . . . you feel good and ready . . . you tie your bib on and go outside . . . you can feel the air on your face, in your hair, and you take energy from this . . . it always feels good to be on the mountain and ready to ski . . . you are happy and focused . . . you step into your skis and head for the lift . . . you can hear the sounds around you and they make you feel good . . . they are familiar . . . you wait in line for the lift and feel the excitement beginning to rise in your body . . . you know how to get those butterflies to fly in formation . . . you know how to use that excitement to give you power and energy.

As you ride up the lift, you begin to check out the course . . . you notice the fall and the position of each gate . . . and you begin to visualize yourself on this course . . . you focus in entirely on the race ahead of you . . . and you begin to make friends with this course . . . you reach the top and get off the lift . . . your breathing is deep and easy as you ski to the top of the course and slowly begin to slip from gate to gate . . . getting to know the top section . . . noticing each bump and slope . . . each gate . . . it's position and width . . . at each gate you visualize exactly how you are going to take it . . . where your line will be and the balance of your body . . . your mind is totally focused on remembering this course . . . and you are aware of your power of concentration . . . you feel strong and ready as you reach the end and head back up the lift to slip the course again . . . this time to focus on the downhill section . . . you think of the course as a whole now . . . its line and fall . . . its tricky spots and angles . . . you know what to do and the strategy you will need . . . it is a good course . . . a challenging course, and you are ready . . . as you slip it a third time, you focus on each gate separately . . . making friends with it . . . remembering how to take each one with the greatest speed and balance.

Now it is time to relax a little, and you head for some free skiing . . . your mind is focused on the course you have just slipped, and while you are free skiing, you pretend you are on the course . . . a few quick gates . . . good speed . . . good balance . . . you begin to get the feel in your body of the first course . . . you are thinking about shinning the gates and being technically sharp . . . you know if your technique is good and you are balanced you will also be fast. You find out your place and head into the lodge to eat and talk with some of your friends . . . this is a good way for you to relax and to stay connected with your buddies and their energy . . . you know how to stay focused on your race . . . your strengths . . . you go back out on the slope . . . you watch some of the other racers, knowing you can learn from them . . . you also know you are here to win and it is important to notice their weaknesses . . . you are a smart racer . . . you are a powerful racer . . . you know you ski to win . . . you remember your affirmations, and you watch, allowing yourself to feel the excitement and energy that fills you when you are about to race . . . this is your sport . . . your place of power . . . you center yourself knowing you are just as good as any skier in the race today . . . they tell you about your power and readiness . . . you are focused and well prepared as you stretch and go through your usual routine of warming up . . . waiting . . . ready.

It is your turn and you stand in the starting gate . . . you are confident and relaxed . . . you breathe deeply centering yourself and focusing on the first two gates . . . you wait . . . and then explode out of the gate . . . eyes forward . . . mind forward . . . you move with quickness and balance . . . always focused ahead . . . feeling strong and powerful, you take each gate as if it is yours . . . you own this course . . . your body is like a well-maintained machine . . . working as one . . . one ski . . . at one with your body . . . your timing is just the way you want it . . . being ready for each gate . . . shinning . . . being in command . . . you move like the wind . . . smoothly . . . easily . . . in complete control and at the height of your technique . . . always focused ahead . . . feeling strong . . . you move through the gates . . . each twist . . . each turn in your control . . . you are fluid as you move toward the finish ahead . . . you power through the last gate and push to pick up speed as you cross the finish . . . you slow . . . turn . . . and stop.

You breathe . . . and wait for your time . . . you can feel the joy and confidence begin to rise in your body as you get your time . . . you know you did your best and you handled that course . . . as you head back to the lodge for a break, you think about what you could do to gain more speed. . . . How are they likely to set up the second course? . . . What techniques can you use to a better advantage so you can pick up a few more seconds? . . . perhaps you discuss the first race with some of your teammates . . . learning from their experience and knowing they are supporting you and you are supporting them . . . you think again of your goals . . . remembering that you are racing to win . . . you have the power and strength . . . and you are ready . . . you go back to the slope.

You slip this new course just as you did the first course . . . focusing on the top section . . . then the bottom section . . . then the course as a whole . . . your heart is light and your mind is totally on the race ahead . . . you feel confident, and your energy is high and under control . . . this one is for you . . . you know this new course inside and out . . . there is nothing that can stop you . . . it is your turn, and you wait in the starting gate . . . centered and focused on the first two gates . . . again you explode out of the chute . . . moving toward the first gate . . . focused ahead . . . you can feel the strength in your body . . . its willingness to give you what you want . . . its readiness to perform at its peak . . . you move smoothly from gate to gate . . . taking each one just as you had planned . . . balanced and smooth, you race from the top section to the bottom . . . using all your technique . . . shinning the gates . . . in control . . . moving like hot fluid toward the finish . . . always focused ahead . . . you know you are the best . . . you see the finish now as you take the last two gates with power and speed . . . pushing . . . moving. You cross the finish and come to a stop . . . you are aware of the people watching and the sounds around you . . . you allow yourself to rest now . . . you get your time and know you gave it your all and you have reached your goal . . . you feel the energy and excitement . . . you are proud of yourself . . . you are proud of the strength of your body and your mind . . . and you breathe and rest.

Slowly begin to let go of the picture now . . . bringing your focus to your breathing . . . gently letting go and remembering your affirmations . . . allow your mind to become empty and to rest. . . . When I count to three, you may open your eyes feeling relaxed and ready and knowing you have everything you need within you to be the best racer you can be.

Kyaking/White-Water Slalom Racing

In the June 19, 1989 issue of *Sports Illustrated,* Jon Lugbill, the undisputed king of white-water canoeing was quoted: "I'm not in this to win world championships. I'm in it because I love it. If I don't win the worlds, if I'm not in the Olympics, that doesn't matter. What's most important is that I gave it a good shot, raised my standards, raised my level."

This attitude is an important one for athletes to consider. The joy of participating in the sport is often the only reason for doing it. Lugbill used goals and modified affirmations from the beginning, just as a matter of course. He seemed to do mental training, as many athletes do, by instinct.

The article goes on: "He set what seemed an almost impossible goal: three world championships. He wrote a '3' on a piece of paper and put it in his underwear drawer so he would see it every morning. He told no one. And, of course, he won in '81 on a tiny, windy creek in Wales, and again in '83 on an Italian river that resembled a rock pile. He surpassed his goal in '87, soaring to his fourth individual title on a fast and powerful river in France.

" 'When I have spare time, my mind thinks. How can I paddle better? It's not just what I find myself thinking about, it's what I want to think about. See, paddling isn't something I *have* to do. You should always do something because you like to do it, something you can devote yourself to and enjoy. It is not worth suffering to get to an end. The means must be enjoyable. . . . I feel you control your mind. You don't let your mind control you. Life is like walking a high wire. If you don't look down, it's fine.' "

Whether it is C-1 boating (a closed canoe where the athlete is kneeling and using a single-bladed paddle), or kyaking (sitting and using a double-bladed paddle), whitewater events require a single-minded purpose, flexibility, and surrender to the flow of the water. In all cases, the athlete is dealing with an outside force that he can never overpower or control.

In interviewing canoeists and kyakers, several topics surfaced regarding the proper mental state of awareness.

1. A safe eddy rule: Look downstream, identify the hydraulics and their effect on the boat; devise a game plan of where you want to go; see self executing the game plan; stay in the moment once you begin the process.
2. "There is nothing in my eyes except what I am running and the path I am on." Concentrate on
   a. Being relaxed, easy, and flowing with the river.
   b. Letting the water have its way.
   c. Putting something on what the river wants.
   d. Surrendering with total control.
   e. Using the river and never opposing it.
3. A technique to use when rolling over
   a. Telling self positive things, leaving no room for fear.
   b. It's a whole process, think: "Roll position, clear the paddle, sweep to the back deck (a front deck to back deck roll), head down, head down, head down. . . ."
   c. Tell self, "I am totally comfortable with 40 to 60 seconds underwater."
   d. Mentally slow it down if you turn over—be free of panic or fear.
4. Positive things to remember
   a. "Boat within yourself."
   b. First run the line in your mind, creating emotional and intellectual safety internally for yourself.
   c. Center yourself.
   d. Draw that line on the water that you have imagined.
   e. Affirmations to use

■ I have great reflexes.
■ I accept and respond quickly to surprises.
■ Let speed be the product of mindless repetition.

5. In a kyak or canoe, you can't be rigid; you must be relaxed, flexible, accepting of wherever you are in the water. You must always have a Plan B (plenty of options); taking your time, with a series of corrective maneuvers. Never, never rush. Always take your time, with care.

Rock Climbing

(This visualization may be helpful to beginning rock climbers or those who experience fear and anxiety before climbing.)

Imagine yourself approaching the rock formation you are about to climb. Look at it with interest, respect, and curiosity. Walk up and touch the rock; let yourself experience its texture; the feel of it; whether it is cool or warm; stand close to it, feeling its presence . . . make friends with this rock that you will be spending time with . . . smell it . . . accept it and allow yourself to acknowledge its power and beauty.

As you put on your gear, do so with care and patience . . . taking your time, making sure everything is correctly done . . . your protection . . . your safety . . . as you begin to get ready to do your climb, take two or three deep abdominal breaths, deep into your belly . . . relaxing your shoulders, centering yourself in the area two inches below your navel . . . feeling yourself to be balanced, focused and ready to go . . . staying centered in your body . . . begin to feel the rock with your fingers and hands . . . exploring it, feeling its energy next to you . . . climbing is an intimate experience . . . one that you share with the rock itself . . . feel yourself balanced on your feet . . . centered in your body . . . trusting the strength in your legs and feet . . . knowing you are strong.

Focus on the rock . . . tuning everything else out . . . just going three to five feet at a time . . . breathe air into any tenseness you may feel in your body . . . exhale any fear or anxiety that you might feel . . . returning your focus to the rock and your body, climbing . . . feeling light, supple, flexible . . . you gracefully climb the rock . . . you are confident, powerful . . . smoothly climbing with a delicate, yet powerful grace.

Your feet feel like Velcro on the rock's surface . . . you place your weight and know it will stay there . . . the rock is helping you . . . it feels solid, warm . . . you and the rock are in perfect harmony and balance . . . you feel its strength in your fingers . . . they are an extension of the rock itself . . . you climb, feeling your center of gravity close to the rock . . . enjoying this communing with a such a powerful entity of nature . . . you feel whole, alive, exhilarated.

You flow with each pitch of the rock . . . flowing from one spot to the next, totally connected with the rock . . . totally absorbed in its energy and grace.

You notice the sounds . . . hearing the rope . . . the carbineers on the rack . . . the sound of the biner when you clip into a piece of protection . . . all the sounds of safety for you . . . knowing you are safe in your climb.

You feel and see you are approaching the top . . . you quickly make the last two moves and you are on top! . . . feel the moment of joy and excitement of your achievement . . . allow yourself to feel the rapture of the moment. Aah . . . deeply breathing oxygen into your body . . . feeling the incredible lightness of being . . . light, free, and living each moment.

If there are others with you, you watch them ascend and reach the top . . . sharing your joy and your mutual success . . . and you begin to think about rappeling down from the top. . . . You begin to check and look at the anchor . . . making sure it's mechanically correct . . . you double check the biners and your harness . . . with a double-back buckle . . . checking that the rope through device is OK . . . you begin to center within yourself again . . . having made sure you are emotionally and intellectually safe . . . physically safe . . . knowing now it will all work . . . you love this moment of leaning out into space . . . you step to the edge . . . feeling the excitement in your body . . . the ultimate moment of trust and surrender . . . you lean far back in space . . . your weight leaning out against the rock . . . the greatest surrender and trust . . . it is good to surrender to the rope . . . you feel the rope through your hand . . . as you descend, the rope begins to feel different . . . less friction going down . . . you watch the rock, enjoying the sensations of doing the rappel . . . feeling light like a spider on a web . . . you feel weightless . . . light and flexible . . . supple and graceful . . . you reach the bottom quickly . . . feeling the incredible rush of adrenaline . . . of another exciting and successful climb.

Allow yourself to come back to your body sitting in the chair, or lying down . . . when I count to three, you may open your eyes, feeling relaxed, refreshed, and ready for the rest of the day . . . one. . . .

Racquetball

Imagine yourself approaching the racquetball court . . . you are looking forward to this match . . . you go inside the court and begin to warm up, hitting the ball against the wall . . . you begin practicing each shot . . . your kill shot in the corners and the low front wall . . . your passing shots . . . your lobs and ceiling shots . . . and your roll out . . . you pause for a moment imagining each shot with an opponent . . . you see yourself doing all the shots flawlessly.

You see and feel yourself as fluid, smooth, and quick . . . with great focus and clarity . . . your body and mind are centered . . . and you are playing well within yourself . . . you begin to pump yourself up mentally . . . telling yourself how accurate your kill shot is . . . how deadly a backhand you have . . . it is your favorite, the backhand . . . you are ready . . . you are quick . . . you constantly seek out and find your opponent's weaknesses.

Your opponent arrives and you warm up together . . . you continue to psych yourself up . . . feeling good . . . feeling confident and powerful. . . . You begin to play . . . you react with fluid and smooth movements . . . concentrating fully . . . playing with power and intensity. . . . You set your opponent up time after time . . . getting in position properly, you have him or her running and making errors . . . you are quick and deadly with your killer shots.

You play on and on . . . once in awhile taking a couple of deep breaths to reestablish your control and to slow yourself down a little when you are serving . . . if you miss shots, you remind yourself to let them go easily and concentrate on the next point . . . if you feel any anger arising, you let that go also; again taking deep breaths and maintaining your calmness and your state of being . . . you say some affirmations to yourself. . . . "I easily let that bad play go. I'm quick, smooth, and fluid. I slow down and concentrate with great focus and intensity."

The end of the game is coming soon . . . you renew your intensity and focus . . . playing aggressively and with great power and control . . . you close out shots easily . . . and you play well within yourself . . . the last point you win easily . . . and it is over . . . you have won.

Allow yourself to enjoy the excitement and satisfaction of a well-played game . . . thanking your body for being strong and powerful . . . for playing so well . . . your mind and body in such good rapport . . . achieving your goal . . . and playing your best.

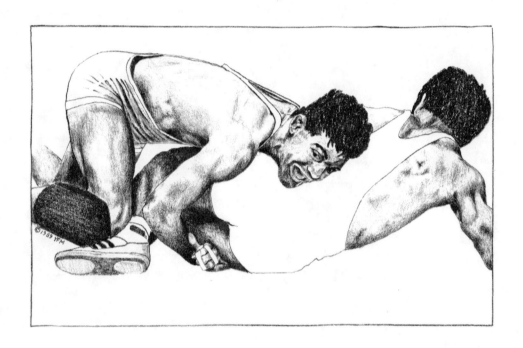

Chapter ■ *Six*

Health and Healing

The heart is the key.

In our culture we are taught to run from our pain, especially the psychological pain. We are encouraged to tough it out, to be a man, to resist, to avoid the unpleasant physical and mental pain of life. The key is opening our hearts to our pain, injury, feelings, thoughts, and dreams—opening, instead of resisting. Stephen Levine, a therapist who works with the terminally ill, talks about opening our hearts to ourselves—to our pain, to our suffering. We live in such judgment of ourselves and each other. Our culture is based on comparison, and while analysis and comparison can be invaluable to us when applied to ourselves and our accomplishments, comparison with others can create much misery in our lives, because we often choose to come up short. **If you must compare, do it in a positive way.** I often tell my clients, "Positive comparison heals; negative comparison hurts."

Before you break the cycle of comparison, you can change how you use it by comparing yourself to others and seeing your value, your uniqueness, and your positives, rather than your negatives. A soccer player I was working with used to torment herself by comparing herself with her teammates, always seeing her weaknesses and how she never quite measured up to her teammates. Rather than trying to break her habit of comparing, I had her compare her strengths with her teammates'. Eventually, by acknowledging the comparison process and substituting affirmations for the negative comparisons, she was able to stop comparing herself to others.

We also spend much time in our lives seeking approval from others. However, the most important approval must come from ourselves. The comparison process enables us to continue an unhealthy cycle of approval seeking. Yes, we want and need acknowledgment; yes, we want and need love; but we often fail to see that these must come from within first, so we can appreciate and accept those things from our families, peers, and coaches.

Resistance

When we open our hearts to ourselves, we are able to open our hearts to others, treating them with respect and acceptance. Likewise, when we are injured or in pain, the more angry we are at ourselves or our body parts, and the harder it is for us to heal. Resistance to pain creates more intensity in the pain. What we resist, we create, exaggerate, or become. The very act of resistance is a powerful, creative force. Resistance is similar to negative self-talk; it creates negativity and a negative power. Bringing the pain or injury into one's heart, literally letting go of the fear and anger around our pain or injury, helps us work with it in a constructive manner. Such acceptance and acknowledgment create an internal climate for healing injury and lessening pain. We are not saying to give up; we are saying merely to stop fighting the pain or the injury. Send it loving energy and acknowledge its importance to you.

For several years I worked with a collegiate sprinter who often was injured. We did a number of visualizations around his injuries, very similar to the guided visualization for healing injury in this chapter. In one section of the visualization, we asked the injury what it wanted. I was continually amazed how his body answered our questions. During one session working with his strained hamstring, we asked, "What does your hamstring need or want from you?" The body's answer was . . . would like more relaxation; more sitting in hot tubs, two to three times a week; getting massages once a week; am getting almost healed; not totally ready yet . . . still not ready for a full sprint.

"What would you like to do?" Answer: . . . want slower workouts; too fast, too soon, "When are you willing to run fast?" Answer: . . . next week; the beginning of next week . . . need another week to run—hard, but not fast.

In a session a week later, we asked, "What's happening?" The body's answer was . . . strained again; not as bad as first time . . . can do strides . . . almost healed . . . don't know how much can take yet. "What do you need from me?" Answer: . . . get relaxed; really tender (sore) . . . before practice, get warmed up really well with warm packs and warm whirlpool . . . and a massage of the area . . . then after workout, be iced.

John had a habit of touching the spot on the hamstring, rubbing it, touching it. His body told him to stop touching . . . just leave it alone . . . except for the heat, ice, and hot tubs . . . otherwise, it just wanted to be left alone.

This was a startling bit of information. I don't know what it meant. My guess is that everytime John touched his hamstring, he had worrisome thoughts and energy or judgment about getting well. John stopped touching the injured hamstring, and we just gave his body what it asked for. John recovered quickly from all his injuries and ran well throughout his college years.

We remind you to ask only if you want to hear the answers and you are willing to do what your body asks of you.

Methods of Healing and Reducing Stress

In cases of pain and injury, we encourage athletes to see qualified medical practitioners immediately. All collegiate athletes have access to the university health center, which is staffed by medical doctors, physical therapists, and athletic trainers. Going to the university health center should be the first step in healing an injury. All the mental methods we discuss are suggested *in addition* to seeing a medical professional. Noncollegiate athletes have their choice of professionals, depending on their locale and the variety of medical practitioners in their area. In the 1980s there has been a huge increase in the number of medical doctors specializing in sports medicine; in addition, more orthopedists are specializing in sports injuries as well. Other medical professionals, who are governed by state licensing regulations and are most often eligible to receive payment from insurance companies, are chiropractic physicians, osteopaths, naturopaths, and podiatrists. In Eugene, with its legions of runners, all are available. Most of these practitioners welcome questions and inquiries about their services. When I began running in 1977, the only sports podiatrist I could find was in San Francisco, Dr. Harry Hlavac. To my joy, Dr. Hlavac made some orthotic inserts for my shoes that I wore for three years. I was so flat-footed I could not run without them. Eventually, Dr. Steven Roy moved to Eugene and established a fine sports medicine practice. I have worn Dr. Roy's orthotics for years and have been able to run seven marathons. Such aids are invaluable to elite and recreational athletes alike. We suggest you see what your town offers and, again, find what's right for you.

In chapter 4 of *The Mental Athlete,* we discussed stress-reduction methods of breathing, meditation, massage, floatation, and relaxation. In addition to those, some interesting newer forms of relaxation and healing are being used in treating athletic injury and in inducing relaxation: acupuncture, rolfing, reiki, and sleep.

Acupuncture

Acupuncture has enjoyed a new-found interest from athletes, looking into everything that might make them better or heal nagging injuries. Acupuncture is an ancient Chinese healing method in which the acupuncturist inserts fine needles into energy pathways in the body. These insertions are used in Chinese medicine to treat numerous illnesses or injuries by opening up blocked energy patterns so that the flow of energy through the body is increased.

Having an acupuncture treatment is an interesting experience. I had ten treatments over a period of three months, working with an exercise-induced asthma condition. The treatments helped considerably: I chose the acupuncture over the inhaling of a steroid that was recommended by my allergist, a traditional M.D. The asthma condition ceased, and after each treatment, I felt a surge of energy in my body. The confounding variable of this process was extreme emotional stress in my life. I was using a number of treatments for the condition, including massage and personal therapy. The asthma was definitely not caused by allergens or any allergic reactions to my environment. I highly recommend acupuncture as an interesting alternative to traditional methods.

Rolfing/Structural Integration

Rolfing was created by Dr. Ida Rolf as a body therapy in the 1930s and became very popular during the human potential movement of the 1960s. Dr. Rolf was a biochemist with a Ph.D. from Columbia University and discovered that the same network of connective tissue that contains and links the muscle system when it's healthy can be used to reshape it when it's been pulled out of proper order. Each muscle and each muscle fiber are enveloped in a connective tissue called fascia. Dr. Rolf's work emphasized working with the fascial system to create more flexibility in the muscles and tendons.

Being rolfed feels rather like getting a deep tissue massage. The practitioner works the muscle sheaths for various muscle groups, in a series of ten sessions of about an hour each, freeing frozen or painful areas. This process results in more pliable and balanced muscles and increased fascial elasticity. Fascia are restored to more healthful balance by returning the muscles and bones to their proper alignments and inducing proper movement. The body returns to more of its original upright and correct posture.

As a runner, I found rolfing particularly helpful in increasing my pelvic flexibility, straightening my legs and knees, and opening up my chest and lower back, resulting in the ability to breathe much more deeply and fully than before treatment. For those who love deep tissue massage, I guarantee you will enjoy the benefits of rolfing. Eugene's premier rolfer, Karen Lackritz, is also an athlete, and she knows how to get the most out of her sessions with athletes. All rolfers are certified by the Rolf Institute in Boulder, Colorado. Rolfers are trained extensively over a three-year period in biological and behavioral sciences, body manipulation, and working with people.

Reiki

Reiki healing was developed in the early 1900s in Japan by Dr. Mikao Usui. Dr. Usui was the president of a small Christian university, Doshisha University, in Kyoto, Japan. He became interested in natural healing methods and did extensive research and reading of ancient doctrines in Chinese, Japanese, and Sanskrit. He finally found in the teachings of the Buddha, in Sanskrit, the formula, symbols, and description of how Buddha healed. After going on a twenty-one day meditation retreat on one of Japan's sacred mountains, he learned how to use the symbols in healing and was able to lay his hands on people to heal them. He began teaching others the natural healing technique of reiki, as well as helping them heal their thoughts. This method has been taught all over the world since the 1930s.

Reiki, rei being ray and ki being the ki or chi of life-force energy, is a hands-on healing method, used by certified reiki master practitioners. Practitioners place their hands on points of the body to open up blocked pathways, enabling the body's energy flow to continue and flow powerfully through the body. Other benefits are increased relaxation and stress reduction and a feeling of well-being. As time goes on, this particular hands-on healing method is gaining widespread use and acceptance throughout the world. The research on hands-on healing methods is beginning to show the effectiveness of human energy transmission and touching on the stimulation of blood flow and circulation in areas of physical injury.

Sleep

In a recent article in *Runner's World,* world-class runners discussed their need for large amounts of sleep during peak competition and workout schedules. Many of the male runners expressed needing nine to ten hours of sleep during hard training or competition. It is becoming more apparent, in reviewing the research on peak performance, that sound sleeping patterns are extremely important in restoring the body and the mind. In working with runners, coaches have reported that if the athletes are getting enough sleep (eight to ten hours per night), injuries are fewer and their susceptibility to infections such as colds and flu are much lower than with less sleep. We believe that in the 1990s more research will be conducted on the immune system, and the relationship of environmental factors and physical training habits will be more clearly delineated. It seems that sleep is as important as diet in curbing injuries and illnesses.

In working with one client, we noticed that after a big race or a very hard workout, he would be more likely to get injured or catch a cold if he didn't take a day or two of easy training. If he kept up a hard schedule after a competition, he invariably sustained an injury or got sick. This also seems to be compounded in runners by low body fat level. Dick Brown, during his tenure as Mary Decker Slaney's coach, would keep a close watch over her body fat level. If it dropped below a certain level, he had found that Mary would invariably get injured. He conducted body fat checks weekly or biweekly to make sure her level was high enough in his formula for peak fitness and wellness.

All of these methods are interesting alternatives for maintaining peak fitness, facilitating healing, and reducing stress. Again, we encourage you to experiment a bit, try some new approaches, and determine what you like and what works for your personal healing program.

In working with athletes, we used the following guided visualizations for inducing sleep, reducing stress, and general relaxation. All can be recorded by you or a friend, for your Walkman. Each should be recorded in a slow voice and cover about a fifteen-minute period. The stress-reduction visualization was successfully used by a number of athletes, including a basketball player, to reframe negative or stressful aspects of the game. Any situation that causes stress in your life can be inserted into this visualization. It has a variety of uses and has been used for fear of flying, speaking in front of a group, taking a statistics test, and various sporting events. See how original you can be in using it in your life!

Sleep and Relaxation Visualization

(This visualization can be used for going to sleep or deep relaxation. *Never* listen to it while you are driving! It is to be used only when you are wanting to go to sleep, preferably in a quiet, safe place.)

Find a comfortable place to lie down; close your eyes; allow your attention to drop down inside; feeling the relaxation in your body and letting go . . . take a deep breath, letting it out with a sigh; **feeling peace and relaxation** come into your body and mind . . . take another deep **breath, and let it go;** begin at the top of your head, imagining relaxation flowing from **the top of your** head; feeling your face relax and soften, feeling the relaxation **going behind your eyes,** relaxing your jaw, your mouth, letting your tongue rest comfortably inside your mouth; imagine your head emptying of all thoughts . . . draining all concerns and cares away, feeling good; begin to feel the relaxation spreading down into your throat; relaxing your neck and feeling the warmth of the relaxation going into your shoulders, down into your arms, into your biceps, into your lower arms, through your wrists, into your hands and fingers; a relaxed feeling, soft and warm; pliable and flexible . . . imagine the relaxation flowing from your shoulders into your upper back and chest . . . going into your sternum and heart center . . . the center of your chest . . . feeling warm and relaxed and open . . . soft . . . down through your solar plexus, relaxing it, feeling at peace in body and in mind . . . feel the warmth of the relaxation spreading down into your belly . . . your abdomen and your lower back . . . into your hips . . . feeling the muscles relax, down into your legs and thighs, through your knees and calves . . . down into your feet and toes . . . all the tension draining out of your body through your feet into the ground . . . so your body is soft, relaxed, comfortable . . . totally peaceful and in harmony.

Begin to think of a time when you were peaceful and relaxed . . . imagining wherever it might have been . . . a place in your mind or a real place where you've been . . . think of a peaceful time when you were relaxed, tranquil, and all was right with the world . . . a sense of happiness, contentment, freedom . . . total relaxation and peace, total inner harmony.

Allow yourself to remember that time . . . seeing the scene . . . the people if there were some with you . . . hearing the sounds or the silence . . . feeling those feelings in your body of peace, harmony, contentment . . . calm, serenity . . . let that whole scene and that whole event come back to you . . . in its entirety . . . the images, the sounds, the feelings . . . of peace and quiet, total relaxation and harmony of body, mind, and spirit . . . allow yourself to be there again . . . allow yourself to feel that relaxation in your body . . . and that peaceful state of mind . . . without worry, without cares . . . just being . . . being peace, being harmony, being tranquility.

Allow yourself to think of a word that represents that state of mind, that state of being . . . it can be any word that represents that state . . . say the word over to yourself, allowing yourself the feeling in your body of peace and harmony and oneness with the world . . . oneness with all of life . . . oneness with your environment . . . imagine seeing your word on a poster, in any colors you want, hanging somewhere in your home . . . or your office . . . saying that word over to yourself . . .

bringing back those feelings of peacefulness and relaxation . . . happiness, harmony . . . knowing you have everything within you that you need to re-create this peace of mind, this peaceful state of being . . . feel your body, light and relaxed, a sensation of floating . . . soft, without resistance . . . letting go . . . your mind being empty and free of thoughts, soft and relaxed . . . at peace . . . begin to think of sleeping soundly and profoundly through the night . . . being in bed . . . relaxing, letting go of all the cares and worries of the day . . . emptying your mind of thoughts, feeling your body totally relaxed and resting . . . softness coming into your body . . . and letting go . . . floating, floating, floating . . . drifting off into sleep, with peaceful thoughts and dreams . . . your body relaxing, regenerating, healing itself, resting itself . . . and your mind taking its rest from thinking . . . into the realms of relaxation and softness . . . and imagine yourself sleeping through the night . . . deeply . . . healthfully . . . and knowing if you do wake up, and even get up, you return to bed, easily emptying your mind of thoughts and returning to sleep, falling asleep quickly . . . welcoming the softness of sleep . . . letting it receive you . . . with love and acceptance . . . feeling safe and secure in the softness of your bed . . . safe from the cares of the world . . . safe and secure, to sleep and reconnect with your higher self and spirit . . . relaxed, peaceful . . . dreaming your dreams in total peace and harmony . . . and knowing you will wake up in the morning when the alarm goes off, feeling refreshed, rested, and ready for the day . . . being grateful for the abundance in your life . . . for your healthy body, for your friends and loved ones . . . for the peacefulness in your life and in your heart . . . knowing you are growing toward fulfillment, happiness, and peace every day . . . allowing your body and your mind to surrender totally . . . and relaxing into sleep, knowing you are safe and secure . . . knowing you are loving and lovable, accepting and acceptable . . . letting go . . . sleeping . . . all your cares and thoughts floating away peacefully like soft clouds . . . floating away . . . at peace . . . relaxed . . . sleeping . . . soundly . . . peacefully . . . with peace in your heart.

Guided Visualization for Stress Reduction

Find a quiet place to sit or lie where you will not be disturbed for about fifteen minutes. Close your eyes and bring your attention to your breathing . . . breathe in deeply . . . hold . . . exhale . . . breathe . . . each time you inhale, breathe in peace and relaxation . . . each time you exhale, breathe out tightness and stress . . . breathe . . . begin to check in with your body, starting with your head and face. Notice if there are any areas of tightness or pain . . . begin to relax . . . allowing the tightness to soften and leave you . . . move slowly to your neck and shoulders . . . letting go . . . lowering your shoulders . . . softening . . . feeling peace and relaxation . . . move your attention to your back and belly . . . letting the peace and warmth in . . . allowing your body to become warm . . . light . . . soft . . . slowly moving your attention to your hips and buttocks . . . relaxing . . . letting go . . . down into your legs . . . your thighs . . . calves . . . and into your feet . . . sending all the tightness and pain out the bottoms of your feet into the earth . . . leaving only peace . . . lightness . . .

softness . . . breathing deeply . . . letting go . . . breathing . . . being at peace . . .
relaxed.

Gently begin to think of a situation that causes you stress in your life . . . it may
be a situation at work or at home . . . let this situation come fully into view . . .
allow yourself to reconnect with it completely . . . notice the people involved . . .
their faces and body postures . . . the environment around you . . . the colors and
temperature . . . the sights and sounds of this situation . . . become aware of your
feelings and body sensations when you are in this situation. . . . What are you saying
to yourself? . . . Notice your tone of voice when you speak to others involved. . . .
Do you feel powerless? . . . Are you afraid? . . . Is there pain involved? . . . Let it all
come back to you now and be completely there. When it is clearly in view . . . when
you feel it deeply inside . . . when you can hear the words and sounds of this situation, begin to form a ball with this picture . . . these feelings . . . all the sounds . . .
maybe it is the size of a basketball . . . or a baseball . . . or a golf ball . . . just a ball
. . . make it a size that will fit into your hand . . . notice how it feels . . . the texture
. . . the weight . . . notice the color and shape . . . hold it in your hand for a moment
. . . it seems so small . . . so easy to handle . . . so light.

Now let it go . . . bounce it . . . throw it . . . roll it . . . blow it . . . away . . . and
watch as it becomes smaller and smaller in the distance . . . notice how it feels as it
leaves you . . . as you release it from your hand and it moves farther away from you.
. . . How does it sound as it moves through the air or along the ground? . . . Allow it
to go . . . give it away . . . become free of it. . . . How do you feel now? . . . What
do you look like now that you have let go? . . . Think of a word that expresses these
new feelings . . . this new look . . . just a word . . . say it to yourself . . . say it again
. . . imagine writing this word on a large poster and hanging it on the wall . . . notice
the colors . . . touch it. . . . How do the letters feel beneath your fingers? . . . Say the
word to yourself and remember how it looks and feels to be free from the stress of
the old situation . . . say it again.

Now experience yourself in this situation again, feeling confident and at ease . . .
see yourself handling the problem and the people with lightness and competence . . .
hear your words and tone of voice . . . your voice is smooth and you feel centered . . . you are clear and focused . . . you are at ease . . . allow yourself to move
through the situation free of fear . . . free of anger . . . free of frustration . . . knowing you can handle any situation with confidence and clarity . . . you are powerful
and flexible . . . you trust yourself and your abilities . . . notice how it feels in your
body to be stress free and centered . . . notice how you look and sound . . . connect
with this new situation fully . . . giving yourself permission to respond and handle
everything just the way you choose . . . with power and intelligence . . . free of
frustration or worry . . . allow yourself to have it all . . . remember your word and
the strength it gives you . . . you are in control of this situation, and you enjoy it . . .
you know that you have everything within you to handle things in a clear and flexible way . . . experience yourself moving through the entire situation . . . step-by-step
. . . word-by-word . . . action-by-action . . . until it is resolved . . . be aware of how
it feels to reach resolution without stress . . . to reach an outcome feeling powerful
. . . centered . . . in control . . . be aware of how you and the others involved

look . . . and what words you hear . . . allow yourself to experience this situation resolved and finished in a clear and clean way . . . and then letting it go . . . letting the picture and feelings . . . the words and sounds . . . become dimmer as they fade away from you . . . as they become smaller and fainter until you are totally at peace and your mind is empty and your body relaxed . . . let it all go . . . remembering how it is to be stress free . . . to be confident and to reach a peaceful resolution . . . allow yourself to be at peace.

Begin to focus on your breathing again . . . inhaling relaxation and peace . . . exhaling any doubt or tension. . . . Breathe in . . . deeply filling your chest . . . exhale slowly and gently . . . focusing only on your breathing. . . . When I count to three, you may open your eyes . . . feeling refreshed, centered, and relaxed . . . one . . . move your fingers and toes . . . beginning to connect with your body . . . feeling relaxed and at peace . . . taking a deep breath . . . two . . . move your head and shoulders . . . reconnecting with the room around you . . . the sounds and the chair or floor beneath you . . . three . . . open your eyes when you are ready.

Guided Visualization for Relaxation

Find a quiet place where you will not be disturbed for fifteen minutes. Sit in a comfortable chair or lie on the floor. Close your eyes. Bring your focus inward and center on your breathing . . . breathe in deeply . . . filling your belly and chest and exhale fully . . . breathe in relaxation and peace . . . exhale tension and worry . . . breathe . . . begin to concentrate on your center . . . an area about two inches below or two inches above your navel . . . whichever feels the most comfortable to you . . . connect with this center . . . this power . . . this strength. . . . Now, begin to feel the energy at the top of your head . . . experience it moving down into your shoulders . . . down your back . . . down through the base of your spine and out the bottom of your feet like roots . . . down through the floor and deep into the earth . . . strong, sturdy roots deep into the earth . . . spreading . . . connecting . . . making you secure and solid . . . continue to focus on your center, feeling the energy and power in that area . . . when you exhale, imagine any tension in your body going deep into the earth through the roots you have established . . . when you inhale, feel the earth's energy coming up into your body through your spine and up into your heart center just behind your breastbone . . . imagine the earth's energy passing through your heart's center and out into the world around you . . . see and feel any uneven, unfocused energy you might have in your body flowing down into the earth to be dispelled as you exhale . . . see and feel the bright earth's energy flowing upward into your spine and out through your heart center into your environment . . . feel the peace and connectedness in your body . . . the lightness . . . the focused awareness connecting you with people and your environment on a deep, confident, and relaxed level . . . as you feel this new found sense of tranquility and of being centered in your body, notice your mind has calmed and you are in control of your feelings and thoughts . . . gently breathing in . . . bringing in new earth energy to your body . . . exhaling through your heart center . . . feelings of relaxation, peace, and being centered spreading throughout your body. . . . Allow your mind to think of a place . . . a beautiful place . . . a place where you are safe and free . . . a place where you feel confident and powerful . . . it can be any place, real or imaginary . . . a meadow . . . a beach . . . a mountain top . . . a hidden waterfall . . . any place that is your place . . . you feel nurtured here . . . you feel beautiful and important here . . . you feel safe and at peace here . . . find a comfortable spot to stand in your favorite place . . . an energy spot . . . and center yourself there . . . quieting your body and your mind . . . being at peace and at one with this spot . . . notice there is a path from your spot . . . follow it with your eyes. . . . As you come to the end of this path, you are aware of a gentle mist flowing along the path coming toward you . . . it is blue . . . experience the blue mist coming toward you . . . enveloping your body in a soft blue light . . . be aware of how this delicate, blue mist makes you feel as it gently moves around your belly and your chest to your heart. . . . What emotions come up for you? . . . What do you feel in your body? . . . You feel peaceful as the mist moves away from you down the path and disappears from your view.

As you turn to look in a new direction, you are aware of a slow-moving green mist drifting toward you . . . you are not afraid . . . you welcome it as it envelops you in a soft, gentle, green cloud. . . . Notice its shade and become aware of how it makes you feel as it reaches your heart with its delicate color . . . it is a soft and healing color . . . slowly . . . slowly . . . you let it go . . . it floats away toward the horizon and out of sight . . . you are happy and feel whole and full of peace . . . as you notice a small pink cloud moving toward you . . . it almost looks like cotton . . . fluffy . . . pink . . . velvety . . . coming to you and filling your heart with tenderness . . . softness . . . compassion . . . lightness . . . joy . . . and love . . . you feel so safe and whole . . . connect with the feelings and sounds that come up for you and sur-render to them as the cloud holds you in its pinkness for a moment . . . then quietly . . . smoothly . . . it moves through your heart and into the distance and is gone.

You stand alone now, calmly . . . waiting . . . a warm glow touches your head . . . moving slowly down through your hair . . . over your ears and eyes . . . golden . . . sunlit . . . warm . . . showering upon you like a gentle waterfall . . . a golden yellow color . . . warmth sprinkling down on you . . . flowing over your shoulders and down your body past your hips . . . down your legs spilling all around your feet like a tissue gown . . . warm and light . . . filling you with wisdom, confidence, and well-being . . . you stand there in the glow and the light . . . aware of your intelli-gence and abilities . . . thanking your body, mind, and spirit for their gifts to you . . . you have everything you need to be, to do, and to have what you wish . . . the gold forms a beautiful, feathery cloud above you, and you feel light and free of the earth beneath your feet . . . allow yourself to float with the golden cloud above you until you become so small and faint that the picture is gone and all is quiet. . . .

Slowly begin to return to the steady pace of your breathing . . . inhaling deeply . . . holding . . . exhaling . . . breathing . . . knowing that any time you need to relax . . . anytime you need to center yourself . . . you need only to think of the colors . . . blue . . . green . . . pink . . . gold . . . and remember your special place of power, confidence, peace, and tranquility.

Begin to reconnect with the room now . . . feel the chair or floor beneath you now as you slowly bring the roots back up into the soles of your feet . . . up your legs and into your spine . . . hear the sounds around you . . . breathe . . . when I count to three you may open your eyes feeling refreshed and relaxed . . . one . . . move your fingers and toes . . . breathing deeply . . . reconnecting with your body . . . two . . . move your head and shoulders . . . coming back into the energy of the room around you . . . knowing you have everything you need to be relaxed and confident . . . three . . . open your eyes when you are ready.

Using Mental Training for Healing Athletic Injuries: Some Case Studies

"Everyone participates in his or her health at all times."

Stephanie Matthews-Simonton
Getting Well Again

One of the most difficult aspects of being an athlete is learning to cope with injuries. An injured athlete may feel himself or herself losing stamina and strength and may begin to believe they are losing their edge. "Because of the importance of athletic performance to many athletes, injury often leads to an attack on the self-image; i.e., they feel sorry for themselves; they exaggerate and catastrophize that their career is ended; they may decrease their motivation and increase their anxiety; they may decide they are injury prone" (Rotella and Heyman 1986). Basically, injured athletes feel out of control of their bodies and, therefore, their training, their performance, and perhaps their future.

In ancient healing and spiritual traditions, the power of a positive mental attitude and the use of imagery were often a major part of the healing process. Researchers are now finding this tradition to be a valid one. Carl Simonton, Norman Cousins, both pioneers in holistic medicine, and the researchers in psychoneuroimmunology (PNI) "have shown that the brain can send signals along nerves to enhance defenses against infection and pump out chemicals that make the body fight more aggressively. . . ." (Wechsler 1987). Though most of today's scientific research is being done with the recovery from major illness, scientists are finding that the same techniques work with the healing of athletic injury and with the athlete's need to be involved in the control of his or her body's process toward health.

The Process

"If you want to recover, you must learn to be tenacious in fighting your disease and hopeful about the outcome. That means undergoing counseling to learn to deal with social and emotional problems. It means setting goals and finding reasons to live. Most important, it means doing mental imagery exercises three times a day" (Wechsler 1987). The sports psychologist may begin by setting physical healing goals with the athlete; for example, to be performing pain free within the next three weeks and to be strong and able to work out with a healthy body in three weeks.

(Time limits depend on the extent of the injury and the doctor's, trainer's, or coach's recommendation.) The athlete should write each goal down as clearly and specifically as possible. For some injuries, it is necessary to write short-term and midrange goals that may have to do with flexibility or preliminary workouts such as physical movement in a pool or hot tub.

Once goals have been written, the athlete's attitude must be confronted, for example, what are the athlete's fears and major frustrations; how does he or she view his or her body; what is the athlete's present level of motivation; has he or she acknowledged that his or her body is injured? "Some view it as a disaster, others see it as an opportunity to display courage, and still others welcome it as a relief from the drudgery of practice or the embarrassment and frustration of poor performance, lack of playing time, or a losing season" (Rotella and Heyman 1986). Once the athlete's attitude has been assessed, affirmations are formed to assist him or her to establish positive mental energy and beliefs about personal control in the healing and strength of his or her body. Affirmations such as "I am becoming stronger and healthier every day," "I am healing my body," "I am healing more and more every day," "My body heals quickly and well," are typical and powerful. Because affirmations are used to counteract negative thoughts and energy that may prolong the healing process, they should be read at least once every day.

"An important element of self-healing is a mental image that projects a positive future outcome. The visualization you imagine stimulates your mind and body and creates a positive intention for healing" (Porter and Foster 1987). As with all performance visualizations, the athlete should begin all healing imagery exercises with a deep relaxation process. A visualization for healing should include the following elements as well as the standard components of all imagery, such as the use of all five senses:

1. acknowledgment of the injury
2. a dialogue between the athlete and the injured part, which includes asking it what it wants and a commitment to giving it
3. forgiveness of the injured part and the body as a whole
4. sending the injured part love and nurturing, sometimes in the form of green, gold, or white light
5. visualizing the injury healing and then whole and healthy

It is also important for the athlete to continue to visualize his/her technique in his/her given sport while the body is healing. We recommend that the athlete continue to attend practice and mentally rehearse each movement, every detail of performance, in order to keep his or her technique sharp and well ingrained while healing is taking place.

Case Study One

In 1985, a masters athlete came to us with a long-term stress fracture. She had been training and competing with this injury for three months until the pain was too great and the fracture had begun to bleed into the surrounding muscle. The doctor had put the leg in a cast and told her not to run for six weeks. She was frustrated and angry.

She was forced to accept that she was injured and had to stop her training and give up her hopes of competing in the national championships.

Her goal was to be walking at least three miles three times a week within five weeks and to be running ten miles a week within eight weeks. She also agreed to change these goals if she experienced continued deep pain or if the doctor found evidence of the fracture at the end of his prescribed six weeks of rest.

She wrote seven affirmations for the healing of this injury on five three-by-five-inch cards and put them around her apartment and on her desk at work so she could see them several times a day. Within two weeks, she noticed her anger began to diminish, and a real sense of control was obvious to her.

For this athlete, imagery became a time for humor and creativity. At first she saw the fracture as a jagged tear in the bone with blood running out like a waterfall. We asked her to let go of that image and to begin seeing the tear healing. She reported seeing little men with brightly colored threads running to the sight and weaving the torn pieces together like a net. Within three weeks she was imaging the fracture as a solid area of white, like the grout between two tiles, holding firmly and strongly. We asked her to experience the bone as whole with no lines or ridges but smooth and healthy. We continued this program with her until she returned to the doctor and he gave her permission to begin running. She then began to imagine the leg being stronger than before and her body running pain free. By the end of five weeks, she was running two miles slowly on a bark path every other day reporting very little pain and was back to her full training by the end of seven weeks.

Case Study Two

This athlete had been working with us on his performance and technique when he became injured with a pulled hamstring. He was a student at the local university and had three midterms that week as well as the collegiate championships in two weeks. His injury occurred at practice. This was a recurring injury. He expressed feelings of wanting to give up, of resignation, and of frustration with his continued inability to stay healthy. He had planned to compete in Europe that summer and was depressed and confused.

After guiding him into a very relaxed state, we asked him to focus inside on the injured area and to ask it what it wanted from him. What was it trying to tell him? He said it wanted to rest, it wanted to be babied, to get a massage, and to be iced. It also wanted him to relax and not to stretch it too much or too hard. It did not feel listened to. He told it that he heard it, and he promised to get a massage and to be more gentle. He also promised to slow down with the stress in his life and to rest. His affirmations were "I am relaxed and creative when under stress," "I listen to my body," "I enjoy resting and caring for my body," "My hamstrings are relaxed and flexible."

We then led him through a visualization of relaxing and healing the hamstring. After two weeks, his hamstring was healthy, and he felt a sense of freedom and control over his body and his training. He competed at top form three weeks after his injury had occurred.

Case Study Three

In March of 1987, a third athlete was referred to us by her physician as a last resort. She had been injured for four and a half months with a stress fracture that had never healed. Every time she went to the doctor, the news was worse. Her ankle had been immobilized for more than two months. Surgery, a bone graft from her hip, had been suggested by an orthopedic surgeon, and acupuncture had been tried unsuccessfully. Nothing was helping, and she was deeply depressed and had been sick several times. All necessary blood work had also been done and her hormones had been checked. She was very angry and irritable and was furious with her body for not healing. She had been doing some visualizing without the help of a tape and found that her mind wandered. We asked her what she was seeing when she did these visualizations. She said she could see the broken bone as it had been in the X ray and there was only one fiber on a corner of one of the pieces connecting the separation. The bone was always broken. She had stopped the visualizations.

Her goal was to be healed and out of the brace in three weeks and able to go to Los Angeles on vacation. She wanted to be pain free and performing by the summer, and she wanted to learn to do healing visualizations. She also wrote two personal goals that she thought would help her body heal. She wanted to learn to take time for herself and to let go of feeling guilty when she took that time.

The most important process for this athlete was her imagery. For four and a half months she had been seeing the bone in her ankle broken and had been perceiving herself as injured and weak. We led her through a guided visualization to become aware of the purpose of her injury and then to experience the bone healing and whole. Instead of viewing herself as having to do everything for everyone, we asked her to experience herself doing things for herself and allowing others to be responsible for themselves. Instead of seeing the bone broken with one fiber on one corner, we asked her to see several fibers growing from both sides of the separation toward each other and knitting together making the bone solid and one piece. When asking the injury its purpose, she reported it was telling her to slow down, to take her time, and to not work as hard as she had before. She continued to say things to herself such as "I enjoy letting other people give to me," "My body is healing and becoming strong," "It is easy for me to make time for myself," "I am comfortable nurturing myself and healing my body." Daily she continued to visualize the bone healing and healthy. A subsequent X-ray one month after our first session showed the bone to be totally healed.

Case Study Four

This athlete had had five surgeries in two years, which had ruined her Olympic hopes for 1984. She was a master of positive imagery, and we asked her how she coped mentally with injuries and surgery and how she kept going in the face of all odds. "In terms of mental training, I imagine the injury getting better, I counsel myself, I get myself to stop worrying. We did formal relaxation sessions in high school and I use it unconsciously now. I do racing in my head all the time. When I'm out biking, I do it frequently; I transform myself."

Being injured so consistently was not easy for her either physically or mentally. She was very upset when her Olympic hopes were smashed. She found that she cried a lot and felt out of control most of the time. It took many hours of talking to her coach and her parents before she began to focus on other goals, other competitions, and other world records. She learned to say to herself, "Look ahead now, you have years ahead of you. Get healthy—just get healthy." After each surgery, she began other physical exercising to help keep herself fit, and she began to visualize. At first, she just visualized her knee healing and being pain free. Soon, her visualizations took the form of performance in a healthy and strong body. Eventually, she began to experience herself at the peak of her competitive ability all pain free and whole. "If nothing else, all this has helped my performing mentally. If I can overcome this, I can take anything anybody throws at me." She went on to compete at the national level two years later.

Conclusions

These four case histories serve to demonstrate the basic presenting issues and the subsequent processes for dealing with the athlete's reactions to injury and his or her necessary involvement in the healing of that injury. Though a tangible, scientifically indisputable bond between the mind's power to inflict and/or heal the body is still in its infancy, research is clearly beginning to show that inner talk, imagery, and positive intent do have a powerful influence in our physical process. "Researchers in biofeedback have discovered that it is possible to control voluntary heart rate, muscle tension, sweat-gland activity, skin temperature, and a wide range of internal physical states normally considered to be under involuntary control by the autonomic nervous system" (Matthews-Simonton, Simonton, and Creighton 1978). Just as mental imagery can produce a state of relaxation or control heart rate, mental images can facilitate and enhance the speed and effectiveness of the healing process.

An athlete can communicate with his or her body using imagery, suggestion, and language to achieve a higher sense of control and motivation whether for performance or healing. Since it is now widely becoming accepted that athletes can use their imagination, mental pictures, and positive self-talk to make their bodies respond with peak performances in competition, it may also hold true for the healing responses of the body. "If the total integrated system of mind, body and emotions, which constitutes the whole person, is not working in the direction of health, then purely physical interventions may not succeed" (Matthews-Simonton, Simonton, and Creighton, 1978). Training the mind to assist in the process of healing is that extra edge, the final piece that creates a whole, ultimately healthy athlete. It is the tool with which an athlete can achieve a sense of control and power when his or her body must rest and mend itself. Research is clearly demonstrating that "the future will demand that injury rehabilitation include both physical and psychological components" (Rotella and Heyman 1986) to assist the athlete in complete health.

A Sample Protocol for Working with Rehabilitation/Injury Referrals

Intake Interviews Athletic history/weaknesses, strengths
Injury history
Diet, sleep, exercise patterns, etc.
Medical history/therapy received
Set goals around injury recovery
Write affirmations for healing and pain
Teach relaxation skills
Lead patient through visualization/imagery

Follow-up Meet every week or biweekly for follow-up
Discuss progress—successes and/or problems
Mental state
Lead through visualization/imagery
Counseling if needed

NOTE: Issues of anger, frustration, etc., come up for patient at various times. These sessions help alleviate stress and give the patient a sense of control over his or her condition and recovery.

Objectives
After four to six sessions, the patient will be able to
Set own goals for recovery
Write affirmations for healing and pain control
Know and practice relaxation and stress-reduction skills
Have a better concentration and focus of attention
Write own visualization if he or she wishes
Be more relaxed
Have a sense of control over their recovery
Practice relaxation in several settings
Cope better with stress

Guided Visualization for Healing Injury

(Begin all visualizations with a progressive relaxation.)

Begin to focus your attention on the injured part of your body . . . become fully aware of its depth and size and shape . . . connect completely with this injury . . . seeing it . . . hearing it . . . feeling it . . . centering on it . . . focusing on it . . . acknowledging its presence within you. Allow yourself to know it totally and completely . . . is it deep? . . . shallow? . . . on the surface? . . . deep inside? Connect with the injury fully . . . allow yourself to feel it . . . see it . . . hear it . . . be fully aware of your injured part . . . acknowledge it . . . know it. . . . When you are fully aware of the injured part, ask it what it is trying to tell you . . . what it needs from you. Listen to what it says. . . . What does it want from you, and what does it want you to do? . . . Listen carefully . . . when it is finished, thank it for its message. . . . After you have thanked it for its message, begin to allow yourself to forgive this injury . . . letting go of any anger . . . hate . . . or frustration you may have felt for it

. . . allowing yourself to forgive . . . to let go . . . to release any negative energy you may have been feeling for the injury . . . send it forgiveness . . . letting go of any resistance you have had for it . . . softening . . . releasing . . . dispersing any negativity into the shape of a small ball . . . see it roll away . . . out of your sight. . . . Slowly begin to send loving and healing energy to the injury . . . releasing the tightness and the resistance in your body . . . imagine the muscle tissue around the injury relaxing . . . softening . . . releasing . . . imagine the injury healing . . . getting stronger . . . and stronger . . . all of the blood coursing through your arteries bringing new food and oxygen to the hurt . . . taking away the injured cells . . . new healthy cells taking their place . . . revitalizing those sore and tender parts . . . the new blood healing the tissue . . . the bone . . . circulating around the injury . . . building new tissue . . . caressing the injured part until it is well and healthy again. . . . Send the injury loving energy for all the times it has come through for you in the past . . . be patient with it . . . knowing it needs some time to heal . . . tell it you love it . . . release any animosity or anger you might have for it. . . . Begin giving the injured area a healing color . . . a beautiful royal blue . . . an emerald green . . . a pale golden color . . . delicate . . . light . . . rich . . . the warm, golden color bathing the injured area . . . healing it . . . loving it. . . . Remembering the love you have in your heart for someone special, feel that love in your heart and body now and begin to connect with this open-heart loving energy . . . allow yourself to send that same feeling of love to your injured part . . . easily . . . gently . . . send warmth and love to this area . . . letting go and softening around the injury . . . telling it how much it means to you and how much you appreciate the work it has done for you . . . send it light . . . send it peace . . . send it healing . . . send it warmth . . . letting go . . . releasing any fear that surrounds it . . . allow yourself to release any tightness you might still feel around the injured part . . . setting it free . . . softly . . . gently let your body be soft and open . . . forgiving and loving.

Begin to focus again on the soft . . . warm . . . peaceful area of your body that is now healing . . . send it strength . . . send it energy . . . send it love . . . imagine a pale golden color surrounding the injured area . . . see it and feel it expanding from the injured area into all parts of your body . . . the warm golden color beginning at the top of your head . . . flowing down through your neck . . . chest . . . into your arms . . . hands . . . fingers . . . through your abdomen . . . stomach . . . into your legs . . . feet . . . and toes . . . see and feel yourself filled with a warm, golden yellow light . . . the color healing your body . . . filling it with love and energy . . . you are healing . . . now allow the image for golden light to slowly disappear.

See and feel the injury becoming flexible . . . strong . . . supple . . . remembering the healing . . . knowing your body will come through for you . . . restoring you to good health . . . again being in an energetic . . . vibrant state . . . full of endurance and good health . . . see and feel yourself performing at your peak . . . happy . . . lively . . . fulfilled and content . . . remembering and saying to yourself some affirmations for healing . . . "I am healing and healed," "My body is healthy and strong," "I am healing quickly," "I am healthier every day," "I am healthy and pain free," "I care for and nurture my body," "My body part is strong, flexible, and healthy," "I am completely healed," "I am performing at my peak."

Begin to reconnect with your present space now . . . bring your focus to your breathing . . . the sounds of the room . . . the smells . . . the feel of your body against the chair or the floor . . . remember you are healing and becoming healthy and whole . . . thank your body as you reconnect with its sensations and the space around you . . . when I count to three you may open your eyes . . . refreshed . . . relaxed . . . alert . . . healthy and at peace . . . one . . . move your fingers and toes . . . becoming aware of the sounds and your breathing . . . two . . . move your head and shoulders . . . feeling soft and relaxed . . . three . . . open your eyes when you are ready.

Guided Visualization for Pain Control

(Begin all visualizations with a progressive relaxation.)

Begin to focus your attention on the area of pain within your body . . . become fully aware of its depth and size and shape . . . connect completely with this pain . . . facing it directly . . . centering on it . . . focusing on it . . . acknowledging its presence within you. . . . Allow yourself to know it totally and completely . . . notice its temperature . . . is it hot, cold, cool, warm? . . . is it deep? . . . shallow? . . . is it sharp or dull? . . . Be aware if it is constant or if it comes and goes . . . connect with the pain fully . . . allow yourself to feel it . . . see it . . . hear it . . . moment-to-moment . . . notice if it has a color . . . if it does, focus on that color. . . . Is the color deep or pale? Does the color intensify or diminish the pain? . . . Be aware now . . . in the present . . . acknowledge it . . . know it . . . feel it . . . see it. . . . Now that you are fully aware of it, ask the pain what it is trying to tell you . . . what message it has for you. Listen to what it says. . . . What does it want from you, and what is it trying to give to you? Listen carefully . . . when it is finished, thank it for its message. . . . After you have thanked it for its message, begin to allow yourself to forgive this pain . . . letting go of any anger, hate, or frustration you may have felt for it . . . allowing yourself to forgive . . . to let go . . . to release any negative energy you may have been feeling for the pain . . . send it forgiveness . . . letting go of any resistance you have had for it . . . softening . . . releasing . . . dispersing any negativity into the shape of a small cloud . . . see it drift away, out of your sight. Slowly begin to soften around the pain now . . . letting go . . . releasing the tightness and the resistance in your body . . . imagine the muscle tissue around the pain relaxing . . . melting . . . softening . . . releasing . . . allow the pain to melt like butter or ice cream . . . becoming smooth . . . give it a healing color now . . . a beautiful royal blue . . . an emerald green . . . a pale golden color . . . delicate . . . light . . . rich. . . . Imagine a person whom you love very much . . . see this person's face before you . . . feel the love in your heart for this person . . . connect with your open-hearted loving energy and begin to allow yourself to send the love you feel in your heart to the pain in your body . . . easily . . . gently . . . send warmth and love to this area . . . letting go and softening around the pain . . . again, send it forgiveness . . . send it light . . . send it peace . . . send it healing . . . send it warmth . . . letting go . . . releasing . . . freeing the pain from the area it has lived in and allowing it to float freely . . . soft . . . smooth . . . light . . . release any fear that surrounds it . . .

allow yourself to release the tightness that holds it . . . setting it free . . . softly . . . gently . . . let your body be soft and open . . . forgiving and loving.

Now begin to visualize the pain getting smaller and smaller . . . be aware of its shape as it floats free and becomes fainter . . . smaller . . . lighter . . . let it grow dim and smaller . . . smaller . . . smaller until it begins to float away from your body . . . release it . . . let it go . . . out of your body . . . out of your mind . . . out of your awareness and into air . . . tiny . . . floating . . . into the mist . . . gone.

Focus again on the soft . . . warm . . . peaceful area of your body . . . sending it healing and strength . . . sending it love and energy . . . you are pain free . . . you have let go and moved into your softness and into your healing . . . allow yourself to rest . . . thanking your body for its strength and its willingness to release the pain . . . see and feel yourself as free of pain . . . rest into your healing . . . your body and mind harmonious . . . quiet and at peace.

Begin to reconnect with your present space now . . . bring your focus to your breathing . . . the sounds of the room . . . the smells . . . the feel of your body against the chair or the floor . . . remember that you are pain free and whole . . . thank your body as you reconnect with it sensations and the space around you . . . when I count to three you may open your eyes . . . refreshed . . . relaxed . . . alert . . . healthy and at peace . . . one . . . move your fingers and toes . . . becoming aware of the sounds and your breathing . . . two . . . move your head and shoulders . . . feeling soft and gentle . . . three . . . open your eyes when you are ready.

Bibliography

Achterberg, J. 1985. *Imagery in healing.* Boston: New Science Library.

Foster, J., and K. Porter. 1987. How to speed up injury recovery. *Johnson & Johnson Athleticare Newsletter,* 3, 1.

Jafee, D. T. 1980. *Healing from within.* New York: Simon & Schuster, Inc.

Locke, S., and D. Colligan. 1986. *The healer within.* New York: New American Library.

Matthews-Simonton, S.; O. C. Simonton; J. L. Creighton. 1978. *Getting well again.* New York: Bantam Books.

Murphy, S. M., and D. Jowdy. 1991. "The Imagery and Mental Rehearsal." In T. Horn, ed. *Advances in Sport Psychology.* Champaign, IL: Human Kinetics Press.

Pelletier, K. R. 1977. *Mind as healer, minds as slayer.* New York: Dell Publishing Co., Inc.

Porter, K., and J. Foster. 1987. *The mental athlete.* New York: Ballantine Books.

Porter, K., and J. Foster. 1987. Who will stop the pain. *World Tennis,* (July): 31–32.

Rotella, R. J., and S. R. Heyman. 1986. "Stress, injury & the psychological rehabilitation of athletes." In J. Williams, ed. *Applied sport psychology.* Palo Alto, CA: Mayfield Publishing Co.

Wechsler, R. 1987. "A new prescription: Mind over malady." *Discover* (February): 51–60.

Williams, J. ed. 1986. *Applied sport psychology.* Palo Alto, CA: Mayfield Publishing Co.

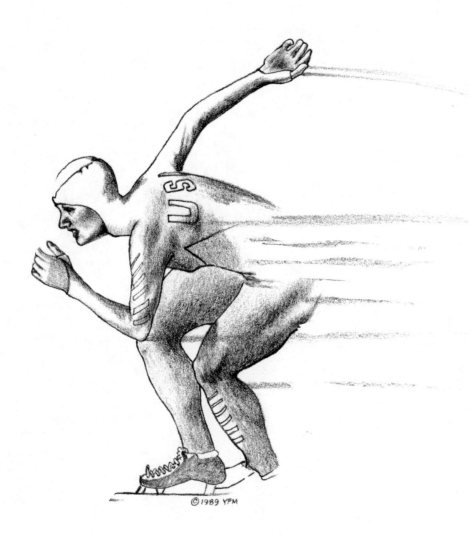

© 1989 YPM

Chapter ■ *Seven*

Unsetting Goals

We cannot force what is not meant
to be. . . .

Unsetting Goals

How do you let go of a goal after having it for months or years? We spend hundreds
of hours visualizing, affirming, and imagining ourselves victorious and achieving our
goals and dreams. What do we do if we don't achieve it all? We learn to **let go and
surrender with style and grace**—easy to say, and sometimes harder to do. In working with both recreational and elite athletes, we counsel them on the letting go process. Yes, you must dream; yes, you must follow your visions; and if after years of
hard work your ultimate dreams have eluded you, you simply let go, acknowledge
your achievements, and go on with life, continuing to seek new pathways and new
ideas and dreams.

The frustration of lost dreams was beautifully expressed by Liz Bradley, a member of the 1988 U.S. Olympic rowing team: ''It is an emotional gamble to set goals
so high: the act of doing so is what draws you along the path, but you are set up for
a big disappointment if you don't attain them. We were fifth. It didn't hurt to not get
the bronze, which is where I realistically thought we should have finished. I really
convinced myself, hook, line, and sinker, that we were good enough to medal. So
much so that I still think it and feel extremely guilty and as if I let myself, my
boatmates, team, country, parents, etc., down. I don't regret having done the mental
training, because it probably got us past the Russians and into the six-boat final.
Maybe we *were* good enough to expect the bronze. How do you find the boundary
between truth and visualization when you raise the latter to such an art? I don't re-

call much discussion of this issue in *The Mental Athlete,* and I think it might be a good thing to address." So it is to Liz Bradley that we dedicate this chapter, with our thanks for drawing attention to this very important concern.

Many world-class or professional athletes retire from competition to pursue new careers in business, education, and health care. They apply their discipline and training to becoming peak performers in careers in diverse fields, some far from the athletic fields of their young adulthood. They have learned and practiced disciplined lives for years; their goals simply change from physical achievement to career achievement.

The following section on training down from elite competition can be applied by any athlete who wants to let go of an unachieved goal and move on to new goals and dreams. Read it and apply it to your own situation.

The affirmations and the visualization, for letting go of a goal, near the end of this chapter will assist you in letting go in a positive and constructive way.

Training Down from Elite Competition

Olympic athletes, especially, often have a difficult time with the letdown or postpartum depression (!) after world-championship or Olympic competition. Many retire from elite competition and suffer from complete mental and physical burnout. After years of intensity and training, this retirement is a retirement from a way of life and a life-style that has formed their waking hours for as many as 15 to 20 years, if they began competing in high school. Realistically, this is a huge loss—a death of a way of life.

Athletes should be encouraged to mourn this death, if necessary. Many may see their retirement as a relief. If it is a death-type loss, it needs to be treated accordingly. Some athletes have described random crying for no apparent reason, sleeplessness, early morning waking, and other symptoms of depression. This is also compounded by retirement from sports that have a high-aerobic base. If training drops to nothing, the body is also reacting to less aerobic exercise and is craving its endorphins! (Endorphins are released during and after exercise and provide a feeling of extreme well-being and satisfaction. They are important in combating depressed feelings.)

Retiring athletes often seem to be suffering from posttraumatic stress symptoms. It is said that the East Germans train down from elite competition both physically and emotionally. In the next few years, the U.S. Olympic Committee will most likely develop guidelines and training programs to help U.S. athletes adapt to life-style changes.

We would suggest a *train-down program* of the following steps:

Physical
1. Gradually reduce workouts 10 to 15 percent weekly for a period of six weeks to two months. Decide on maintenance exercise, to give your body some exercise and to stay in recreational shape.

2. Investigate alternative exercise programs that may be cross training or perhaps a completely new sport(s) to enjoy as a recreational athlete.

3. Eat a healthy, low-fat, high-complex carbohydrate diet with adequate protein intake to maintain fitness, to give you plenty of energy, and to keep your weight down while doing less exercise.

4. Sleep for at least eight hours a night. Even though you may feel there is no reason to sleep so much, your body has worked hard for years. The emotional and physical exertion has been extreme, and your body may feel the need to rest and relax for several months.

5. Get massages biweekly or more often to induce relaxation and peacefulness in your body. It will help to nurture your body in a simple, pleasurable way.

Mental/Emotional

1. Write a journal after the Olympics, etc. for one to two months—daily or every other day—with your moods, feelings, ideas, and insights. This will serve to get your feelings out of your body and onto paper. The journal may turn out to be important to you in later years.

2. Talk with friends and colleagues about what you are feeling; if they are fellow athletes, ask them how they are feeling and what their plans and ideas are.

3. Get some personal counseling if you think it might be helpful. Talking with a professional, particularly a knowledgeable sport psychologist, can help you get things out and let you know that your problems and concerns are reasonable, rather than weird and unacceptable.

4. Make a list of what you gained and learned from your experiences, your successes, what you are happy with—all the positives.

5. Make a list of regrets. Make a process for acknowledging your feelings; be willing to forgive yourself and to let go of your regrets and shortcomings. Burn it, bury it, or throw it away. This small ritual can be helpful in letting go of your sorrow or negative feelings of disappointment or anger.

6. Go for career counseling and for information about what you might want to do next.

7. Write affirmations around letting go of this cycle of your life; affirmations about forgiveness of yourself can be very helpful in your letting go process.

8. Record and listen to the visualization in this chapter. It can help you acknowledge your feelings, let go, forgive yourself, and open up a space emotionally for something new to come into your life.

If we hide or deny our feelings, they're with us forever. It's only by letting them go that we can be truly free. And it's only by experiencing them that we can let them go.

Affirmations for Letting Go of a Goal/Forgiveness

I let go of my goals for _____ and open myself to new possibilities.

I acknowledge my strengths and learn in the process of going for my goals.

I did the best I could do in striving for my goal.

It is easy for me to let go of the past and to look toward the future.

I am enjoying the present.

I am taking care of myself, resting, and relaxing.

It is time for me to move on to new challenges.

I find new things to inspire and challenge me in new ways.

It is OK for me to feel sad or depressed. I am mourning the passing of a way of life for me.

I am proud of my dedication and achievement in my competitive years.

I acknowledge myself and my abilities.

Being ___th in the world is a fine achievement.

I am proud of myself and the goals I achieved.

We all did the best we could do during the competition.

My future is filled with abundance and prosperity.

I trust and believe in myself.

I let go of the past and move on.

I forgive myself with love and acceptance.

My mind and body are at peace.

I am grateful for
  my healthy body.
  my good mind.
  my fitness.
  all the support I received from my family, teammates, friends, and coaches.
  my achievements and honors.
  my energy and creativity.
  the opportunity to compete at world-class levels.
  the abundance in my life.

Visualization for Letting Go of a Goal

Find a comfortable place to sit or lie. Close your eyes and take a deep breath . . . holding it and letting it go. . . . Allow yourself to begin to think about your athletic accomplishments . . . what you have done over the last five years . . . begin to see, hear, and feel your great competitive moments . . . in all their entirety . . . allow yourself to remember one of your peak performances . . . see the people who were there with you . . . hear all the sounds of that performance . . . feel the feelings in your body of the peak performance . . . the excitement, the excellence . . . the confidence and the power you felt . . . remember it all . . . and begin to acknowledge yourself, your performances . . . your abilities . . . your strengths . . . knowing you were good, you were powerful, and you were talented in what you were doing . . .

you deserved to be on those teams and to win and to accomplish what you achieved . . . remember it all . . . knowing you were worthy of it all . . . feeling good and whole and complete . . . acknowledge your successes . . . being proud and knowing you did the best you could . . . begin to allow yourself to let go of those memories . . . feeling your body and mind release them . . . sending them off into the air around you . . . seeing them fade slowly away into a beautiful golden light . . . letting them go gracefully and with love and appreciation in your heart . . . gratitude for the experiences, the friends, and the places you visited and competed in . . . appreciation for the richness of your athletic life . . . allow yourself to let go of it with love . . . letting go easily and without effort . . . and allow yourself to forgive yourself or others for any mistakes that were made during your last performances . . . saying, "I forgive you, (saying your name). . . . It was OK to make some mistakes . . . you are forgiven . . . it is over . . . it is time to go on to new things. . . . I love you, accept you, and forgive you . . . it is OK, and you are OK . . . it is OK to let go" . . . and imagine yourself looking into a mirror, into your own eyes . . . saying, "I forgive you . . . " and knowing it is time to forgive and let go . . . let all the images fade into a golden light . . . and feel your mind and your heart being open and receptive . . . allowing yourself to make room for something new in your life . . . allowing yourself to be open . . . open-minded . . . openhearted . . . allowing the space in your mind and heart to be open to new possibilities and new dreams . . . enjoy this new and open feeling . . . knowing it is OK to wait for something new to come in . . . perhaps now, perhaps later as you are doing some other activity, something new will come in . . . just know you are now preparing yourself for new adventures . . . a new you and a new life . . . knowing that all the learning you received by being a competitive athlete prepared you for many other aspects of your life . . . acknowledging again what a gift it was to have had your opportunities . . . begin looking forward to the future with trust and anticipation . . . knowing and trusting that you will receive . . . and that you will be blessed by some new and unexpected adventure . . . trusting the continuing process of abundance and prosperity in your life . . . being open and receptive to the process of change.

Imagining the golden light surrounding you, protecting you . . . knowing you are safe . . . trusting yourself and trusting the process of change . . . begin to become aware of your body sitting in the chair or lying down . . . and when I count to three, you may open your eyes, feeling alert, awake, and ready for the rest of the day or evening. . . . Knowing it is OK to let go of the past and to look toward your future . . . with anticipation and excitement . . . knowing you have within you everything you need to be, to do, or to have what you want in life . . . knowing you are flexible, able to receive, and let go gracefully . . . one . . . move your hands and feet . . . taking a deep breath . . . letting it out . . . two . . . move your neck and head, stretching your shoulders and neck . . . and three. . . open your eyes when you're ready . . . feeling alert and awake.

What Next? Life After Athletics

After turning into a recreational athlete and maintaining a fitness level that is satisfying to you, begin to explore new ideas for careers. You may want to go back to school or to take a vacation or time off from any structured or disciplined activity. It is helpful to take R & R (rest and relaxation) sometimes lasting anywhere from one to six months or more. We believe it is important to give yourself permission to take this time out to help you in your transition from your previous athletic life-style to a new career path. Be gentle with yourself and give yourself some time and space to make this important change.

Most colleges and community colleges have excellent career counseling services. Check your local colleges to see what they have to offer. Some interesting books to read might be

> *Do What You Love, and the Money will Follow,* Marsha Sinetar, Paulist Press, 1987
> *Growing a Business,* Paul Hawken, Simon and Schuster, 1987
> *Work with Passion: How to Do What You Love for a Living,* Nancy Anderson, Carroll and Graf Publishers, Inc., 1984

Whatever you choose, allow yourself to take your time and be selective in your choices. It is OK to experiment to find out what is the right choice for you. Enjoy the process of finding a new path and direction for your life. Your patience will serve you well. Be willing to take your time and have fun with your new adventure.

Our greatest growth is in the striving, rather than in the achieving of our goals.

Judy Foster

Chapter ▪ Eight

Fear and Anger

Feel the fear and do it anyway.

—Susan Jeffers

Fear

Fear can be a unique underlying motivator or destroyer in our lives. Our fear often stops us from achieving what we desire and creates self-doubt and confusion in our minds. Many of us become paralyzed, terrified, immobile, and sick with dread when we are fearful. Fear can turn us into victims, feeling overwhelmed, weak, and helpless. We may feel empty, debilitated, and lost. And what are we afraid of? Of losing face, looking stupid, looking like a failure to others. We are often afraid of ourselves, our own power, success, failure, love, hate, rejection, death, and life—or simply the unknown.

In a recent workshop, we discussed common fears about success and what success meant to us. To see how you look at success, take a few minutes now to write down quick answers to the following questions: (We thank Wings, Inc. for the use of these questions.)

1. How do you know when you are succeeding?
   a. How does succeeding feel to you? (Be specific.) _____

   _____

   _____

b. What do you say to yourself and to others when you are succeeding or feel successful? _____

_____

_____

c. What do you look like when you are succeeding? What do you look like when you are successful? _____

_____

_____

2. When you are successful, what information do you receive from family, friends, peers, and the universe at large? _____

_____

_____

In looking at your answers, see what things represent success to you. Is acknowledgment important? Is it self-satisfaction, what other people say to you, the excitement of winning, the energy you feel, the money you make? It is important to know what is important to you in achieving success and your goals.

And what do you say to yourself? Do you acknowledge your successes, or do you continue to raise the bar on yourself? Is your win ever good enough? Do you pat yourself on the back after a win? Or are you self-critical and judgmental? Sharing your joys and sorrows with your friends and family can help make you feel proud, fulfilled, and supported.

My answers to question 1a were receiving acknowledgment from others; a feeling of self-satisfaction, excitement, and energy; receiving enough money to live the lifestyle I enjoy; and being able to do work I love doing.

Personally, I enjoy sharing my successes with my friends and family. When I am afraid or doubting myself, I look to them for support and encouragement. I allow myself to be vulnerable with them, being open with all my feelings, both positive and negative. I trust they love me for who I am, not what I achieve or don't achieve.

From the workshop several common fears emerged about success and money. Some of these were

If I have a lot, I'll be shallow, stuck on possessions, and materialistic.
When I was a child, people often bought things for me and used money for power, control, and manipulation.
My fear is not having enough of anything—money, love, affection.
Being successful takes a lot of time and effort.
In order to be successful, I must sacrifice something.
I'm not good enough.
I should be doing something other than what I am.

I can't do it good enough.

I'm afraid that if I'm as successful as I can be, I'll end up alone.

There is not enough for me.

These are powerful, negative belief systems, which keep us from success and achieving our dreams. In order to counteract negative belief systems, they must be identified, and affirmations written to reframe the negative thinking that surrounds them.

My own **fears of success** are

1. _____

2. _____

3. _____

4. _____

Now write **four affirmations to counter your fears.** (For example: If your fear was "I'm afraid that if I'm as successful as I can be, I'll end up alone," two affirmations might be "My success draws wonderful, loving people into my life," "I enjoy my success with my partner and my friends.")

1. _____

2. _____

3. _____

4. _____

Risk

As we discussed in chapter 1, in order to achieve, it is important to learn to risk and to do new things. If you want to create success in your life and deal with your fear, it helps to go *toward* the fear instead of avoiding it. Please understand, we are not advocating that you do dangerous or unsafe activities! Fear is a healthy emotion when it comes to physical danger. The fears we are discussing are fears of our feelings and emotions, not of physical safety. And with these emotional fears, it is helpful to acknowledge them and to decide to do something about them.

Risk is the ability to take chances. In the dictionary, risk is defined as exposing to danger. No wonder it is so hard for some of us to risk! Leaders and peak performers see risk as taking a chance and trying something new and different. The year Babe Ruth hit the most home runs, the other little mentioned fact was that he also had the most strikeouts. He was willing to risk failure, losing face, etc., to achieve a record that stood for decades.

Try this exercise to see how you think and feel about the word risk. Take a couple of minutes and close your eyes, quieting your mind and breathing deeply. Look at this page with the word risk in the center, and begin quickly and without much thought to write whatever pops into your mind about risk.

RISK

Keep writing until you know you are finished or about five minutes. What have you written? These words will give you an idea about your own belief systems around risking or taking chances.

When we did the exercise, this is what came up for us: heart pounding; it's OK to let go; breathe deeply, calm body; allowing myself to be seen, to be vulnerable and open; doing something different; asking for what I want; putting self on the line; soften heart center; OK to lose face; self-confidence; feeling the fear and doing it anyway; reaching, striving, growing, accelerating; mental/emotional risk; there's a difference between danger and fear; nothing to lose; visualize self getting what you ask for; and letting go if you don't.

In her book, *Feel the Fear and Do It Anyway,* Susan Jeffers says, "Pushing through the fear is less frightening than living with the underlying fear that comes from a feeling of helplessness." We agree. The terror and anxiety that come from avoidance is much worse than the action we can take in doing something different.

Making a short list of all the things you are afraid of in a competitive situation helps you acknowledge and recognize your fears. For instance, one of our athletes wrote: afraid of looking stupid, losing to someone below me, losing my scholarship, what people will think of me if I lose. Another wrote: afraid of falling off the beam, of losing, of looking bad, of blowing my dismount.

These fears were counterbalanced with the following affirmations:

I look good when I perform.
I have total focus and concentration during my routine.
I give back to others the responsibility for their own opinions.
I play well and powerfully against someone who is not as good as I am.

I win easily over less-talented players.
I am a confident and powerful player.
I am worthy of my scholarship.
I deserve my scholarship, and I am good enough to have it.
I am powerful and in control on the beam.
I let go easily of any fear I might feel.
A little fear excites and motivates me.
When I feel fear, I turn it into excitement.
My dismount is precise, powerful, and excellent.
My dismount is one of my most powerful moves.

In dealing constructively with your fears, remember to do this process:

1. **Acknowledge** the fear, the setback, or the emotional feelings.
2. **Breathe** deeply three to five breaths.
3. **Relax** your shoulders, neck, stomach, abdomen.
4. **Say or write** affirmations to counteract the fear.
5. **Visualize** dealing with your fear from a place of power and control.

Sometimes the process of risking is as important as the outcome. Often it is what we **learn** by trying something new, rather than what we **achieve**. The following visualization may help you to control your fear of the unknown or a particular fear you have in competition.

Guided Visualization for Dealing with Fear in Competition

Find a comfortable place to sit or lie. . . . Begin to breathe deeply . . . taking a deep breath, holding it . . . and letting it go with a sigh . . . breathing in . . . and letting it out . . . breathing in energy . . . breathing out peace . . . relax your shoulders . . . your neck . . . soften your abdomen and stomach . . . and begin to feel yourself to be centered, whole, and balanced . . . begin to imagine gold, white, or pink light coming into the top of your head, down into your body, coming out through your solar plexus . . . feel your solar plexus to be powerful and strong . . . with the light flowing out of it . . . feeling and seeing the light from the top of your head . . . flowing through your body and out through your solar plexus . . . feeling relaxed . . . powerful . . . and with a flexibility and suppleness around your solar plexus . . . imagine it pulsating with the passage of this energy from the top of your head and through it.

Begin to acknowledge your feelings of fear . . . remembering the list you made . . . or a situation or risk that causes you to feel fearful . . . and as each fear comes up . . . acknowledge it and thank it for making itself known to you . . . take some time to think of each fear . . . acknowledge it and say to it, "I thank you, and I welcome you (and think of the fear), and I let you flow through me," . . . and let yourself imagine the fear flowing through your solar plexus and flowing out through the middle of your back . . . just passing through, as if you were transparent . . . the fear flows in and the fear flows out . . . there is no place for it to stay in your body . . . it is just flowing through you . . . moving on through your solar plexus as a light breeze . . . feel your solar plexus to be strong and flexible . . . letting the fear pass through it, without pain or anxiety, just as if you were watching or feeling a soft breeze . . . continue to imagine the light flowing down from the top of your head out through your solar plexus . . . feeling strong, powerful, and centered.

Begin to say your affirmations about your fears. . . . "I belong here. . . . It is OK to make a mistake. . . . I learn from my mistakes. . . . I let go with ease and grace. . . . It is OK and I am OK. . . . It is easy for me to let go of self-criticism. . . . I nurture and take care of myself. . . . I am proud of myself and my accomplishments. . . . I trust myself and my abilities. . . . I am strong and powerful. . . . I am able to let go of my fears easily. . . . I just do it!!"

Begin to imagine yourself handling the situations you fear in a calm, comfortable, and powerful way . . . . see, hear, and feel yourself succeeding . . . handling your anxiety . . . feeling powerful and in control . . . feeling your solar plexus to be strong and flexible . . . knowing you are good enough and are worthy of your accomplishments . . . feeling your strength and power . . . acknowledging your fear and letting it go . . . going on to succeed . . . to achieve your goals and dreams . . . knowing you have what it takes to be successful and to overcome any obstacles, including any fear you might have or feel . . . you *are* good enough . . . you are worthy of respect and achievement.

Slowly let the images and feelings fade, remembering you have everything within you to be, to do, or to have what you want in life . . . knowing you are enough and you deserve the best. . . . When I count to three, you can open your eyes . . . feeling strong, powerful, and confident . . . one . . . take a deep breath . . . letting it out . . . two . . . stretch your neck and shoulders . . . three . . . open your eyes when you're ready.

Affirmations for Fear and Self-Doubt

Psyching Yourself Up

I am ready!
I am hot!
I hang in there.
I just do it!

Perseverance

I am persistent.
What I have to say is important.
It is easy for me to keep going.
I am patient.
I am aggressive and well respected by
    teammates and peers.

Handling Rejection

I belong here.
It is easy for me to hear no.
I ask for what I want easily.
I let go of any upset when I hear
no.
I handle rejection easily and turn it
    into a learning experience.
I am patient.
I learn from these experiences.

Reframing/Letting Go of Losses

It is OK to make a mistake.
I learn from setbacks.
I let go with ease and grace.
It is OK, and I am OK.
I am patient.
I find it easy to let go of self-criticism.
I nurture and take care of myself.

Advocating for Self

I am important.
What I say/need/want is important.
I deserve _____ .
I am worthy of respect.
I trust and respect myself.
I am proud of myself and my
  accomplishments.
It is easy for me to ask for what I
  want.

Feeling Overwhelmed

I am centered and relaxed.
I am strong, powerful, and centered.
I listen easily.
I am peaceful and harmonious in
  the midst of chaos.
I work on an even pace emotionally.

Handling Success

I take time to enjoy my successes.
I acknowledge my successes.
  (List them occasionally so you
  can remember them.)
This is fun!
I know I am successful when . . .
I nurture myself when I am busy.
I let in the praise of others.
I deserve to succeed.
I acknowledge and appreciate
  myself.
I handle success with grace and
  style.
I am a successful and respected
  athlete.

Asking for What You Want

I ask for what I want clearly.
This is important to me. I would like

_____ .

It's OK to let go of what I want.
I release attachment to the outcome.
Hearing yes or no is OK.
I am patient.
I am straightforward in asking for
what I want.
I deserve to have what I want.

Stressed Out/Handling Stress

My top priority is making sure I
  take an hour/day for myself to
  nurture myself.
I breathe deeply and fully.
I am important to me.
I see and use stressful situations as a
  challenge.
I deserve rest and relaxation.
I am patient and relaxed.
I do one thing at a time, with care.

Fear of the Unknown

I welcome abundance and prosperity
  into my life.
I am creating a highly successful
  athletic reputation for myself.
I am creating a hugely successful and
  prosperous athletic career.
I am ready for whatever comes my
  way.
I trust the process.
I move mountains easily in the next
  six months.
I am building my athletic security
  every day with every task I do.

There is **acceptance and success** in just being out there. By **letting ourselves be seen,** by **taking risks** to do something different, we grow. Avoidance just doesn't work, and it makes us miserable by turning us into victims.

Successful people are the ones who turn *everything into fuel* for growth and self-development.

—James Newton

Anger

Reflect for a moment on how anger makes you feel . . . feel the anger in your body . . . Where do you feel it? Is it in your heart? . . . your chest? . . . your mind? . . . Feel the heat of the anger in your chest . . . constricting, tightening your chest and body . . . feel the pain that anger brings to your body and mind. . . .

Such were the words I heard in 1977 at a retreat. They were spoken by Stephen Levine, the author of *Healing into Life and Death.* I had never before thought much about anger. These words were the first part of a guided meditation on forgiveness and letting go of anger. I was struck by the power of the meditation and how badly my body felt when I imagined feeling anger.

Anger is a natural process, one to be expressed and observed. A small amount of anger can be very motivating and a powerful force in athletic achievement. The problem with using anger as a motivator is that most of us have great difficulty controlling it. When we are really angry, anger controls us, and we often give up our personal power and integrity when we lose it.

It is important that anger be expressed and released from our bodies. Unexpressed anger can turn into illness or uncontrollable rage, enslaving our bodies and minds. Anger has become a major issue in the past ten years in athletic competition. Because of top tennis players like McEnroe and Connors, young players are having fits of anger, which most of the time simply interfere with their playing and get them into trouble with officials. We have spent many hours counseling players in controlling their tempers.

We believe that Connors and McEnroe are in control, even when they are angry. They seem to use anger as a vent for aggression and to distract their opponents. Unfortunately, the younger players are using them as role models for anger, but these young athletes are not in control of themselves on the court and end up furious with themselves. This fury serves no better purpose than to blow their concentration and win them penalties rather than points.

In counseling athletes, we work with them to help them express their anger in settings other than athletic competition. The steps mentioned in acknowledging fear also apply to anger.

1. Acknowledge your anger and feelings.
2. Breath to calm yourself—three to five deep breaths.
3. Relax your shoulders, neck, stomach, and abdomen.
4. Say and write affirmations for controlling anger.
5. Visualize.
6. Later, go home or somewhere safe, and get the anger out of your body: by beating a pillow; by chopping wood; by screaming in a private place, in

your car with the windows up; by writing all of your feelings on a paper and burning it—whatever you need to do to let the anger go and to get it out of your body in a constructive way.

Many people in our culture are what are referred to as conflict avoiders. Conflict avoiders are in massive resistance to anger and avoid conflict at all costs. They become placaters and are terrified of confrontation. Many see anger as being out of control of your emotions, which is unacceptable; they may believe anger is bad; they may have a lot of shame or guilt around anger and its expression. They may think that any emotions that look out of control such as crying or being angry are totally unacceptable. Such belief systems often result in disassociating from one's emotions and true feelings and eventually in illness.

Those of us who overexpress anger may be doing so in order to manipulate our environment to create safety or protection for ourselves. Some believe we make people angry to make them feel guilty. In any case, **every time we get angry at someone, we give up our personal power and integrity.** Anger can be expressed without dumping all over the person we are angry with.

Often anger is a result of feelings of resentment that we may harbor for friends or opponents. Resentment often is the killer of friendships and relationships, when anger is unexpressed and ignored. Resentment binds us, keeps us down, creates feelings of powerlessness, and holds us back from our achievements. Feelings of resentment can make us withdraw, withhold information, blame others, feel trapped, and become victims. Part of us shrinks inside, our hearts close, and we feel hurt and pain.

Take a couple of minutes to write down quickly what thoughts and words come to mind around the word **anger.** Write the words on the page with anger in the center.

ANGER

In doing this exercise, you will uncover some of your belief systems around anger. When we did the exercise, our words were: in the way; overwhelming; useful; fear; power; active; it works for a while; look like jerks; I'll show them!; I will be victorious!; I'll get them!; out of control; movement; motivation; aggression; rage; loss of control; feels better than hurt or humiliation; it goes outward instead of inward; hurting; violence; focused; concentrated; look stupid.

These words represent a number of feelings that athletes express about anger and its expression. It is important to remember:

We are not these feelings; these are simply things we do and feel.

Anger in Competition

Two athletes we worked with had major issues around anger on the court. Both were young men; one played tennis and one was a basketball player. They were both sixteen. After three sessions each, both had good control of their tempers during games and tournaments.

The basketball player, Eric, found success by focusing on his strengths and saying and remembering affirmations about his strengths, as well as a few about letting go of anger and missed shots. The following affirmations were helpful to Eric:

I'm a smart player.
I'm the best defensive player on the team.
I'm real aggressive.
I'm a good team player.
I've got a good positive attitude!
I'm quick and fast.
I mentally let go of missed shots easily.
I play more aggressively each game, especially on offense.
I am as relaxed in games as I am in practice.
I am calm, cool, and collected on the court.
I easily forgive myself for missed shots.
I have good concentration and focus in the game.
I stop worrying about what people think.
I let go of what people think about me.
I have fun playing.

The tennis player, Shane, would get furious with himself if he started to lose or miss shots. His negative self-talk was cursing at himself, talking to himself saying, "Dummie, hit the ball right! You're playing like ___. You can't lose to this joke." If he got mad, he would stay mad and end up blowing the match. Affirmations that helped Shane were

I forgive myself for missing a point.
I encourage and support myself with my talk.
I let go of mistakes and focus on the next shot.
Between points, I let go of the last point and think about the next shot.
I play aggressively and well, especially if I'm behind.

I think positively during a match.
I am mentally tough in each match I play.
When I'm ahead, I play even more aggressively.
I love playing well, and I have fun playing.
I am calm, cool, and collected on the court.
I have Andre Agassi's attitude.
I am a cool dude.

Personal Anger Awareness

Take a minute or two to think about your sport and what things make you angry
when you are playing or competing.

1. I get angry when

    a. _____

    b. _____

    c. _____

    d. _____

2. How I am currently dealing with my anger during competition:

    a. _____

    b. _____

    c. _____

    d. _____

3. How I would like to constructively handle my anger in competition:

    a. _____

    b. _____

    c. _____

    d. _____

4. Five affirmations to help me handle my anger in a positive way:

    a. _____

    b. _____

c. _____

d. _____

e. _____

The following visualization may be helpful to you in reframing and releasing any anger you are experiencing in competition. As with all visualizations, select one of the relaxation sequences to quiet your mind and body before the visualization process.

Guided Visualization for Dealing with Anger in Competition

Find a comfortable place to sit or lie. . . . Begin to breathe deeply . . . taking a deep breath, holding it . . . and letting it go with a sigh . . . breathing in . . . and letting it out . . . breathing in energy . . . breathing out peace . . . relax your shoulders . . . your neck . . . soften your abdomen and stomach . . . and begin to feel yourself to be centered, whole, and balanced . . . begin to imagine gold, white, or pink light coming into the top of your head, and down into your body, coming out through your solar plexus . . . feel your solar plexus to be powerful and strong . . . with the light flowing out of it . . . feeling and seeing the light from the top of your head . . . flowing through your body and out through your solar plexus . . . feeling relaxed . . . powerful . . . and with a flexibility and suppleness around your solar plexus . . . imagine it pulsating with the passage of this energy from the top of your head and through it.

Think of the last time you were angry in a competition or practice . . . or of the list you just made on anger. . . . Begin to acknowledge any feelings of anger you might have during competition or practice . . . remembering the list of things that make you angry . . . and as each item of anger comes up . . . acknowledge it and thank it for making itself known to you . . . take some time to think of each angry thought . . . acknowledge it and say to it, "I thank you, and I welcome you (and think of being angry); my anger is welcome here; you are welcome here and I acknowledge you and let you flow through me," . . . and let yourself imagine the angry feelings flowing through your solar plexus and flowing out through the middle of your back . . . just passing through, as if you were transparent . . . the anger flows in and the anger flows out . . . there is no place for it to stay in your body . . . it is just flowing through you . . . imagine yourself surrendering to the flow . . . the anger moving on through your solar plexus as a light breeze . . . and feel your belly and abdomen to be strong and flexible . . . letting the angry feelings pass through the area above your waist, without pain or anxiety, just as if you were watching or feeling a soft breeze . . . continue to imagine the light flowing down from the top of your head out through your solar plexus . . . feeling strong, powerful, and centered.

Begin to say your affirmations about your anger . . . "I let go of my anger easily . . . I am in control of myself on the court . . . I am powerful and centered. . . . It is easy for me to forgive myself . . . I easily let go of mistakes or missed shots . . . I am calm, cool, and collected . . . I am mentally tough . . . I am focused and concentrated . . . I encourage and support myself . . . I am a positive player." Begin to imagine yourself handling your anger in a calm, comfortable, and powerful way . . . see, hear, and feel yourself succeeding . . . handling your anger . . . feeling powerful and in control . . . feeling your solar plexus to be strong and flexible . . . knowing you are in control and are worthy of your accomplishments . . . feeling your strength and power . . . acknowledging your anger and letting it go . . . going on to succeed . . . to achieve your goals and dreams . . . knowing you have what it takes to be successful and to overcome any obstacles, including any anger you might have or feel . . . you **are** good enough . . . **you are** worthy of respect and achievement . . . you are safe and in control . . . **you are powerful.**

Begin to remember a time **when you were** totally confident and in control of yourself during a competition or in practice. . . . Allow yourself to see, feel, and hear the events of that time . . . let all the images come back to your awareness . . . feeling the feelings of pride, joy, freedom . . . all the power and strength of that time . . . your own self-approval . . . self-acceptance . . . that feeling of well-being and a job well-done . . . the feelings of competence and confidence . . . perhaps of you helping your teammates or them helping you . . . working together as a team . . . allow yourself to experience that time again . . . seeing, hearing, and feeling the events . . . and think of a word that represents those thoughts and feelings . . . saying the word over to yourself . . . knowing that word will bring back all of those feelings of confidence and control. . . . And remember you can say that word to yourself anytime you feel angry, and the anger will dissipate easily, and you will experience feelings of confidence, power, and control . . . easily dropping any anger you might feel . . . becoming confident and powerful, focused and in control. . . . Remember your word . . . the word that transforms anger into confidence and control. . . . Knowing you can say your word anytime you wish to remember these positive feelings . . . (pause). . . .

Slowly begin to let the images and feelings fade, remembering you have everything within you to be, to do, or to have what you want in life . . . knowing you can acknowledge and control your anger anytime you wish . . . knowing you are worthy of the best . . . remembering your word.

When I count to three, you can open your eyes . . . feeling strong, powerful, and confident . . . one . . . take a deep breath . . . letting it out . . . two . . . stretch your neck and shoulders . . . three . . . open your eyes when you're ready.

Fear and anger are two strong and powerful emotions. If we open to these feelings and are comfortable in acknowledging and expressing them, we can overcome most mental obstacles in our journey toward success. What we move toward and through, we overcome; what we resist, we may intensify, exaggerate, or become.

There is enough for me and I am worthy of all the success and abundance that I receive.

Chapter ■ Nine

Youth Sports—Working with Young Athletes

Do's and Don'ts for Parents

Probably since the beginning of sports history there have been parents who were enthusiastic, shouting, supportive, critical, loving, pushing, caring, and demanding, on the sidelines or in the stands. Most of the time this is crucial to the performance, good or bad, of the child's athletic endeavor. After working with young athletes, their parents, and their coaches, we were asked to come up with a list of what works and what doesn't work for the parents of aspiring young athletes. The following are the most powerful do's and don'ts for parents to support their child in the most positive and beneficial way.

The Do's

1. Allow your child to be interested and to want to play whatever sport he or she chooses. Provide the opportunity of many choices and support his or her choice even if it is not yours. Support your child's choice to play no sport when he or she is the most comfortable with that option.

2. Teach your child to respect his or her coach. Do this primarily by showing respect to the coach yourself. It is vital to the child's progress and performance that he or she listen to and trust the coach's advice and instructions.

3. Be willing to let your child make his or her own mistakes and learn from them. When your child makes a mistake, ask what they think they could have done differently, what they learned from the experience, and if they would like any feedback (not criticism or blame) from you—what you saw, what you think they might have done differently, and what you think they might have learned.

4. Be interested and supportive, light and playful, understanding and open-hearted. Be accepting and tolerant of your child's learning process and his or

her physical abilities. Acknowledge and enjoy your child's participation and successes—even the small ones.

5. Model flexibility of your own opinions. Be willing to be wrong and move off your position. Listen to the other side of the situation and let go of the need to be right or in control.

The Don'ts

1. Don't try to relive your youth through your child. Just because you wanted to be, or were, a hero on the football field or in gymnastics does not mean *that* sport will be your child's choice. Accept that your child may not excel in that or any sport.

2. Don't blame the equipment, coach, other players, referees, or even the weather if your child or the team does not do well or win. Blaming others teaches nonaccountability to kids. They do not learn to look at what they could have done differently or learn from their mistakes if they learn to blame others.

3. Don't push, push, push. Children who are pushed beyond their capabilities may lose their self-confidence, become resistant and resentful toward their parent, become unsure of themselves and their abilities, and stop trying. They may also exhibit a disturbance in eating and/or sleeping habits.

4. Don't expect perfection or tie your ego or image to your child's performance. Perfectionism is a very hard expectation to live up to. Laying guilt on a child because their performance made you look bad is highly destructive. Your child is not responsible for your ego or your reputation in the community.

Remembering this simple list may assist parents in remembering that youth sports are to be enjoyed by children as well as parents. Most children play sports because they have fun playing. When sports become work and drudgery, children lose interest and some of the joy in growing up. Remembering to be a little less serious about life helps all of us enjoy athletic competition.

Top Issues of Young Athletes

In our work with young athletes, in the ten-year to eighteen-year range, we began to notice a similarity in issues, regardless of what sport they played. After trust was established, we began to work with their core issues. The following list represents the main issues of male and female athletes from ages ten to eighteen:

1. Focus and concentration
2. Learning to visualize
3. Stopping negative self-talk
4. Controlling anger on the field/court
5. Precompetition anxiety and fear
6. What other people think of them

Actually, many of you adults reading this chapter will probably say, "Those are my issues too!" and they may well be. After we have been functioning in the world for a while, we learn to do some of these tasks. Children are very vulnerable and impressionable, and many haven't learned yet to deal with self-doubt, peer pressure, or authority. There is an inner child in all of us who struggles with these issues. Perhaps we should all let our inner child come out to learn with us the nuances of solving these problems.

Tips for Working with the Six Top Issues

We have found that one of the best ways to improve concentration and focus is to have an athlete listen to a guided visualization of ten to fifteen minutes on a Walkman, with eyes closed and sitting in a quiet room. This mental focus on listening to a voice and imagining visual and physical responses to his or her sport teaches the child to focus and refocus constantly. Our minds wander constantly, grasping at each new idea or thought that comes up. Listening to guided visualizations brings our attentional focus to one spot, and we learn to mentally track for longer and longer periods of time. Before we learn to track, we must do a minisurrender—surrendering to doing *nothing* but sitting and listening for ten to fifteen minutes, without going to sleep.

The process of focusing can be facilitated by the nostril-breathing process of holding the right index finger over the right nostril and breathing through the left nostril for thirty seconds to a minute. This accesses the right brain, slows down left-brain thinking, stops mind chatter, and facilitates right-brain processing.

If the athlete is between eight and thirteen, an even shorter visualization time period is recommended—perhaps ten minutes or less at the beginning. Also, when attempting to teach the five-step program to young athletes, sessions should be no longer than thirty to forty-five minutes each. Keep them interested and on target— simple and quick, in short segments.

When working with young gymnasts, we found they responded best to watching only short parts of our videotape of *The Mental Athlete* (a total of thirty minutes in length) at each session. We usually showed only ten minutes at the beginning of each session and talked about one or two steps. We took time to teach them simple relaxation procedures first, before we embarked on more complex tasks of visualization techniques.

In my work at developmental camps at the U.S. Olympic Training Center, with athletes fourteen to twenty years of age, the best method was to do two sessions of one to one and a half hours of general lecture, goal writing, visualization, and questions and answers about sport psychology. These were followed by individual sessions of one hour apiece with each athlete. The athletes were very receptive to the individual attention and had an overall understanding of what the process of mental training was all about. These sessions received very high ratings in the evaluations of the camp. The athletes received needed individual instruction, as well as a confidentiality that group process does not allow. They reported they had benefited greatly from this information and process.

As for the six top issues, the processes for addressing them can be found in the individual chapters in this book. Learning to visualize and positive self-talk are covered in chapter 3, dealing with anger and fear in chapter 8, and what other people think is discussed in a number of different sections throughout the book. The process is the same for youth athletes as for adults; the only difference is the teaching is broken down into smaller chunks. And remember, *no one can be forced to learn this process.* There must be a willingness to change and to do something different in order to create the space for improvement. If the leaders of the team are supportive of mental training, other team members will listen. The more the mental edge is discussed during sports coverage, the more attention it will receive from young athletes. Using mental training is a matter of exposure and awareness. It's OK to go slowly in implementing a mental training program; some athletes will love it, and some of the ones you think would benefit most will never look at it. Great measures of patience, tolerance, and acceptance by the coach and parents are necessary in this process.

A Sample Talk Given to a High School Soccer Team in Boston

(This is an example of a simple thirty-minute talk for young athletes.)

How many of you watched the Olympics?

(Many raised their hands.) What did you notice regarding talk about mental training or mental preparation? (Much discussion about what was said about the mental edge, etc., of Olympic athletes.) We discussed different events and how athletes were using sport psychology in their training and competition.

Elite athlete survey in 1984

We discussed the survey we conducted in 1984 of elite athletes and their use of mental training techniques. The "seven traits of champions" that we found in our survey were they (1) let go of losses; (2) never saw themselves as losers even when they lost, (3) went for the win, not to place second; (4) analyzed losses for learning, (5) used visualization often, especially before competition, (6) let go of the past and looked to the future; and (7) had total belief in themselves and their abilities.

The most important aspects of sport psychology in high school

If athletes were to use only two or three processes of mental training, the most important would be (1) setting goals for themselves for the next year or so, (2) listening to what they say to themselves (negatively and positively), and (3) learning to use mental imagery and mental rehearsal (visualization) processes.

If your best friend said to you what you say to yourself, you'd never speak to him again!

What we saw yesterday in your game that you might improve

1. Lapses in intensity—you were flat-footed a lot.
2. The other team came out really aggressively in the second half. You did that in the first half, but not the second.
3. They encouraged each other a lot—yelling and clapping for the team when they were on the sidelines and when they were playing on the field.
4. You rushed some of your shots too much when you were going for the goal.
5. Loss of concentration near the end of the game—you were getting tired and you showed it.

What can you try to change?

1. No hesitation before a shot; commit yourself to the shot you're taking—this is different than rushing the shot. You can take your time and then commit yourself with strength and follow-through.
2. Let go of anger quickly and easily. (You often came from a position of "it's not fair." So what? You just have to let it go and go on.) How do you let go of anger on the field? Breathe; walk or run away; don't give your opponents the satisfaction of seeing your anger; and play hard instead of fighting hard with your words or body.
3. Anticipate what you're going to do in the lag times of the game.
4. Increase your focus and concentration by watching the team carefully and encouraging your teammates with "let's go" statements.
5. Come out hustling in the second half.

How can high school athletes use sport psychology to play better?

1. In the last half hour of the game, if you're tired, use your positive self-talk and affirmations—"I'm strong . . . I'm fast . . . I'm powerful." Also talk more between yourselves—encourage other team members and congratulate them on good shots.
2. If you lose a game, analyze your game for what you did right; acknowledge yourself for doing it right; analyze for what you did wrong and work on it during the next week's practice; and let go of the loss and focus on the next game.
3. Practice setting up more intensity shots under pressure in practice. Practice with people "in your face"—not every day, but for a day or two to try different things to see what works and what doesn't.
4. Use visualization and imagery practice to imagine yourself playing your position as well as you'd like to play it—doing things right; having a lot of speed; having good energy for your team; and having strength and endurance—really put yourself out there.

Cautions About Selecting a Club or Coach for Young Athletes

In the spring of 1989, Shelly Sanford, a sportswriter from the Austin (Texas) American-Statesman, contacted us regarding an article she was writing on the coach-athlete relationship. Her article described a number of cases of coaches having sexual contact with their minor athletes. While this is a somewhat rare event, sexual abuse and exploitation in our culture are a growing concern. It is unclear whether more athletes are coming forward with this problem or whether it is becoming more prevalent. Her examples are frightening; they describe a problem most of us would rather not think about.

Apparently, in some sports, young girls as young as nine years old have slept with their coaches. Rachel, nine, slept with her coach for four years before her parents discovered her coach, Sam, in bed with her. He left the state but later returned to coach elsewhere.

"Young girls, who aspire to become world-class athletes, are placed in the care of a coach they believe will help them reach their goal. The result is generally a strong bond that develops between the athlete and the coach through an intensive daily workout program and competitive road trips."

Without becoming overly paranoid, what can parents do to prevent such occurrences? It is important that the coach be trusted and receive respect from parents and children alike. Much, of course, depends on the integrity of the coach. According to a former teammate on the team with Rachel, "The horrible thing is that some of the parents of the kids on the team were blaming Rachel. That was the reaction. This guy was having nine and ten year olds spend the night with him—the whole relay team. Everyone said to my mother, 'You are being a busybody.' They gave my mother a hard time. The signs were all there. The problem is the authority figure. I don't think a child should be put in a situation where an older man is putting his hands on her shoulder, or where she is sitting there in a bathing suit, and that makes the child feel uncomfortable. Kids don't know what is OK and what is not OK. Parents are remiss who don't let their kids know about the bad things out there."

Jill Sterkel, assistant head swimming coach at the University of Texas at Austin, stressed an increase in parent's monitoring their child when under a coach's care. It gets down to the bottom line of coaching ethics and personal responsibility of all the adults, both coach and parents. The consequences of such incidences can ruin careers or cause much emotional stress in the future, especially for young women. The youngsters often have no idea how to deal with such situations. When the matter of hero worship comes up, the problem is compounded.

We would like to suggest a few guidelines to parents of young athletes, especially young females.

What Parents Can Do When Sending a Child to a Program

1. Choose club or coach carefully by getting expert opinions about the club or coach.
2. Ask for references.
3. Talk to parents of children enrolled and ask for a list of a few who no longer attend the school or belong to the club. Find out why their child is no longer enrolled and what they think about the coaching their child received.
4. Establish from babyhood a trust between you and your child—the creation of good communication and trust between parent and child is essential. Trust

your child and what he or she tells you. It is important to believe your child and what you are told. Your child should trust you enough to tell you the truth. Make sure your child is telling the truth and not trying to get even with a coach for other reasons. Quietly collect more information about the coach and the situation described by your child, getting as much objective information as possible.

5. Instill in your child a feeling of self-trust and a knowledge of what is uncomfortable touching by others.

6. If kids are spending the night, make sure there are at least two adults present.

7. Don't be paranoid, just be careful. Children need to learn trust of others. In youth sports, hero worship is a common and normal response. Relying on the coach's integrity is essential. It is also your right to get good information about the coach and the program from other parents.

8. It might be helpful to read the guidelines from sexual abuse programs on what to tell your child about inappropriate touching from strangers, family, or friends.

9. Communicate with your child about touch. Any touch that a child receives that is scarey, confusing, or to be kept a secret should be talked about with you. The child should never be shamed or embarrassed by you for disclosing this type of information to you. Receive your child with love and acceptance.

10. The most important question about touching is: who is the touch for? The child or the toucher? Obviously, it should be for the child. Children need to be touched and nurtured, and even at a young age, they can feel when someone touches them if it is OK or not. All of us, when touched, respond with either relaxation to the touch or with a tightening in our bodies. Children can learn the difference and can sense what is safe and what is not.

11. Recommended books for children on touching are (a) *A Very Touching Book: For Little People and Big People* by Jan Hindman. McClure-Hindman Associates, P.O. Box 208, Durkee, OR 97905; (b) *Something Happened and I'm Scared to Tell* by Patricia Kehoe ($3.95). Parenting Press, Seattle, Washington; and (c) *Loving Touches: Positive Caring Kinds of Touching* by Lory Freeman ($3.50), Parenting Press, P.O. Box 15163 Seattle, Washington, 98115 (1-800-992-6657).

12. Any coach who uses corporate punishment or who verbally abuses his athletes should be avoided.

While these guidelines may not solve all the problems, they may give parents peace of mind and some feeling of control over this issue. As parents, we want to be careful, yet still give our children a sense of trust of others and a feeling of well-being in their world.

Chapter ▪ *Ten*

Sport Psychology for the 1990s: A Glimpse into the Future

Applied Sport Psychology

What we mean by applied sport psychology is the using and teaching of mental training skills—hands-on experience by athletes in using the principles and concepts of sport psychology research. Visualization, self-talk, affirmations, imagery and rehearsal, goal setting, mental log keeping, relaxation skills, focusing, and concentration are among the concepts taught in applied sport psychology.

In the next five years we will see much more general acceptance of sport psychology and mental training by traditional coaches. Many more team-sport coaches, such as football, basketball, and baseball, are now using sport psychologists with their teams, as well as referring individual players to the "mental skills" coach, for example, the sport psychologist. It is important that coaches remain open to the feedback of their athletes. Often, the more autocratic coach is unwilling to hear any negative feedback at all. Sometimes the attitude is "I'm the coach, and what I say goes. If you don't like it, you can quit." As this attitude changes or softens, there will be more willingness on the coach's part to hear what might be new and helpful information about what is working and what isn't. More trust between coach and athlete is established, resulting in better communication patterns.

With this general acceptance, more coaches are and will be learning mental training skills that they will teach to their athletes. Much of the work I do as a sport psychologist is educational. Mental skills are easy to learn and somewhat easy to pass on, after a suitable practice period. It is helpful for an outside expert (the sport psychologist) to come in and teach some skills; then the coach can continue reinforcing and using the skills on a daily and weekly basis with athletes. The sport psychologist can be more time effective by working with individuals and doing introductory sessions for teams and athletic departments.

The 1990s will also see many more individual athletes working with a sport psychologist on a one-to-one counseling basis. Often this takes the form of the "presenting problem" being sports performance and eventually turns into general counseling sessions on many different issues in life, school, etc. One sprinter I worked with said to me after a couple of months, "Is this supposed to affect my life too?" He found that the mental training was filtering over into his schoolwork and his personal relationships in a very positive way.

In working with teams, sport psychologists may find themselves developing a team-building approach similar to the team-building models used in business settings. In business team-building sessions, there is an emphasis on discussions of accountability (no more blaming of others or self), building agreement and commitments, dealing with resentment and expectation, letting go of resentment and getting on with the task at hand, group problem solving, ways of improving communication among team members, and mutual team goals. The sport psychologist's function would be that of a facilitator and information presenter. The facilitation process would be of upmost importance, in order to keep communication between team members and coach open and nondefensive.

In counseling, we are hearing from and seeing more and more recreational athletes. They are simply interested in improving their personal performance and enjoyment in their sport—usually tennis, golf, running, soccer, basketball, and volleyball. These are people who most likely were not athletes in college or high school. Most are white-collar workers and professionals, who have the discretionary income to seek services. They are every bit as enjoyable to work with as collegiate or elite athletes. They are pleased and sometimes thrilled with their improvements. They are an enthusiastic and interested group, and I would encourage other sport psychologists to say yes to them if they have the time to work with them. It's fun.

Lastly, we believe there will be more "mind/body/spirit" emphasis in sport psychology in the next ten years. With the research being done in psychoneuroimmunology (PNI), there are more and more indications that the immune system is definitely influenced by what we think and feel. Our emotions and feelings play a big part in our physical health, illness, and wellness.

We must be careful not to tread too closely to the religious overtones of what spirit means. When we refer to spirit, we mean something inside that is nourished emotionally by what we think or do. Nourishment of that spirit is important for joy and personal satisfaction in life. It can be something as simple as reclaiming the joy and fun we had when we first started competing in our sport. We believe it is important to preserve this original fun and personal satisfaction of playing the sport. When an athlete loses the original fun of playing, he or she is going to quickly burn out. Personally, we believe in the development and balance of the whole person, rather than just individual parts.

Athletic Departments in Universities and Colleges

In 1988, we saw the first hiring of a paid staff sport psychologist on the administrative team of a university athletic department. As the ranks of sport psychologists grow, more and more have been working on a consultant basis with collegiate athletic teams and athletes. Although there are more than just one, Pennsylvania State University was one of the first, if not *the* first, major university that designed a position for a full-time staff sport psychologist. The level of collegiate competition being what it is, in the 1990's we will see a dramatic increase in these positions.

As this use of sport psychologists increases, more and more teams will be willing to acknowledge their use of psychological services. There will continue to be a rise in the positive image of these services, and the "head case" label will hopefully become obsolete.

The athletic departments will also begin to promote sport psychology clinics and seminars for the public or high school athletes (following NCAA guidelines, I am sure) to enhance their public relations images.

Workshops for trainers and coaches will become commonplace and part of the athletic department program. The athletic department will support and encourage the use of the sport psychologist's services by teams and individual athletes. They will also drop the label of head case and will begin emphasizing peak performance assistance from the sport psychologist.

Youth Sports

As the public awareness of sport psychology increases, through television coverage of sporting events, more interest will develop among high school athletes. We have been approached by a number of high school coaches to give workshops for their teams. In the next ten years, the teaching of mental training techniques will become commonplace in high schools and with very young athletes, especially in sports such as diving, swimming, and gymnastics. As competition and quality athletics increase in high schools, coaches will also be looking for their new competitive edge, which will turn out to be sport psychology. Following collegiate examples, high school coaches will begin using mental training techniques with their teams. The coaches probably won't have to convince their athletes of the importance of mental training. In our work, we have found that athletes at the high school level are very interested in how to use these techniques. They do not want to know the details of research; a little background of why it works, especially examples, is fine with them. Most are bored with the research information. Even college athletes don't want research; they want the bottom-line information of how to learn and perfect their skills.

As we mentioned earlier, athletes in the ten-year to fourteen-year age range will be learning mental training skills. We have had the experience of working with very young gymnasts, some as young as eight. As a caution to other sport psychologists when working with a very young child, a basis of trust must be established. Many simply clam up around a grown-up. It is better to work with them, if possible, while they are being physical and moving. There is always the danger of peer teasing, however, if they are seen working with you unless you are working with a whole group of them individually. Then it is OK. Also, being introduced as the visualization coach or mental coach is much less threatening. And it is much better not to use Dr. in front of your name; Coach Smith is best. After working in that capacity during their training, then the one-to-one private session has a better chance of working.

Sport psychologists may be doing more teaching of dos and don'ts for parents. We developed a list of dos and don'ts when working with younger athletes, mainly because of what we observed in parents' behaviors during competition. The dos and don'ts are in chapter 9, Youth Sports. We believe it is extremely important for parents to model good athletic behaviors, especially those of not blaming the coach and are of respect for the coach. Otherwise, team morale and performance are seriously undermined.

Much of the work of the sport psychologist in youth sports may center around issues of focus and concentration, self-confidence, anger control, pregame anxiety, and fear in competition. In our work with young athletes, most concerns deal with these issues. We spend most of our time teaching them how to visualize/image; to focus and concentrate; to deal with anger on the court or in the game, which may interfere with their performance; and to talk to themselves. In the teens, negative self-talk is the number one enemy of self-confidence and positive self-image. Once we find out what they say to themselves, we start working with some affirmations to begin more positive thinking. At that age, they are so worried about what other people think. One of the most useful affirmations they can use is "I give back to others the responsibility for their own opinion/feelings/thoughts." They find that the more they focus on their game, the less time they have to worry about what other people think.

Organizational Development Skills

At the annual meeting of the Association for the Advancement of Applied Sport Psychology in October, 1988, I attended a session for members of the U.S. Olympic Sport Psychology Registry.

Dr. W. R. McKelvain talked to us about a new and interesting concept of the use of sport psychologists' services—organizational development. We have used it in business consulting with corporations, both in facilitation and group process work. He said that he sees sport psychologists working more and more with professional teams and front offices of the teams. Many of the organizational skills used by business consultants will be used with these professional teams. There seems to be a need for facilitating the communication between players, coaches, and front-office staff. In addition, we can see group-dynamic skills being useful to the sport psychologist. Many of the topics in team-building sessions would be relevant, as well as communication skills, conflict resolution, building agreement, and problem solving. Coping with stress issues would also be important. Dr. McKelvain, the consultant to the U.S. gymnastics team, sees organizational development consulting as innovation—a way of initiating and sustaining change. Organizational development consultants are often seen as change agents—as those who initiate change, as well as teach others how to adapt to organizational change. With the changing face of athletics in the next ten years, it would behoove us to get more training in organizational development and change.

In addition, any sport psychologist working with professional teams will find it essential to have more experience and information about substance abuse issues. This is an important issue for pro teams and is getting to be a huge problem on college campuses as well. All of us need to update our knowledge and skills in substance abuse for our work in the next decade. Basically, there will be more organizational skills needed by sport psychologists working with national governing bodies of sport (such as the TAC, USTA), pro teams, and athletic departments to assist in organizational functioning, mediation/communication, and resolving team issues.

In-Service Training of Traditional Psychologists, Counselors, and Social Workers

At the popularity of sport psychology has increased, there has been more interest from traditional therapists in being trained to help athletes. Soon the sport psychology community will also be faced with decisions about whether to allow training and certification of these "outside" therapists. Because of our book *The Mental Athlete*, we have been contacted by a number of psychologists and counselors looking for training in working specifically with athletic issues. This interest will continue to grow, and sport psychologists will have to decide how they want to proceed with the licensing and training of psychologists, counselors, and social workers who were not originally trained in sport psychology and counseling.

There are many pros and cons to this issue. There is the fundamental split between sport psychologists who were trained in physical education departments versus those who were trained in psychology programs. Different sport psychology programs at various universities are usually located in either physical education or psychology departments. There is a peaceful geniality between the groups, and a tolerance and an acceptance. The entrance of traditional therapists could create either a holistic climate or a more divisive one.

The conflicts that arise will be derived from one of two viewpoints: prosperity or poverty consciousness. Let me explain. With a prosperity consciousness, the belief system is one of believing that there is enough prosperity for all, a belief in abundance, cooperation and networking, and positive comparison. With a poverty or scarcity consciousness, people believe there is not enough to go around; they are not going to get enough; they can't do enough; they must be in competition with everyone; and if comparing themselves, they often come up lacking. Since sports are based on competition, albeit healthy competition, these belief systems and issues may clash in the licensing and training arena.

Training and Certification of Sport Psychologists in College and University Programs

The issues of psychology-versus physical education-based programs will continue. We hope to see the continuing peaceful coexistence of these programs with the stimulating interaction of the past fifteen years. At conventions, where such issues are frequently discussed, there has always been pleasant and enjoyable discussion and sharing of ideas and research. In the 1990s, which may be a period of immense social change, we look forward to even better communication between many diverse groups and to conflict resolution that can serve as role models for the content of our teaching and training.

In intern training, we believe it is important that upon leaving the university with a doctorate the new sport psychologists have a firm basis in applying their skills as well as being proficient in research. We have heard from a number of graduate students throughout the country who are looking for places to work hands-on in counseling athletes and in teaching mental training skills. Many of these students are excellent in research design and implementation, yet know little about working with a client in a counseling situation. We believe that research is very important for our field, and we think that balance is necessary in preparing the quintessential sport psychologist. They need the people skills (right brain) to go with the research skills (left brain). Both belong in the graduate school curriculum.

U.S. Olympic Committee Sport Science

In the next ten years, the influence and importance of sport psychology will grow in the sport science program of the U.S. Olympic Training Center. It will become more apparent how important mental skills are in training Olympic athletes. There will continue to be developmental programs in Olympic sport for the pre-Olympians between the ages of eight and twenty. More and more developmental camps will have sport psychologists on staff to teach mental skills to young athletes. The sport psychology program will continue to conduct research programs and to grow stronger with each passing year. We have had a slow, but significant start; we believe that in the next ten years sport psychology will come into its own in the Olympic training program.

After the 1988 Olympics, a seminar program was started for former Olympic athletes to help them look at career options after their athletic careers were finished. The CAPA program (Career Assessment Program for Athletes) sponsored five seminars in different areas of the country to offer career adjustment assistance to athletes. In 1989 an Olympic Job Opportunity Program was established to continue this work. They help Olympic athletes develop new career ideas before they are finished with their competitive years. This program will continue to grow in the 1990s.

Summary

We think it is important for us, as psychologists and athletes, to remember that although mental training skills may be simple they are extremely powerful. What we set as our goals, what we say to ourselves, and what we see and don't see are vitally important to our success. In an interview one week after her fall in the 1984 Olympic 3000-meter race, Mary Decker Slaney was asked if she visualized as part of her training. Had she seen herself running in the Olympics? She said she had dreamed about it and visualized it for months. Then she paused and said, "But I never saw myself finishing the race."

Chapter ■ *Eleven*

Sport Psychology/Mental Training Programs for Team Sports

A Sample Sport Psychology Program for University/College Athletic Departments for Team Sports

In January, 1988, Pennsylvania State University hired a full-time sport psychology specialist, Dr. David Yukelson, to work in the Academic Support Center for Student Athletics. This position was a staff position, not regular faculty, and it was funded by the Athletic Department. Dr. Yukelson uses a holistic approach with athletes that emphasizes improving the self-esteem of student athletes. The program promotes balance—working with the whole athlete, in academics, athletics, his/her personal life, and socially. The Center has a team approach and provides the services of five counselors, a freshman-orientation specialist, and a career development specialist. Dr. Yukelson's work includes working with twenty-eight teams and approximately 800 athletes in the athletic department.

His team educational presentations discuss goal setting, commitment to excellence, mental training, concentration techniques, and focusing. His first year was spent in developing rapport with athletes and teams, developing trust and interest in learning motivation and performance enhancement techniques. In addition to performance enhancement training, Dr. Yukelson helps the individual reconcile his or her role as both a student and an athlete. The issues of most interest to the student athletes were mental training and performance enhancement based on time management, assertiveness, learning to express their needs without others taking it personally, and interpersonal communication. His time is spent counseling four to five athletes a day; attending as many practices as possible; checking in with the sports medicine staff regarding student athlete injuries and rehabilitation; consulting with coaches; and giving educational presentations to teams and other interested groups. He was most likely the first full-time sport psychologist hired by a university athletic department.

In late 1989, Arizona State University hired a full-time sport psychologist as part of the administrative staff, under the direction of the Student Health Center's Chief of Mental Health, and located in the Department of Intercollegiate Athletics. In the 1980s most sport psychologists in universities were employed as faculty members in either psychology or physical education departments. As we discussed in chapter 10, the 1990s will be a time for the hiring of more sport psychologists in administrative positions in collegiate athletic departments. These psychologists' prime function will be working directly with student athletes and teams.

The job functions we describe were taken partially from a job description from ASU. The responsibilities of this position are a good example of the direction that sport psychology professionals will be taking in the next ten years in collegiate athletic departments.

The sport psychologist in the athletic department

1. performs mental/behavioral health assessments for student athletes
2. provides therapy/counseling for athletes, as appropriate
3. refers athletes to other services on campus as needed
4. serves as a sport psychology educator to athletic teams, coaches, and individual athletes
5. coordinates the educational, consultation, and public relations components of the Applied Sport Psychology program
6. teaches one course per semester on applied sport psychology, a psychological skills training course
7. assesses need for and organizes sport psychology seminars for coaches, athletes, and staff
8. conducts workshops and other outreach activities in the community
9. maintains involvement with related research and teaching activities in academic departments such as Health and Physical Education, Psychology, and Counseling
10. coordinates education/training programs such as EDGE (Education Development Growth and Effectiveness—a videotape program in mental training and sport psychology principles)
11. supervises and helps select graduate assistants to teach the other sections of the psychological skills training course

In 1989, of the 600 athletes in the athletic department at ASU, about half took the psychological skills course. Seven sections per year were taught. Dr. Dan Landers, a professor in physical education, was primarily responsible for developing this outstanding program at ASU, after his arrival in 1981.

Both of these programs were very unique in 1989 and provided guidelines for other major universities in the use of sport psychologists on an athletic department staff.

Examples of Existing Mental Training Programs for Teams

High School Program in Football

Gary Stautz has been the head football coach at Gresham High School (a suburb of Portland, Oregon) since 1981. Gresham is an AAA team in Oregon. In 1987 and 1988 Coach Stautz began using sport psychology and mental training techniques with his team. In 1988 and 1989 their record was 12–1, and they lost in the semifinals of the state finals to the eventual state champions.

In 1987 they were 5–5 and lost the first round of the playoffs, trying third in the league. In 1988, the team decided they wanted to improve their win-lose record and they were tired of the team dissension of the previous year. The juniors from 1987, as returning seniors, decided to do "mental stuff" to get more serious, to have fun, and to promote team unity. They were committed to doing something different and to work on their mental game along with their physical training.

Coach Stautz, a long-time teacher and counselor, worked with goals, affirmations, and visualization techniques with the team. In 1988 spring training, they started with writing team and individual goals and how to achieve them. Their main team goal was team unity. The linemen and backs would have what they called "Hogs' Night Out," where they competed to see who could eat the most! The athletes spearheaded this and had a good time. Everyday in spring training they did something in terms of their mental game, looking at where they were and what they needed.

They talked a lot about being good; they had good talent; and they began to believe they had a great chance to do well. They discovered that in their previous year's team goals they had only wanted to get to the playoffs. Very few players wrote down that they wanted to be state champions. (This is similar to athletes who want to make the Olympic team. They never go farther in their heads and usually lose in the first round at the Olympics.)

In spring training, as a team they

1. watched highlights of well-executed offensive plays (selecting their own music to go with it—rap, etc.)
2. each received their own video to watch at home for inspiration and improving skill level
3. watched tape, learned from it, visualized themselves in their position
4. wrote team and individual goals for the coming season, plus offense and defense goals

All of these affirmations were printed on a two by three inch laminated card for each player to carry in his wallet and to read every day. In addition, each player had a copy of the general affirmations that were written on an eight and a half by eleven inch sheet distributed to each player.

The 1988 Gresham football team affirmations were

Our (my) great efforts lead to consistent execution.
We (I) intensely control all short-yardage situations.
We (I) take pride in winning the turnover game.

Positive things happen because we work hard and believe in each other.
I put the individual aside and strongly promote team unity by my actions and words.
We (I) minimize fumbles by carrying the ball properly.
We (I) reduce mistakes with positive concentration and intelligent play.
I know my assignment for each play and situation.
We (I) enthusiastically block downfield for each offensive play.
We (I) take great pride in opening holes for running backs.
We (I) run with reckless abandon, crush tacklers, and earn the hard yard.
We (I) fire off the ball with great quickness and power.
The passing game succeeds due to superior pass protection, well-placed throws, and confident catches.
We (I) powerfully dominate the line of scrimmage.
We (I) make the key interception and fumble recovery.
We (I) intimidate opponents with a relentless pass rush resulting in sacks and rushed throws.
We (I) always make the technically sound tackle.
We (I) show great effort in pursuing to the ball in the correct manner.
We (I) continually contain and stuff the run.
We (I) electrify the crowd with exciting kick returns.
WE ARE THE 1988 MT. HOOD CONFERENCE CHAMPIONS!

The major affirmations for the team were

Our great efforts will lead to consistent execution.
We intensely control all short-yardage situations.
We take pride in winning the turnover game.
Positive things will happen because we work hard and believe in each other.

Coach Stautz worked individually with each player before the season, filling out a form he developed with the following information for each player:

Football Information Form

Name_____

Height_____ Weight_____/_____ Date_____

Position: Offense_____   Defense_____   Special_____

This year: _____

_____

_____

Role next year _____

_____

_____

Team goals: _____

_____

_____

Individual goals: _____

_____

_____

Bench_____ Squats_____

Cleans_____ 40 yd._____

Off season: _____

_____

_____

Leaders: _____

_____

_____

Drugs and alcohol: _____

_____

_____

College Y/N _____ Football Y/N _____ Accum. GPA _____

During the season, on each Thursday's practice before Friday's game, Coach Stautz had each player (for a total of about twenty minutes)

1. visualize positive things
2. visualize great plays
3. do a miniguided visualization—thinking about the game, seeing self doing well

4. run a play, position by position, briefly blocking, moving, hole there, backs getting ball, etc.
5. have defense think about an off-tackle play, doing it, thinking how to stop it, etc.

Each player had a copy of the video and watched the defensive and offensive plays from previous games, for inspiration and game plans. On the video, the players had given the coach rap music, "Eye of the Tiger," "Rocky," "Footloose," and other music, to include on the sound track for the plays. They felt the music they had personally picked was inspiring and uplifting to listen to and improved the motivation they received from watching the video. They also read all their affirmations once each day.

In addition to these activities Coach Stautz spent time with different groups of players such as the offense, defense, the running backs and wide receivers, and the quarterbacks. Each of these types of players needs to play with a specific emotional state of mind and must be worked with differently. The quarterback needs to be stable, ready to play, calm, cool, and collected. The defensive linebackers need to "breathe fire, be hot, light their hair on fire, and just play football!" The offensive linemen and linebackers "do battle, and have to have their wits about them." The backs need to be aggressive enough to make tackles and still be aware of what is happening on the field. Each player learns what the right emotional pitch is for him. Before each game, the quarterbacks are with Coach Stautz; the rest of the groups are with different coaches, getting ready for the game.

In talking to Coach Stautz, we asked how the team dealt with the pressure each week. He said, "We took one game at a time. We (the coaches) tried to stay loose and have fun, to get the work out of the kids. We put our concentration on the task at hand. We really believe in the team aspect. We always believe we still have a chance even when things aren't going well. We did a lot under adversity. Even when we were the underdogs, we played hard. The team belief factor is: We can do it as a team. We prepare for each game." How did he deal with the press and pressure as they continued winning? "We were ranked in the top ten almost every year; we were league champions four out of seven years. We're pretty used to the press and TV. Basically, we just ignored what the press said and just worked on our goals each week."

In his opinion, what were the major issues of individual football players?

1. Self-doubt (not believing in themselves and that they could do it)
2. Trouble visualizing their own individual good plays
3. Mental patience—when things go bad, the ability to hang in there and turn things around
4. Trouble visualizing good team plays

"We have a big five rule—we call it reacting to the big five. In the five minutes after we score, or in the five minutes after they score, how do we want to do it? We play with NO LETUP. We had a tough schedule. We won several games in the last minute, and one we won in overtime. Even when we were behind, the kids believed they were going to win. They were able to concentrate and come through in the crunch.''

How did they deal with the loss in the semifinals? ''It was tough. We had dominated the whole game. They felt good about how they had played, but they were really disappointed. Our attitude is basically, the sun's going to come up tomorrow. Life isn't always fair. We should have won, but we didn't. We just tried to let go and remind ourselves of how well we did during the whole season. We try to keep a perspective for the kids and to put games in perspective to life.''

College Football Programs

A large university program on the west coast began using a counselor to teach sport psychology and mental training concepts, beginning with the incoming freshmen recruits. Over a four-year period, the team improved considerably, and the comments of the coach in the media became more and more positive as the years passed. The process of this more-limited program consisted of an introductory lecture in the fall to the whole team and work on goals and visualization techniques. The counselor was available throughout the season and the year for individual counseling.

Each class (freshmen, sophomores, etc.) sets up goals for each year, and individual goals are written. The head coach was skeptical at first but, as time went on, became more impressed with the results. Much of the work of the counselor entailed mediation between players and coaches. This can be valuable assistance and, in this case, furnished important information and feedback to coaches. The coaches and players respect the counselor.

In an interview with one of the team members, we asked what he would do to improve the program. He said he would

1. Work more with the injured players. This is absolutely imperative. Your mind is doubting that you can play up to strength again. Your mind is asking, ''Are you the player you were before the injury?'' Players need the mental training in believing they are as fit as ever after they are healed.
2. Divide the team by offensive, defensive, line, linebackers, running backs, and the backfield. It would be very effective to do visualizations that are very position specific and to prepare audiotapes for individual positions. It would be most effective for a particular individual in a specific area.
3. Do a more thorough job of educating people on how powerful the mind is. ''I believe the mind is at least 70 percent of football. A lot of guys still think it is brute strength and talent. It's much more than that. A lot of them are still so-so about it. They don't understand it.''

Dr. Bill Straub, a professor of Exercise and Sport Sciences at Ithaca College in New York, worked for two years teaching mental training techniques to the football team at the State University of New York at Cortland, a Division III school. Dr. Straub started by teaching a one and a half-hour workshop in mental training to the team. The training included relaxation techniques, concentration skills, goals, and cognitive restructuring. After the workshop, the team voted on whether to include mental training in their program. They voted 90 percent yes. This was a simple way to get consensus and support of the team. His program consisted of

Mental training one hour each week for the entire team

Individual intervention/counseling for those interested (Of the sixty players the first year, fifteen saw him personally.)

Developing a psychological warm-up tape for individual players (to be used during warm-up for distractions)

Audiotapes made for individual players on peak performance, mastery, coping with what ifs, handling anger

Helping coaches give better feedback

Videotapes of game segments for motivation—selected out five clips where they played well; three to four where they needed improvement

Team building—dealing with issues of jealousy, team unity, letting go of petty distractions, team commitment to doing well

Relaxation training and how to visualize

Working with offense and defense separately

Developing slogans around winning, distributing a bumper sticker—Cortland Red Dragon Football: The pride is back!

The year before he started working with the team, their record was 1–9. The first year, their record was 5–4. The second year, they had a 9–0 season, their first undefeated season ever. They lost one game in the playoffs. The team turned around a defeatist attitude in two years. They set goals such as winning is consistently reaching your goals. They set short-term goals—hold to ___ yards rushing and passing—and individual goals in effort and perfection—working hard, achieving a standard of excellence.

The football psychological consultant at Arizona State University is Earl Edwards, a former NFL lineman, who played for the Buffalo Bills and the Cleveland Browns and retired in 1979.

Edwards has a contract with the football team, through the athletic department, to do individual counseling with the players. He teaches relaxation training, records individual audiotapes for training, and position tapes. He does goal setting, visualization training, mental training for improving technique and pregame routines for dealing with lost confidence and nervousness. He began working with the team in the fall of 1986. He only worked with one player the first year; however, that player was instrumental in helping the Sun Devils win the Rose Bowl that year.

All these examples represent the beginnings of the use of mental training in traditional team sports. We will see many more in the 1990s as coaches become more familiar and comfortable with mental training methods. Each coach and sport psychologist can experiment with various forms of these programs to discover what fits their specific team. These programs also can be applied to team sports other than football.

Proposal for a Sport Psychology/Mental Training Program in Football or Basketball at a University/College

I. First year of the program
   A. Conducting training and sport psychology sessions
      1. Coaching staff
      2. Athletic trainers
      3. Team members
         - Introductory session for whole team
         - Group sessions for defense, offense
         - Minigroup sessions by positions, or groups of positions
   B. Individual counseling sessions with top thirty players (at least one session; more if desired/needed)
   C. Group sessions for freshmen athletes and redshirts
   D. Meetings with coaching staff on what's working and what isn't
   E. Weekly group meetings before each game—what need to work on; what we did right, wrong on Saturday; team and individual goals for the next game; visualizing technique, etc.
   F. Any other meetings, counseling, etc., as needed
   G. Working with injured players to develop goals around healing injury and coping with being injured
II. Second year and beyond
   A. Coaching staff training—coaches' and team goals for the year
   B. Continued training in sport psychology/mental training
      1. New coaches, trainers
      2. All incoming freshmen and redshirts
   C. Weekly or biweekly meetings with coaches to keep updated on progress; problem solving
   D. Weekly group meetings before each game (one or two)
      1. Analyzing mental aspects of last game
      2. Mentally preparing for the next game
   E. Group sessions for offense and defense
      1. Goal setting for team
      2. Goal setting for each player
      3. Visualization process
   F. Individual counseling for top thirty players or more (at least once, more if desired)
   G. Working with injured players about mentally coping with pain and injury; making goals for healing and recovery

This type of program is always under the control and supervision of the coach. In the implementation of such a program, content of individual sessions is confidential between sport psychologist and player. However, the athlete is always free to discuss whatever he wishes from the session with whomever he chooses. The psychologist is ethically required to keep confidentiality agreements regarding clients. The coach is the key person in charge; the purpose of the sport psychologist is to facilitate morale, team cohesion, and communication between coaches and players. The sport psychologist strives to create balance, cooperation, and team unity and best functions as an additional member of the coaching staff, for example, the mental training coach.

This program can be modified for use in a high school program also. Coaches may find it useful to use this program as a model, adding or deleting whatever they wish to develop a comprehensive program for their own school or district.

Appendix A

■

Guided Visualizations

Guided Visualization for the Boston Marathon

(Begin all visualizations with a progressive relaxation process.)

It is Monday in Hopkinton . . . you are milling around with the other runners . . . knowing where the starting line is and beginning to focus on the twenty-six miles you are about to run . . . you feel perfectly ready and prepared . . . you had to qualify to be here . . . you had to be one of the best . . . be aware of the weather . . . the total environment as you get ready . . . notice the colors and sounds . . . the runners stretching and striding . . . and experience yourself as you begin to warm up . . . to stretch and move . . . focused . . . confident and ready for the challenge ahead . . . feel it in your body as you do your strides . . . readying yourself . . . breathing deeply . . . you take off your sweats and stretch a few more times . . . easy . . . relaxed . . . warm . . . you move to the pace marker where you had planned to start and find a good spot . . . you breathe deeply and remember that you have trained well . . . you are fit and ready . . . you have rested well and nourished yourself and you are ready . . . waiting for the last minute instructions and the sound of the gun . . . you remember your goals and your affirmations . . . you are relaxed and focused . . . you are strong and prepared . . . you are happy to be here and to meet the challenge.

You hear the gun and you begin . . . pushing and jostling, finding your space . . . it is mostly downhill these first few miles, and you know you have to be careful . . . you know you want to keep a steady pace . . . even and comfortable . . . downhill can be hard on you even in the beginning . . . you relax into a planned pace for now . . . breathing easy and caring for your body as you stride over the downgrades and up the slight rolling of the road . . . you notice the barren trees along the roadside and you realize that spring is not quite here yet . . . you begin to have a little room around you now as you and the other runners find a good pace and rhythm . . . you pass the two-mile mark and you check your time . . . running easily . . . a few more little hills and then you will pass some reservoirs . . . you like this area . . . the water makes you happy . . . you begin to look for some of the landmarks that are familiar and let you know that you are doing well and are on pace . . . like the Framingham sign that stands out in front of you as you go by telling you that you only have a few more miles until you reach Framingham . . . you know that when you get to Framingham you will have finished the first 10K . . . the first six miles . . . see yourself as you come down past the reservoir in Asland . . . you get your time at five miles. . . . How is your pace? . . . Are you too fast or too slow? . . . Just be aware and make any adjustments you feel are necessary at this point . . . check in with your breathing, knowing you are relaxed and all is going very well . . . you reach Framingham and the scenery changes . . . lots of small shops . . . the road winds and your body leans as you come to the old railroad station and complete the first 10K. . . . How do you feel? . . . Check in . . . as you pass the Happy Swallow Cocktail Lounge on your right . . . you knew it would be there . . . it is an old friend . . . you move smoothly . . . easily . . . into the seven-and eight-mile stretch where the road is flat and you give yourself permission to rest while relaxing into a good pace . . . making time . . . using the flatness to your advantage . . . moving out . . . stretching . . . feeling good and strong as you approach Natick . . . running powerfully . . . you go through Natick . . . past the ten-mile mark . . . you check in again . . . breathing easily . . . settling into this faster pace . . . past the twelve-mile mark . . . moving . . . striding . . . the road is flat and you are in control . . . having fun . . . feeling good . . . you know what's ahead . . . Wellesley . . . and the girls . . . the first crowd you know you can count on . . . cheering . . . waving . . . ready to give you new energy and make you smile . . . and you will have reached the fifteen-mile mark . . . more than halfway . . . you begin to look forward to it . . . there's a huge American flag as you enter Wellesley Square . . . you have passed the college now . . . a church and graveyard go by . . . you have eased your pace a little now . . . resting . . . gathering strength . . . taking energy from the crowd . . . you notice the beauty of the town . . . the colors . . . and come back to focus on the race you are running . . . check in again. . . . Are you taking enough water? . . . Monitor your body . . . caring . . . nurturing . . . listening . . . knowing you are fit and ready for the whole race . . . you have prepared well and you feel good . . . relaxed . . . in control.

You are well into the third 10K now . . . and you are passing the Nike store . . . one of your favorite areas . . . everyone out in front of the store . . . yelling . . . urging you on . . . giving you support . . . you smile your thanks and keep moving . . . on pace . . . in stride . . . feeling good . . . moving into the big downhill into Newton . . . catching your breath . . . breathing . . . caring for your knees . . . your calves . . . resting . . . supporting your body . . . monitoring . . . down into Newton . . . through Newton . . . on Route 16 . . . heading for Highway 128 knowing you must go up and over . . . notice the big green highway sign . . . not much of a crowd . . . you are heading toward Woodland Park and the seventeen-mile mark. . . . How do you feel? . . . How are your inner thoughts and quiet talk? . . . You have made it almost seventeen miles . . . you are proud of what you have done . . . your body is holding up its end of the deal . . . thank it as you run smoothly . . . mile eighteen . . . nineteen . . . feeling strong and relaxed . . . breathing well . . . easy . . . you turn onto Commonwealth Avenue . . . this is the fun part . . . this is the last 10K . . . this is where the big crowds are . . . lining the street . . . they make you smile . . . remember your goal for the last 10K as you approach Newton Town Hall . . . it is a beautiful building . . . you feel good . . . you know that right after the town hall you will have gone twenty miles . . . the homestretch . . . you also know that Heartbreak Hill is ahead . . . you have prepared for this . . . you know this hill . . . you have made it your friend . . . your body is ready for the change . . . ready to lean . . . to push forward . . . to change its position and work in a different way . . . this will change your energy . . . and focus . . . it is very pretty at the bottom of Heartbreak Hill . . . the houses are big . . . well kept . . . and there are some flowers and a huge crowd . . . you lean into the hill . . . you are working now . . . the change is good, and you are having fun making this hill work for you . . . it is different than the rest of the course . . . it is important to conquer this hill . . . you are confident and in control . . . you push . . . up and up . . . pulling with your arms . . . feeling strong . . . powerful . . . putting you whole self into it . . . you can see the cameras and scaffolding at the top . . . they are going to take your picture . . . up you go . . . pumping . . . moving . . . staying in stride . . . knowing you can make it . . . remembering your goal . . . saying good things to yourself . . . notice how it feels to have your picture taken and see the funny policeman . . . you've made it to the top . . . allowing yourself to rest now . . . getting your breath . . . moving downhill . . . taken care . . . thanking your body . . . relaxing into an even pace . . . changing your stride . . . being gentle with your legs . . . gathering your strength . . . time for Beacon Street now . . . the crowd is rowdy . . . having fun . . . you settle and focus . . . be careful . . . you talk to your legs . . . caring for them . . . keeping them loose and easy . . . you are on your way home . . . into Cleveland Circle and turn . . . leaning . . . watching for the trolley tracks . . . you work the turn . . . feeling strong . . . enjoying the lean of your body . . . onto Beacon Street . . . it's easy now . . . you remember your strategy . . . you begin to feel the excitement growing in your body . . . new energy . . . only a couple of miles to go as you pass the brownstones on either side of the road . . . coming back to your form . . . back to your breathing . . . finding the energy you need . . . it's downhill . . . it is easy . . . you see the Citgo sign . . . down you go . . . past the church . . . you are near the last two turns . . . one right . . . leaning . . . hearing the crowd . . . leaning left into the last turn . . . now you can see the "Pru" building . . . you are almost there . . . the finish line is ahead . . . the crowds seem to be everywhere . . . yelling . . . cheering . . . waving . . . you feel strong . . . kicking . . . running hard now . . . picking up on the energy of the crowd and the knowledge that you have done it . . . you have run the race . . . the scaffolding in front of you . . . the building in front of you . . . the finish line in front of you . . . running . . . flying . . . under the scaffolding and down the long stretch . . . slowing . . . coming to a walk . . . relaxing and trying to catch your breath . . . you slowly become aware of what you have just done . . . what you have accomplished . . . the joy . . . the exhilaration . . . the fatigue . . . the peace . . . you breathe . . . you have reached your goal . . . your body and mind gave you all . . . you smile . . . thank your legs . . . your lungs . . . your arms . . . your mind . . . let the success in . . . let the tiredness be . . . let the pain be . . . let the joy come . . . let yourself rest. . . . Experience yourself walking into the square . . . cooling off . . . your breath coming easy now . . . resting.

Come back to your body sitting in the chair or lying on the floor now . . . focus on your breathing . . . breathe deeply . . . slowly letting go of the picture and reconnecting with your present space . . . allow the feelings of accomplishment and joy to linger . . . make them a part of your being as you become aware of the sounds and feel of the room around you . . . breathe in deeply . . . exhale . . . knowing you can call up those feelings any time you choose . . . at the count of three, you may open your eyes . . . refreshed . . . confident . . . ready . . . one . . . move your fingers and toes . . . breathing easily . . . two . . . fully connecting with your body . . . moving your hands . . . feeling new energy and peace . . . three . . . open your eyes when you are ready.

Guided Visualization for Butte to Butte

(This is a 10K race in Eugene, Oregon.)

Take a quiet moment, close your eyes, and center on your breathing. Breathe in deeply and hold it for a moment, letting go and allowing your mind and body to relax and become empty and peaceful. In hale . . . hold . . . exhale.

Move your awareness inside and notice if there are any areas of tightness or places where you feel sore or uncomfortable . . . begin on your most dominant side and check in with each muscle group . . . if you feel some tension or soreness, acknowledge it, send it some energy and peace and let it go . . . move your awareness from side to side and from head to foot, acknowledging any tension or tightness . . . any pain or discomfort . . . sending care and warmth . . . and letting go. Return to your breathing anytime you find it difficult to let go or move beyond some pain or tension. Recenter yourself and then go back to that area and let it go . . . allowing it to relax and become soft . . . allowing yourself to relax . . . quiet . . . let go . . . and open.

Begin to see yourself arriving at 43rd and Donald. See the starting line and notice the crowds of people and hear them talking among themselves . . . allow yourself to connect with all the sights . . . the sounds . . . and the energy of this festive and fun 10K race . . . the colorful T-shirts, the fun runners, the serious competitors . . . feel the nervousness in your gut . . . that old familiar feeling . . . you know it is your normal preoccupation with a race . . . remembering that the minute you start, you will be in control and will relax.

As you start your warm-up routine . . . your stretching . . . jogging . . . moving . . . take pleasure in those special moments in your life . . . all the times you reached your goal and id your best . . . see yourself doing your strides . . . the strong, powerful movements of your legs stretching out . . . your body feels good . . . it feels strong. Both your mind and body are anticipating this race . . . you are looking forward to it . . . you know how good it feels to run hard and how good you feel at the end . . . that sense of euphoria and feeling of accomplishment . . . you know it is always worth it . . . the nervousness is just part of the game and part of the way you play . . . you acknowledge it and let it go . . . let it slide away and come back to focus on your routine.

Experience yourself getting ready to start the race . . . you are completely focused within, and you are taking your last few strides . . . stretching out . . . feeling your muscles warm and supple in your body. Take your place at the starting line . . . hear the instructions and announcements over the microphone . . . this is such a great race . . . you wait . . . and then you hear the sound of the gun.

You take off . . . you are familiar with the course . . . feel all the people around you . . . bumping, breathing, some still talking . . . you know some of them . . . you have your eye out for certain runners . . . you know who they are, and you know what your strategy is . . . feel your body moving easily as you begin the gentle climb toward "the hill" . . . you've trained for this hill, and you know you are strong and fit . . . the hill is one of the things that makes this race so great, and you look forward to conquering it in style . . . up and up you go . . . finding your space in the crowd and moving in a rhythm that is good for you . . . your legs feel powerful, and your arms pump and pull you up as you move smoothly, beating this hill . . . using it to your advantage . . . you lean forward and dig a little deeper . . . pushing yourself to the top and over . . . heading for the one-mile marker . . . you are excited now and focused on your breathing . . . finding a steady rhythm of inhaling and exhaling . . . feeling strong . . . you turn left onto Fox Hollow as you hear your time . . . check in with your body. . . . Are you on schedule? . . . Did you go out too slowly or too fast? . . . Makes the necessary adjustments as you head down Fox Hollow . . . using the gentle slope to regain your pace and your breath . . . enjoying the rewards of downhill running . . . you become aware of the weather on your skin and the sounds around you . . . you notice the crowds along the road cheering you on . . . it feels good to run downhill. As you pass the two-mile mark and head for the intersection of West Amazon and Hilyard . . . you remember that there is water there, and you check with your body to know if you are ready for some fluid . . . your body feels strong and free . . . you are well prepared for this race . . . your body is warmed up now and comfortable in the pace you have set for the next three miles . . . your legs move smoothly and with ease . . . you feel light and in control . . . you run through the three-mile mark . . . hearing your time . . . feeling smooth and strong . . . you bend to the right onto Hilyard and settle into the long straight fourth mile . . . there are many people lined up along this part of the course . . . you know you can take energy from them and their enthusiasm . . . this is one of your favorite races . . . this is fun . . . the four-mile mark is coming up . . . this is an important place in the race . . . you move along picking up the pace just a little . . . you listen for your time as you run through the four-mile mark . . . you come to 19th and make a sharp turn to the left . . . feeling strong as your body leans into the turn . . . two miles to go . . . you remember your strategy and check in with your body . . . you are ready for these last two miles . . . you are strong and fit . . . your legs feel powerful and light . . . you turn right onto High Street . . . it's a straight shot into the park now, and you pick up your pace . . . lengthening your stride . . . feeling confident and in rhythm . . . you keep your focus and concentration . . . heading for the five-mile mark . . . you run past the aid station, grabbing some water and moving with hardly a change in your stride . . . you remember your goal for this race . . . you remember that you have trained well . . . you know you can do it . . . less than a mile to go as you run over the railroad tracks and notice the crowd at the 5th Street market . . . you've had some good times there, and you think about the great food as you run into the park . . . picking up speed you pass the six-mile mark . . . your time is just where you want it to be . . . you are heading for the finish line now . . . you push your body . . . lifting your knees and pumping your arms . . . it feels good to move this fast . . . your body is like a well-maintained machine moving with unlimited power . . . you bend to the left . . . leaning . . . sprinting toward the clock and the finish . . . people are everywhere now but you are focused and moving fast . . . you can hear the cheering . . . you feel the joy rising in you . . . you fly across the finish and into the chute.

Begin to slow now . . . coming to a walk and allowing yourself to catch your breath . . . you can feel the enthusiasm inside, and you begin to hear your friends yelling at you . . . they are excited . . . you are pleased and proud of your race . . . you let yourself walk and warm down now . . . talking to your friends . . . feeling good and feeling spent. You know you ran a good race . . . you had fun and you achieved your goal . . . now it's time to rest and enjoy the energy around you and the rest of the day.

Begin to let your image go . . . allowing your mind to become quiet and peaceful . . . focusing again on your breathing . . . breathing in fully . . . exhaling gently . . . you feel relaxed and refreshed . . . you are ready . . . when I count to three, you may open your eyes knowing you have everything within you to achieve your goal . . . one . . . move your fingers and toes . . . coming back to the space you are sitting or lying in . . . two . . . move your head and shoulders . . . reconnecting with your body . . . feeling refreshed and ready to run Butte to Butte . . . three . . . open your eyes when you are ready.

Guided Visualization for the Houston/Tenneco Marathon

Experience yourself standing in the crowd at the beginning of the course . . . look around you. On your right is the tall Tenneco building . . . it is a perfect day for a marathon . . . the temperature is in the 40s or low 50s . . . no rain . . . you feel the coolness on your skin . . . you are ready . . . muscles feeling good . . . trained . . . warmed . . . at their peak . . . you stand at your minutes-per-mile mark . . . noticing the crowd and aware of the noises and the occasional body contact . . . for a moment it is quiet . . . last-minute instructions . . . you are aware of the excitement in your body and the anticipation in your breathing . . . you center your body and energy and listen.

The gun sounds and slowly you begin to move within the crowd as if you were all one body . . . you feel fresh and ready . . . all the excitement and preparation is centered into one focus . . . one purpose . . . one goal . . . you are moving smoothly

. . . the crowd has thinned now as you approach the first mile mark . . . everything feels right . . . you are strong . . . your first mile is just the way you wanted it to be . . . you turn onto Texas Street noticing the Texas Commerce Tower on your right . . . you smile inside . . . you are so ready . . . so fit.

Your breathing is even and deep . . . your stride smooth and easy . . . you are beginning to settle into your body, and you find your perfect pace as you pass the second mile mark . . . you are on Crawford Street now and begin to think of the fifty-yard slope onto the bridge . . . runners begin to crowd in as the road narrows . . . you can feel the jostling and bumping . . . you hear the pounding of feet . . . as you run across the bridge, you notice the city off to the left and right . . . your body position changes again as you run down off the bridge into old town and take a quick left onto Hogan . . . it felt good to lean . . . your stride is powerful and even . . . you are comfortable . . . the neighborhood is Hispanic now and you notice Los Toros restaurant and wonder if they serve good Mexican food . . . you feel good and are pleased with your splits . . . you pass the three-mile mark and then the four, feeling strong and in control.

You lean left again as you pass the five-mile mark and hear your split . . . this is Main Street . . . you think for a moment of all the towns that must have a Main Street as you run smoothly past the large crowd on the corner and approach the water station . . . you grab a cup, drinking as much as you can without changing your pace . . . your race is going well . . . you reach the underpass striding down into it . . . hearing the echo as other runners yell and feet pound around you . . . up you go still running through the old part of town . . . you notice the overpass above and lean slightly forward as you immediately begin the steep climb up the bridge spanning the river . . . your body is happy to change its position . . . to work a little harder . . . to reach the top and run past the University of Houston buildings and down off the bridge . . . slowly you remind yourself . . . centering . . . resting . . . easing your breathing.

It almost seems sudden as you run onto Texas again and into more modern buildings . . . you notice First City on the left and Palais Royal . . . Burger King is on the right . . . your belly is happy and comfortable . . . you are not hungry . . . you have taken good care of your body . . . six miles . . . you have almost finished the first 10K . . . you smile . . . it is going even better than you had hoped . . . your stride is easy and you feel confident and powerful. Elgin street is coming up . . . you turn left and see Main Bank on your left . . . smoothly you turn right onto Crawford and then onto Almeda . . . it seems as if restaurants are everywhere . . . you are maintaining a good, controlled pace and are aware of the trees . . . Texas Medical Center and then right onto McGregor . . . there's Hermann Park and now AMI Park Plaza hospital . . . you dismiss the images as your turn left onto Main Street again . . . leaning . . . striding smoothly . . . breathing evenly . . . moving . . . focused on the race and your well-trained body . . . you run past the fountain and down the avenue under the canopy of the overhanging trees . . . it is cool.

You are in the medical center proper now . . . people and patients are watching from windows . . . another aid station . . . you replenish your body . . . and are aware of the music . . . the entertainment and sounds of fun . . . you feel good as you turn onto University Street lined by beautiful homes. Rice University is on your right as you head down University into the shopping center . . . the crowd is huge . . . it gives you energy . . . it pleases you . . . another water station . . . more music . . . the Poorman's country Club . . . and shops . . . you are well into the second 10K, and you check in with your body . . . breathing even . . . legs strong . . . arms comfortable and easy . . . feet happy . . . everything looks affluent and you feel affluent . . . as you run past the light at the wide intersection and notice the police station on your right.

You take a right into Weslayan . . . down a short stretch and into the Plaza . . . more water and good music . . . you are happy and confident . . . you are having fun and run over the railroad line taking a sharp left into West Park . . . you lean into the turns feeling strong and using them to gather your power and change your body position . . . it feels good . . . you feel good . . . under the freeway and along 59 Feeder and under the freeway again making a right onto Post Oak toward the fantastic fountain . . . the Transco Tower shoots like a needle into the sky . . . music . . . Post Oak . . . tall glass buildings and the three blue towers at the end—a left turn onto San Felipe, and you know that you are more than halfway home . . . everything is working smoothly . . . no pain . . . no doubt . . . no fatigue . . . you are in control, and you maintain your pace . . . and concentrate.

Running smoothly past Chimney . . . Fountain View . . . Potomac . . . you run . . . turn . . . stride . . . breathe . . . you're on Woodway now and feel the breeze and the road under foot as it dips down . . . past the Inn on the Park and the Swiss Chalet sign . . . over the bridge . . . under 610 loop and into the trees . . . quiet . . . you center on your breathing and the peace as you run gently up and then down under the railway bridge . . . reaching the Memorial Park running track . . . it is empty . . . you remember the hours you spent training . . . speed work . . . pushing hard and settle back into your pace . . . it is the eighteenth mile . . . one 10K to go . . . you are proud you still feel strong . . . you have been passing some people the last mile or so and this has given you more energy . . . more water.

You take a right onto Shepherd and left under the overpass into the final four miles . . . people seem to be everywhere and you become aware of their cheering and shouting . . . and you remember the dips coming up around the parkway and notice the skyline past the water fountain that looks like a ball on the left . . . steady . . . smooth . . . strong . . . there's the freeway system again . . . under and through the park feeling the excitement of near completion . . . you have worked hard for this . . . these last six miles are the most important . . . you have remained strong even when you felt a little tired . . . maybe a little tight . . . you let go of it and focused on your breathing and the smoothness of your stride . . . your inner talk was positive and supportive . . . and you maintained your pace . . . now you have only about two hundred yards to go . . . you hold it together as you turn left onto Smith . . . you pick up the pace . . . you lengthen your stride . . . you feel as if you are going to fly . . . you can see the clock . . . hear the crowds and feel the thrill of your accomplishment . . . your feet fly over the finish line as you punch your watch.

You have done it!!!!! . . . You slow . . . begin to walk . . . to catch your breath . . . someone comes to help you . . . you thank them but move on your own aware of the clapping and cheering . . . you keep moving savoring the moment . . . the feeling of joy . . . the quiet of your body . . . resting . . . breathing. You thank your legs . . . your arms . . . your lungs . . . you feel like a winner, and you are proud . . . you are a strong and beautiful runner . . . and now you allow yourself to rest.

Guided Visualization for the Pittsburgh Marathon

Find a quiet, comfortable place to sit or lie. You will need about ten to fifteen minutes. Sit comfortably in the chair with both feet flat on the floor and relax with your hands at ease in your lap and your back against the back of the chair. If you are lying on the floor, rest with your arms at your sides, legs fully extended, and your back flat. Begin to relax . . . close your eyes and focus on your breathing . . . center your body parts and clear your mind . . . imagine your center of gravity and power to be located about two inches below your navel . . . you feel calm and balanced . . . inhale deeply into your diaphragm . . . hold it for a moment . . . and exhale from your belly to your chest . . . inhale . . . hold . . . exhale . . . empty your mind . . . allow any random thoughts to pass through as if they were on a river . . . feel your body and mind letting go . . . inhale . . . hold . . . exhale.

It is the morning of the marathon . . . you have trained well . . . you have nurtured your body and mind, and now you are ready for the marathon you have looked forward to for months . . . you are near the starting line beginning to warm up . . . you notice the weather and the environment around you . . . you are aware of the colors and the sounds and the feel of the people near you . . . you know you can handle anything that may come along during this race . . . you begin to warm up . . . moving . . . stretching . . . running a few yards and back again. You can feel the excitement in your body and the readiness of your mind . . . you notice if any of your friends are nearby and then bring your focus back to preparing for the start . . . you take off your warm-up shirt and stand ready at your speed marker in just your racing clothes . . . you breathe deeply . . . centering and focusing your mind and body . . . waiting for the sound of the starting gun . . . you can hear the announcer and then the hush of the crowd.

The gun sounds and the crowd begins to move . . . slowly you move forward finding room to get into your pace and lengthen your stride . . . you know the first seven miles or so are basically flat, and there may be a tendency to go out too fast . . . you are prepared for this possibility and have learned to pace yourself . . . running well within yourself and your strategy . . . down Butler Street you run as the crowd begins to thin . . . finding your pace . . . creating your space . . . you are feeling strong and light . . . you are glad the race has begun and that you are moving . . . from time to time you notice the people around you . . . their colors . . . their movements . . . once or twice maybe someone bumps you and you feel the warmth of their body . . . you feel the ground beneath your feet and the air on your face . . . it feels good . . . you are in control knowing you are ready for the challenge and the fun of this marathon and the goals you have set for yourself . . . you reach the first mile mark and hear your time . . . you check it with your plan. . . . Are you a little too fast? . . . Perhaps a little slow? . . . You make the corrections in your stride and pace . . . feeling strong and powerful . . . feeling light and smooth . . . you take a slight left turn feeling your body lean a little and head for the two-mile mark . . . running through that . . . bending left again and then right; you are on Penn Avenue running through Lawrenceville . . . you notice the renovated shops and restaurants as you go through the four-mile mark . . . you check in with your times and your body . . . all is well . . . you are running smoothly and well within your pace now . . . there is plenty of room around you though people are running with you . . . you are focused and your breathing comes easy . . . you take a sharp right turn to the 16th Street bridge, which is flat and easy to cross . . . you are now on the north side and go through mile five and take a left onto Ohio Street . . . it feels good to lean into the turns, and you think about making them your power play . . . you are having fun . . . as you lean right off of Ohio and then left onto Commons and then left again . . . . and then right to the six-mile mark . . . you practice this power play game . . . you hear your time and lean right again as you pass the six-mile mark and head for Western Avenue where you bear left . . . you are strong and smooth . . . the first 10K is finished and you are right where you want to be . . . feeling fresh and energized . . . ready and focused, you lean left through the seven-mile mark and onto the West End Bridge . . . running across the Ohio River is always a good experience . . . the water gives you a sense of power and flowing just like in a race, and you take energy from it.

You take a sharp left turn onto Carson Street . . . now you have a long straight run . . . you know there is a slight upgrade to the Fort Pitt Bridge ramp and then a fairly steep, short downhill . . . you look forward to this change in the course . . . it gives your body a chance to be in a different frame . . . you have been careful to pace yourself, and you feel confident you can handle this change. As you go through the nine-mile mark, you begin to prepare mentally for the hill you know is coming up . . . you have trained for this hill and you look forward to the challenge. You have some strategy for this part of the race, and you feel in control as you pass the ten-mile mark and head for the hill.

Hospital hill begins to slope gently beneath your feet after you cross the Birmingham Bridge . . . you feel your body willing to lean forward just a little and your arms move to help . . . you know you won't need to change your stride as you focus on the power you feel as you continue up the gentle slope . . . you feel strong and ready for the last 30 percent of this hill . . . your body responds well to the slope, and your mind is focused on your breathing and your power . . . you lean forward as the hill rises more sharply . . . pumping your arms and staying in your rhythm . . . your body feels tough and strong . . . you know you can make it and you keep your focus . . . you crest this hill at Magee Hospital as the road levels out and becomes basically flat . . . you breathe deeply . . . calming your body . . . setting back into your usual running form and pace . . . that felt good . . . you connected with your strength and endurance, and you feel confident and powerful . . . you thank your legs and arms for their good job and their health as you lean left onto South Craig Street and then right onto 5th Avenue toward the thirteen-mile marker . . . almost halfway and your stride is smooth and light . . . you have settled back into your planned pace your breathing is in rhythm with your body and you feel in control and happy.

The next six miles are basically flat, and you begin to notice the neighborhoods and you can hear the crowds . . . you notice the weather on your skin . . . you have been certain to take plenty of fluids along the way and though you know you have run more than fourteen miles now, you feel ready for the next twelve and are confident of your strength and endurance . . . you remember your affirmations "I am a strong and powerful runner. I am well trained and ready for this marathon. I enjoy running within my pace and pushing myself to the finish." You are happy and all is going well as you turn right onto Penn Avenue and run smoothly through the fifteen-mile mark . . . you run through more neighborhoods and pass more crowds . . . you enjoy the energy they give you and the occasional change of scenery . . . your stride is still smooth and light as you pass a couple of runners . . . notice their breathing and bring your focus back to your form and breathing . . . part of you is amazed as you pass the eighteen-mile mark and run through Penn Circle . . . that was fast . . . you acknowledge your energy and strength as you head up Highland Avenue toward Wellesley and Highland Park . . . the nineteen-mile mark is coming up, and you know you are about to start the last 10K of the race . . . this is the most important part of the race and sometimes the most difficult . . . you are prepared . . . you have trained for this last leg of the marathon and your mind and body know just what to do . . . you also remember that these last six miles or so have a gentle roll to them, and you know you can take care of your legs when you run downhill . . . you turn left onto North Negley Avenue . . . leaning . . . feeling your body respond . . . knowing you are headed home . . . through the twenty-mile mark you run . . . hearing your time . . . preparing for the home stretch . . . you feel the course beginning to rise and fall as you move along toward Walnut Street and the Shadyside shopping district . . . you are bringing your focus inward now . . . concentrating on the next five miles ahead . . . you are aware that you have worked hard and you acknowledge that you will be glad to rest . . . you also know you are in control and feeling strong and prepared for the last few miles . . . you pass a couple more runners, and this gives you more energy and helps you think positively about your strength and endurance . . . you are heading for the twenty-two-mile mark now at the corner of Liberty and South Millvale . . . the next two miles are downhill . . . you talk to your legs . . . letting them know you will be careful and you are depending on them . . . you make your stride easy as you begin to run down . . . feeling light on your feet . . . being gentle on your ankles and knees . . . the Kerotest Building is ahead . . . the twenty-four-mile mark . . . the ground levels out beneath your feet and becomes flat . . . you thank your legs and remain focused on your breathing and form . . . just a little over two miles to go. You know the last two miles are flat and fast all the way to Point State Park.

You can now see the Burgh's skyline beckoning to you . . . you connect with your rhythm and stride . . . soon you will pick up the pace just a little . . . you acknowledge the tiredness and know it is a good kind of tiredness . . . already you begin to feel the pride and enthusiasm of what you are about to accomplish . . . you run smoothly through mile twenty-five and bend slightly to the right and finally onto

Penn Avenue . . . the noise from the crowd picks you up and seems to move you along without effort . . . you can feel the excitement and the joy beginning to wash over you . . . you can see the colors of the finish line and the numbers on the clock as you draw nearer and nearer . . . three hundred yards to go . . . your pace is fast . . . you are almost sprinting . . . your body moves on its own and your mind feels empty and relaxed . . . you fly over the finish line . . . hearing your time and knowing you can stop now and walk and breathe and enjoy.

You move slowly through the chute and into the crowd . . . you allow yourself to calm down and begin to feel the full impact of your success . . . you let it all in . . . the noise . . . the park . . . the colors . . . the smells . . . the feel of your legs, arms, lungs, heart . . . you connect with your whole being.

Let yourself rest now . . . taking your time . . . enjoying the crowd and your friends . . . thanking your body for its health, its strength, its endurance, and its willingness . . . you have reached your goal.

Come back to your body sitting in the chair or lying on the floor now. Focus on your breathing . . . breathe deeply . . . slowly letting go of the picture and reconnecting with your present space . . . allow the feelings of accomplishment and joy to linger . . . make them a part of your being as you become aware of the sounds and feel of the room around you . . . breathe in deeply . . . exhale . . . knowing you can call up those feelings any time you choose . . . at the count of three, you may open your eyes . . . one . . . move your fingers and toes . . . breathing easily . . . feeling refreshed . . . two . . . reconnect fully with your body . . . move your shoulders and head . . . feeling new energy and peace . . . three . . . open your eyes when you are ready.

Bibliography

■

Bennett, James G., and James E. Pravitz. 1987. *Profile of a winner.* Ithaca, NY: Sport Science International.

Benson, Herbert. 1975. *The relaxation response.* New York: William Morrow & Co.

Chopra, Deepak. 1989. *Quantum healing: Exploring the frontiers of mind/body medicine.* New York: Bantam Books.

Cook, David L., and Ray Tricker. 1989. *Athletes at risk: Drugs and sports.* Dubuque, IA: W. C. Brown.

Davis, Martha; Elizabeth R. Eshelman, and Matthew McKay. 1982. *The relaxation and stress reduction workbook.* Oakland, CA: New Harbinger Publications.

Fadiman, James. 1986. *Be all that you are.* Seattle, WA: Westlake Press.

Gallwey, Timothy, and Bob Kriegel. 1977. *Inner skiing.* New York: Random House.

Garfield, Charles A., with Hal Z. Bennett. 1984. *Peak performance: Mental training techniques of the world's greatest athletes.* Los Angeles, CA: J. P. Tarcher.

Gawain, Shakti. 1978. *Creative visualization.* Berkeley: Whatever Publishing.

Hansen, Mark Victor. 1981. *How to achieve total prosperity.* Newport Beach, CA: Mark Victor Hansen, Associates, Inc.

Harris, Dorothy V., and Bette L. Harris. 1984. *The athlete's guide to sports psychology: Mental skills for physical people.* New York: Leisure Press.

Horn, Thelma. 1991. *Advances in sport psychology.* Champaign, IL: Human Kinetics Press.

Houston, Jean. 1982. *The possible human.* Los Angeles, CA: J. P. Tarcher.

Jeffers, Susan. 1987. *Feel the fear and do it anyway.* New York: Harcourt, Brace, Jovanovich.

Kubistant, Tom. 1988. *Mind pump: The psychology of body building.* Champaign, IL: Human Kinetics Press.

Levine, Stephen. 1979. *A gradual awakening.* New York: Anchor Press/Doubleday.

Levine, Stephen. 1987. *Healing into life and death.* New York: Anchor Press/Doubleday.

Loehr, James. 1986. *Mentally tough.* New York: Evans.

Loehr, James, and E. J. Kahn. 1989. *Parent/player tennis training program.* New York: Penguin.

McCluggage, Denise. 1983. *The centered skier.* New York: Bantam New Age.

Mahoney, M. J. 1979. *Self-change: Strategies for solving personal problems.* New York: W. W. Norton & Co.

Mahoney, M. J. 1989. *Human change processes: Notes on the facilitation of personal development.* New York: Basic Books.

Marks, Linda. 1989. *Living with vision.* Indianapolis, IN: Knowledge Systems.

Nideffer, Robert M. 1985. *Athlete's guide to mental training.* Champaign, IL: Human Kinetics Press.

Orlick, Terry. 1980. *In pursuit of excellence.* Champaign, IL: Human Kinetics Press.

Orlick, Terry. 1986. *Psyching for sport: Mental training for athletes.* Champaign, IL: Leisure Press.

Porter, Kay, and Judy Foster. 1987. *The mental athlete.* New York: Ballantine Books.

Schwarz, Jack. 1977. *The path of action.* New York: E. P. Dutton.

Suinn, Richard, ed. 1980. *Psychology in sports: Methods and applications.* Minneapolis, MN: Burgess Press.

Syer, John, and Christopher Connolly. 1984. *Sporting body/Sporting mind.* New York: Cambridge University Press.

Williams, Jean M. 1986. *Applied sports psychology.* Palo Alto, CA: Mayfield.

IMPROVE YOUR PERSONAL BEST!

with

Customized Guided Visualization Audiotapes by Kay Porter, Ph.D.

Let Dr. Porter create a customized audiotape to meet your personal needs —
for a specific sport, event, or topic. Possible areas include:

- Improving your job performance
- Letting go of stress in your life
- Improving your athletic performance
- Achieving personal power and peace of mind
- Increasing your self-confidence

- Achieving your highest goals
- Healing injuries/controlling pain
- Psyching yourself up to achieve your best
- Relaxation and breathing for mind and body

Each tape is approximately 15 minutes long and includes a guided visualization and positive self-statements (affirmations) to develop positive thinking patterns and eliminate negative beliefs about performance.

Enclose $25.00 for each tape, plus postage and handling:

$2.50 for 1-3 tapes
$3.50 for 4-6 tapes
$6.00 fpr 7-9 tapes
$8.00 for 10 tapes

Send check or money order to:

Porter Performance Systems
P.O. Box 5584
Eugene, OR 97405

Or call (503) 342-6875

_____ tapes at $25.00 each = _____ + postage/handling = _____ TOTAL

NAME_____

ADDRESS_____

CITY_____STATE_____ZIP_____

PHONE_____

GUIDED VISUALIZATION AUDIOTAPES

The champion trains the mind... conditioning, strengthening, and developing it so it is focused, positive, and concentrating on fulfilling a goal. Kay Porter, Ph.D. leads you through guided visualizations for individual and team sports. What the mind imagines, the body produces.

Guided visualizations for team sports:

• Team Building
• Football
• Basketball
• Baseball/Softball
• Soccer
• Volleyball

• Dealing with Anger and Fear in Competition
• Healing Injury and Pain Control
• Stress Reduction and Relaxation
• Goal Achievement/Powerflow
• Letting Go of a Goal

Guided visualizations for individual athletes:

• Dealing with Anger and Fear in Competition
• Healing Injury and Pain Control
• Stress Reduction and Relaxation
• Goal Achievement/Powerflow
• Going to Sleep

• Tennis
• Golf
• Triathlon
• Skiing (Alpine)
• Track/Running
    -800/1500 meters
    -3000 meters on track/cross country
    -5000/10,000 meters cross country/road racing
    -marathon

Check the tapes that you want to order.

Guided visualizations for team sports:

_____ Team Building
_____ Football
_____ Basketball
_____ Baseball/Softball
_____ Soccer
_____ Volleyball

_____ Dealing with Anger and Fear in Competition
_____ Healing Injury and Pain Control
_____ Stress Reduction and Relaxation
_____ Goal Achievement/Powerflow
_____ Letting Go of a Goal

Guided visualizations for individual athletes:

_____ Dealing with Anger and Fear in Competition
_____ Healing Injury and Pain Control
_____ Stress Reduction and Relaxation
_____ Goal Achievement/Powerflow
_____ Going to Sleep

_____ Tennis
_____ Golf
_____ Triathlon
_____ Skiing (Alpine)
_____ Track/Running

Send check or money order to:
Porter Performance Systems
P.O. Box 5584
Eugene, OR 97405

Or call (503) 342-6875

Name_____

Address_____

City_____State_____

ZIP_____ Phone_____

Enclose $12.00 for each tape, plus:
$2.50 for 1-3 tapes
$3.50 for 4-6 tapes
$6.00 for 7-9 tapes
$8.00 for 10 tapes

For multiple orders, combine the above list for postage rates.

_____ + _____ postage/handling = _____

TOTAL AMOUNT ENCLOSED $ _____

YOUR MIND MAKES THE DIFFERENCE!

Through the easy access of video, you can learn mental training for peak athletic performance with the **Mental Athlete** videotape by Kay Porter, Ph.D. and Judy Foster.

Developed in consultation with Olympic champions and other elite athletes, this 30-minute video presentation shows you step-by-step how to:

- Identify your negative thought patterns and retrain your mind to think in positive ways in competition and training.

- Set realistic short- and long-term athletic goals.

- Develop positive self-statements (affirmations) about your training and competition.

- Learn relaxation, concentration, and visual imagery skills.

- Psych yourself up or calm yourself down in competitive situations.

- Overcome mental blocks and problems in competition.

- Develop your own mental training log to help you track your progress and identify areas in need of special mental preparation.

The champion athlete visualizes being a winner long before the competition. He or she trains the mind — conditioning, strengthening, and developing it so that it's focused and completely concentrated on fulfilling the goal of those endless days of physical training. Gaining the mental edge with the Porter/Foster five-step method from their best-selling book, **The Mental Athlete**, this book/video combination can help you overcome many of the psychological roadblocks holding you back from your own championship performance.

PLEASE SEND ME:

_____ **Mental Athlete** videotape(s) at $65.00 each   _____Beta   _____VHS

NAME_____

ADDRESS_____

CITY_____STATE_____ZIP_____

Account #_____

Expiration Date_____Signature_____

All orders must be accompanied by P.O. number, check, or money order. Make checks payable to:

Method of payment:

❏ Check or money order

❏ CHARGE

    ❏ VISA
    ❏ M/C
    ❏ AMEX

Wm. C. Brown Publishers
Trade & Direct Group
2460 Kerper Boulevard
Dubuque, Iowa 52001
Or call TOLL-FREE 800-338-5578